# Novel Configurations

Allan H. Pasco

# Novel Configurations
# A Study of French Fiction

Stendhal
Balzac
Zola
Gide
Huysmans
Proust
Robbe-Grillet
Saporta
Cortázar
Ricardou

Summa Publications, Inc.
Birmingham, Alabama
1987

Copyright © 1987 Summa Publications, Inc.
Printed in the United States of America




ISBN 0-917786-50-5
Library of Congress Catalog Number 86-63079

*Pro Dallas conjugi sed tantum sit Deo gloria.*

# Table of Contents

The Introduction considers fictional patterns, indicating
the theoretical principles that guide the essay, and, of
course, introduces what follows. Each of the book's
chapters is intended to advance understanding of a significant novel which was chosen because it makes use ot a
typical structuring device. Taken together, I hope these
novels will illustrate a new system of fictional classification,
one which will be useful in defining and illuminating the
basic configuration of the genre and in coming to terms
with some of the interesting innovations of our own
century.

Stendhal's fine novel is used to illustrate the concept of
closure with thorough analysis of the work itself. *La
Chartreuse de Parme* also exemplifies the most common
variety of fictional structure: that organized around a
sequence or process.

This chapter surveys the problem of overture, before
drawing attention to an important kind of opening at
work in Balzac's *Gobseck*. The novella provides an example
of those creations where, because narration is subordinated
to description, the reader is encouraged to neglect action
and, instead, form a static image of the whole.

These pages continue and develop the proposition that
*Gobseck* and *La Chartreuse* illustrate the two conceptual
categories into which all fiction may be placed: structures
of process and image. *Germinal*, Emile Zola's masterpiece,
illustrates a complex kind of process novel where the
action or armature consists of a series of allusions to
certain Greek myths and to the story of the New Testament
Church. The novel employs the most common, thus
dominant, novelistic pattern. Like the works previously
discussed, it is then endomorphic (from the Greek for
"within" and "form," a word which suggests internal
organization).

Russian Formalists believed that any time an aesthetic device becomes clearly established in readers' minds, it would be attacked by the next generation of artists. In the fifty years at the end of the nineteenth and beginning of the twentieth centuries, such major artists as Gide, Huysmans, Proust, and Joyce indicate awareness of and fatigue with the patterns previously discussed. This chapter analyzes Gide's *L'Immoraliste* to demonstrate how the endomorphic novel was subverted.

This portion of the study stresses two novelistic strategies: positive and negative narration. While in most novels the reader's attention is focused on what is taking place "out there," in *En rade* the objective events have importance only insofar as they reveal the protagonist's inner development. Huysmans's text is like those strange hollows archaeologists found in and around Pompeii. Only when some clever person thought to fill the empty spaces with plaster of Paris and chip off the shell of hardened lava, did they discover the forms of dogs and men writhing in the agony of death by burns. Negative narration has become a particularly important device in the recent novel. More important, perhaps, is the way *En rade* joins other works of its day by revolting against the accepted conventions of fictional patterns.

While displaying mastery of well-worn devices, Proust's masterpiece exploits a revolutionary, new pattern. It establishes numerous sign-systems within itself, any one of which suffices when apprehended by the reader to give *A la recherche du temps perdu* structure. The novel thus resembles what mineralogists call a "paramorphe," that is, a structure formed by changing the physical characteristics without changing the chemical composition. In this sense, Proust's novel is paramorphic. By whatever extension the reader may consciously—or more probably, unconsciously—chose, the work will achieve form.

In the "Conclusion," *A la recherche* serves to review the concepts of action and inaction, process and image, open and closed structure, positive and negative narration, and patterns which I have termed endomorphic and paramorphic. The paramorphic structures exploited by such modern artists as Calder and Jean Ricardou, Marc Saporta, or Julio Cortázar suggest that this particular kind of pattern has considerable significance to the modern novel.

# Preface

THE FOLLOWING PAGES HAVE SEVERAL PURPOSES: first, each of the essays is intended to advance understanding of a significant novel. In addition, each work was chosen because it exemplifies the configurations of novels, wherever and whenever they originated. And, finally, the study of these novels provides the basis for a new system of fictional classification, one which may be useful in defining and illuminating the basic structures of the genre and in coming to terms with some of the interesting innovations of this century. As David H. Richter wrote, there might be "a small, finite number of possible 'shapes' into which a fiction may be formed, few enough so that we can guess at a novel's form by creating and discarding hypotheses until we find one that fits."[1] This book represents an inductive attempt to suggest the outlines of such a limited system. While I have not started with theory, rather with novels themselves, and though I do not end with sociology or psychology or one of the other social sciences, rather with an interpretation and its significance to the novel in general, if I have been successful, the value of the following work will be apparent to anyone acquainted with both the novel and critical and narrative theory.

As I consider what I have written here and where I have been in the intellectual journey that produced the volume, I am most aware of what I owe others. I have attempted to give specific credit where appropriate, but all too often major influences are mentioned only in passing, if at all. I have been particularly remiss in regard to those Anglo-American New Critics, Russian Formalists, and Structuralists whose work has formed me through the years; nevertheless, to enumerate adequately my obligations, many of which predate this particular project, would overburden the already extensive documentation. I do, however, want to say that I am particularly grateful to the novelists and critics who met me in the quiet of my study and challenged me to rethink the presuppositions and conclusions that had comfortably guided me for years. I have not always agreed with those whom I read; my debt for stimulation is no less real.

In addition, I want to mention Roy Jay Nelson who perceptively read an early version of chapter 5, Robert J. Niess who gave invaluable assistance in working up a draft of chapter 4, Emile Talbot who helped me with chapter 2, Djelal Kadir whose hand is also evident in this chapter and who provided excellent advice for other portions of the text, and David Lee Rubin who has followed this project almost from its inception. Professor Rubin has read all of it at least once and has done me the kindness of bringing numerous weaknesses and failures to my attention. Those flaws that remain will doubtless mark the places where I did not follow the counsel of these excellent readers. Finally, because an early version of chapter 3 was published in *Texas Studies in Literature and Language,* 20 (1978)—used by permission of the University of Texas Press—and several paragraphs in *The Virginia Quarterly Review*—©*The Virginia Quarterly Review*—a portion of chapter 4 in *French Review*, 46 (1973), 739-49, much of the textual analysis of *L'Immoraliste* (ch. 5) in *The Romanic Review*, 64, 3 (May 1973), 184-203 (copyright by the Trustees of Columbia University in the City of New York), and a significant portion of chapter 7 in *Contemporary Literature,* 18, 1 (1977)—copyright by The University of Wisconsin Press—I wish to thank the various presses and journals for permission to include them. I am also grateful to Alfred A. Knopf, Inc., for permission to quote from Wallace Stevens's poem, "The Idea of Order at Key West."

# Chapter 1
## Introduction

IT SEEMS TO ME THAT REALLY GOOD CRITICISM must be able to situate the work under consideration in its epoch. I would hope that it also furthers understanding, while revealing an intimate awareness of significant literature in the critic's own time. However subordinate critical writing may be to the artistic works it analyzes—and I make no claims for criticism as an independent art form—it must show an openness to recent artistic creations and then encourage a bridge between the then and now. I recall a raging argument about whether Calderón (or was it Goethe?) had anything worthwhile to say to readers of today. It was a gathering of cordially antagonistic critics of divergent views. Marxism, Structuralism, the New Criticism, the Geneva school, and literary history had all had their say when Paolo Cherchi took advantage of a pause. "Well, yes, I suppose so, but whatever the case, you and I can't read Dante well if we haven't read Borges." I agree.

The current project began after a long period of immersion in recent fiction. I had just finished reading an article which came very close to suggesting that Zola's novels are irretrievably dated, with little or nothing to say to modern readers.[1] I knew my expectations and, consequently, my way of reading had been changed by the time I had spent in García Márquez, Thomas Pynchon, and Michel Butor, but I had trouble believing that Shakespeare, Dante, or Balzac no longer offered me anything. Just as the work of truly great painters of the past is enhanced by the greater appreciation modern artists have given us for color and space, one would think something similar would happen to our perception of the wonderful novelists writing in nineteenth-century France. In short, I planned to concentrate on whether or not older fictions could content my newly formed exigencies.

As I read and studied, however, I found myself increasingly drawn to what seems to me a revolutionary change in the ways some novels are formed. Such an innovation is not surprising. Novelists have from the beginning indulged in novelties. Still, the character of this change has importance, and my project changed. In the following pages, though I shall spend considerable space pointing to the similarities between "former" and "new" novels, I do so not to demonstrate that the "new" is "not so new after all" but to emphasize what appears to be an extraordinarily significant innovation.

Following such theorists as E. D. Hirsch, Jr., I posit the reliability of novelists' texts, and I respect a text's historically recoverable verbal meaning.[2] I consequently seek to justify and validate my interpretations by indicating their correspondence with the texts in question. In the essays that result, I provide translations— my own unless otherwise stated—of the texts quoted. References are, however, included to facilitate returning to the original works.

Vocabulary has proven a serious problem. Not only has the concept of structure become no easier to deal with since Cleanth Brooks pointed to some of its problems back in the 1940s,[3] but terminology seems regrettably vague and controversial. Clearly, the physical composition of printed pages in books is of little interest to those seeking a better grasp of novels' ideational configuration, form, or shape, or structure, or pattern—each of these terms has its adherents and detractors. Philip Stevick, for example, proposes jettisoning "the word structure altogether, [which] whether we wish it to or not, carries with it connotations of economy, symmetry, accountable proportion, organic form."[4] Stevick is perfectly correct about this meaning. In the end, it provides one justification for my retaining the term: as I shall use it, the Aristotelian qualities of order, size, wholeness, economy, and form are indeed implied. "Structure" has another advantage. Thanks to substantial agreement among linguists, it has once again gained a relatively stable definition.

The ideational creation that I call structure may be invented out of whole cloth by readers and imposed upon a chaotic aesthetic object. It may be around an absence (I think of Godot who does not, and indeed for structural reasons must not, come in *En attendant Godot*—1953). It may still elude today's readers, but any novel capable of bringing aesthetic satisfaction to its audience has structure, by which I mean—I take Emile Benveniste's definition—"the arrangement of a whole by parts and the demonstrated solidarity between the parts of the whole which are mutually conditioned."[5] As Benveniste goes on to argue, "Each of the units of a system is thus defined by the totality of the relations that it sustains with the other units and by the oppositions it enters into. . . . In reality, the parts . . . may only be determined within the system which organizes and dominates them as they are related to each other. They have no value except as elements of a structure. The system must first be freed and described" (ibid., p. 21). "Each system, being composed of units which are mutually conditioned, are distinguished from other systems by the internal disposition of these units, disposition which constitutes its structure" (ibid., p. 96). Edgard Varèse perceptively warns against viewing structure "as a point of departure, a pattern to be followed, a mold to be filled. Form is a result—the result of a process."[6] And, while it is possible that this organization be "the very movement by means of which the essence comes alive,"[7] one can nonetheless describe particular structures, at least after having completed the reading.

Such a reading suggests both a knowing reader and an in-depth analysis that is adequate to the systems existing latently in the novel. It should permit producing a description faithful both to the original text and to the subsequent abstractions that will be used in grouping classes of novels. It also takes into account the text's significant relationships: I think of size, position, order, context, arrangement, grouping, while considering distance, amount and degree of linking with contiguous or distant elements, narrational point of view and reliability of focus, tone, analogies, inversions, rotations, reversals, polarities and contradictions (what Varèse calls "alternate and opposite correlative states"). Even on adding synecdoche to this list of possibly significant relations, it is far from complete. It does, however, suffice to suggest the importance of textual *inter*relations; in the case of oppositions, the relationships established are extremely strong and affect the entire system of the work. No text is truly autonomous. All depend on conventions accepted by both writer and reader. Nonetheless, the networks of significance within texts are of superior weight in determining which extratextual matters pertain.

There are several other requirements for the readings I shall advance. Following in this respect Hjelmslev, among others, they must be self-consistent, or free of internal contradiction; they must be consistent with the novels in question; and they must be as simple as possible.[8] For obvious reasons, the most important of these criteria is faithfulness to the text. And, as Kermode says, "[T]he text to interpret is the one the author would have recognized as his own."[9] While the analysis needs include only those elements that cannot be easily subsumed to other components, and thus strive for simplicity, it must incorporate enough material to make the next step of abstraction possible. To say, for example, that *Madame Bovary* is a work about a woman who overdosed on Romantic novels may be true, but it is not adequate, for it leaves out far too many relationships.

The resultant interpretation must also give the material for worthwhile generalizations that are consistent with each other. An analysis of such a novel as Huysmans's *En rade* (1887) should make it clear that the fictional events import only to the degree that they reveal the changes taking place in the hero. The plot then concerns the psychological reality of the main character, not what he sees. If the analysis clearly makes this point, comparison with a recent novel like Robbe-Grillet's *La Jalousie* (1957) becomes a simple matter. There, also, the external reality functions to present the narrator's obsessions.

Adequate interpretation requires close attention to those elements that are repeated, since, as Valéry said, "*Form* is essentially tied to repetition."[10] It is by repetition that the novelist indicates which aspects of his work signify, which elements should then predominate in the critic's analysis. In short, the reading should highlight those features which distinguish one text from another, while permitting the assignment of abstract or classifying characterizations to each.

Ideally, such classifications would be inclusive, that is, they would cover all novels, past, present, and future. I have no such pretentions for the system of classification I shall propose in the following pages. Pragmatically speaking, prediction of future developments in art seems an unrealizable dream, and I consequently stress only the endomorphic novel (from the Greek *endón* or "within" and *morphé* or "form"), the vertebrate novel whose structure is internal. Still, there are signs on the horizon of another variety. I shall discuss it in regard to Proust's *A la recherche du temps perdu* and other novels in the last two chapters.

Nor is the classification I offer the only one available, though the drawbacks of other, current systems may indicate certain advantages for what I propose. Perhaps most important, they do not stress what seems to be a major area of current innovations: structure. While many recent novelists have turned their backs on characters that resemble human beings, for instance, we continue to discuss "character novels." Terminology which does not help readers see the most important features of present-day literature fails significantly to be as helpful as desirable.

The need for a more useful set of terms and concepts has encouraged several important critics to approach structure from the standpoint of function. Burke proposed "that a poem's structure is to be described most accurately by thinking always of the poem's function. [We then assume] that the poem is designed to 'do something' for the poet and his readers, and that we can make the most relevant observations about its design by considering the poem as the embodiment of this act."[11] Unfortunately, function— whether what Burke terms the subject, or tragic, comic, satiric modes, or whatever—does not direct attention toward the salient efforts of recent writers. It does, however, have the virtue of consistency, that is, in application, it does not mix apples and garlic, the practice of too many classificatory systems in the arts.

It is very common to find the same critic, in the same study, indeed, in the same sentence, categorize novels by referring to radically different constituent parts or approaches: "Ideological, psychological, and realistic novels predominated between the two wars," one might find, for example. There is nothing wrong with categorizing according to manner (ironic, satiric, precious, scatological), subject (Jewish, philosophical, gothic, mystery), goal (ideological, feminist, socialist, didactic), major device (epistolary, picaresque, allegorical, character) or other characterization (third person, autobiographical). Any of these classes can be helpful when applied consistently. My major reservations have to do with the lack of interest in structure and in the seemingly endless classifications. While it may be useful to refer to adventure, detective, rustic, erotic, pastoral, scientific, popular, populist novels of romance, ideas, manners, or action, one begins to doubt the usefulness of a taxonomy which could develop a distinct term for many if not most individual novels. Systems of classification must be capable of grouping constituent elements conveniently, while current practice bears an uncomfortable resemblance to those languages which have separate ideograms for each thing or concept.

At the same time, of course, one must beware of confusing the classification with the reality of the novel. The term used for a class is at best an appropriate analogy. Recent criticism, so preoccupied with the theories and methods of other disciplines, provides numerous examples of systems which, though applied with undoubted good will and the best of intentions, distort the text they were meant to illuminate. Any time one deals with one object in terms of another the risk of deformation exists. Jean Starobinski even wonders "whether the phenomena that psychoanalysis talks about are not *constituted* by the very manner with which it elaborates its own discourse."[12] The only protection against distortion is to consider the work in its own nature and to refuse to refer it to some other art or discipline. This, as much as humanly possible, is the practice of the following pages.

One more stricture, and I have done with caveats. As I have read recent critical theory, I have frequently wondered at its distance from the actual novels, poems, plays, which seem to me the stuff of criticism. While not everyone will consider this a flaw, I view my task as more directly related to literature. To assure that it remains so, I have tried to draw all my theory from specific literary texts.

With these thoughts in mind, I am free to begin developing a way of viewing the "normal," "classical," "traditional," or "former" novel. This is the concern of the next three chapters. No one would deny that recent novelists have been busily innovating. The problem is to understand exactly what those innovations are. I believe the most important literary contribution of the last century concerns structure and structuring, but, in order to make this claim, I must outline a new optic for viewing the way novels are ordinarily put together. Looked at from the point of view of structure, what seems basic has to do with the internal configuration of most novels. The inner nature is indeed such a fundamental fact of fictional pattern that we usually take it for granted. Perhaps only when artists begin to subvert what tradition views as foundational do we recognize how important those foundations have been to us. Of course, fiction has no rafters, no load bearing walls. With all due respect to Proust, who compared his masterpiece to a cathedral, novels are not buildings. But there is a certain similarity, since, in the place of ridges and capstones, joists and buttresses, fiction has plot, character, action, theme, setting, image, rhythm. Most novelistic works take one or more of these devices and use them as the central framework around which the fiction is organized. Most are structured internally. And these, then, are the works I call endomorphic, for, as previously mentioned, the term "endomorphic" suggests "inner form." The word thus serves to group all novels, new and old, which have some sort of internal backbone or frame to give shape to the creation.

As my first specimen, I choose Stendhal's *La Chartreuse de Parme* (1839). It provides an almost perfect example of the most common of endomorphic structures, what some critics have called "vertebrate" (because such novels are formed around sequential plots or sequences that constitute their spines). I prefer to call works of this variety "process novels." While most such fictions are centered on an action, the term will admit to its category any novel which uses a sequence of whatever type—whether plot or no—as its principal organizing device. In addition to indicating the way the novelist laid out the work, the term "process" suggests how a reader must appreciate it. If he attempts to arrest the movement, the development, the sequential nature of the work in any way, he has seriously distorted the creation and taken it for something it is not. In short, he has refused the conventions accepted by the author and, implicitly, by the work. While nothing says that readers are obliged to accept an author's rules, those of good will, it seems to me, do so.

La Chartreuse has long been criticized for its imperfect conclusion. I disagree, but in discussing the problem, and explaining why my opinion differs, I am able to take a brief foray into the problematics of "closure" and "overture." Closure, or the way novels communicate a sense of completion, is especially important to me and to my efforts because it provides the backdrop against which to consider those novels which seem to open up at the end, rather than to reach a definite conclusion. I take the term "overture" from Umberto Eco, though he is not alone in his usage. It is particularly useful in that it does not just indicate continuation of the fictional events, it suggests that the work is in itself, and as a whole, an initial movement in a much larger symphony. Usually, such creations provide stimulation for a reader's creativity. When successful, they cause him to imagine the themes, events, or characters spinning webs in future worlds.

La Chartreuse de Parme, and, in the succeeding chapter 3, Balzac's Gobseck (1830-35) provide meat for this discussion. The latter work also illustrates fiction which, in opposition to sequential, "process novels," does not need to be conceived through time. Though internally structured, or endomorphic, it is not sequential, at least not in the way it is configured as a whole. It does have plots, but such action does not constitute the primary means of its organization. Unlike La Chartreuse de Parme and other process novels, then, it need not be appreciated as a series or development through time. Its action is arrested and subordinated. Rather than narration, the quality one normally expects to prevail in fiction, the work is predominantly description. In short, Gobseck (and many other Balzacian novels) presents the reader with an image of society. Once the reading is completed, the reader may—and I think should— conceive it instantaneously as an image. I consequently label it and other similar examples "image novels." In contrast to novels of action, where plot reigns supreme, one might say it is a novel of inaction.

In a sense, the terms "process" and "image" are arbitrary. I could have developed or adopted terminology from the concepts of narration, plot, or metonymy, on the one hand, and description or metaphor, on the other. The advantage of "process" and "image" consists in their appropriateness at the several levels of creation, whether the text or the reader's re-creation. Just as "process" can refer to the development taking place in the work of art and "image" the evocative, textual sign, so both terms are properly used to refer to mental phenomena. "Process" may be used for the particular, systematic changes taking place in the human mind during cognition, while "image" may be the sensorial, emotional, or intellectual complex represented in the mind. Such complexes may be conceived in an instant of time. In short, "process" and "image" may indicate either the aesthetic object or the reader's own representation.

Zola's *Germinal* (1885) provides an opportunity to test the vocabulary developed in the preceding chapters. It is a rather complex kind of process novel, which, in addition, exemplifies a variety of openness that differs from that found in *Gobseck*. The central armature consists of a series of allusions to certain Greek myths and to the story of the New Testament Church, ending with the kind of prophetic utterance typical of Old Testament prophets. Zola seems to be saying that mankind will either change his ways or civilization as we know it will end in a blazing holocaust. Consideration of *Germinal* leads to a discussion of the variations possible in image and process novels. This fourth chapter concludes my attempt to circumscribe the "traditional" novel. I could go on at more length and cite many more examples, but I think the essential outlines of the "normal" work of fiction are clear.

Whenever a prevailing aesthetic model becomes so obvious as to be easily grasped, it is only a matter of time—and a short time at that—until artists mass against it. By the end of the nineteenth century, the revolts against the novel were many and varied. *A rebours* of 1884 might be picked as the opening salvo of a fictional revolution which took the reader to the far edge of what was acceptable, but such points are always subject to considerable discussion. Flaubert's dialogue novel, *La Tentation de saint Antoine* precedes it by ten years, and it was far from alone. What can, however, be said is that the fifty years or so at the turn of the century were marked by raging attacks and counterattacks, manifestos and declamations, and occasionally bizarre attempts to go beyond what was apparently perceived as an aesthetic dead end. Huysmans and Flaubert were but parts of a rather large movement. The Symbolists struggled to create a new, more evocative language; Galdós, Mark Twain, and others strove with varying degrees of seriousness to confront reality with the ideal and, thus, rise above both to some higher plane; Mirbeau pushed bad taste in subject matter to levels that had not been approached since Sade's insane *Les Cent-Vingt Journées de Sodome* (ca. 1785); Zola took early insights of crowd psychology and created fictional mobs which take on a personality and individuality of their own. More and more artists attack the limits of the novel and other art forms.

Few writers can match André Gide's awareness of this aesthetic controversy and of the history, state, and potential of the novel as it was then constituted. W. Wolfgang Holdheim demonstrates, in his excellent *Theory and Practice of the Novel: A Study on André Gide* (Geneva: Droz, 1968), that Gide clearly understood the degree to which his works implicitly comment on the novel. He subjected language, imagery, and structure to extraordinary pressure, both by forcing them to bear unusually heavy significance and by putting them into seemingly irreconcilable oppositions. His *L'Immoraliste* of 1902 provides an excellent example of the revolt against the established canons of fictional practice. It seems to show that Gide was conscious of the patterns I have outlined in preceding chapters and of the fact that something new was needed. Perhaps that is why he set process structure in direct opposition to image structure, action against inaction. Certainly, it indicates an admirable comprehension of the status quo and a desire to subvert common practice. That in itself is enough to make Gide a precursor of the New Novel. I think, however, that this was the limit of Gide's contribution. He was extraordinarily perceptive; he was an outstanding technician; he created a number of marvelous masterpieces; and his artistic prowess combined readily with clear-headed awareness to produce an unerring satirical eye which seldom missed its mark. Still, unlike Huysmans, who was a great innovator, he was a magnificent revolutionary, skilled at tearing down, though somewhat wanting in his ability to create novel forms on the rubble of the old. Shaping a new world is not always as easy as taking part in a successful revolt.

Mallarmé's influence on Gide was, I think, limited to improving his critical abilities. The result of Huysmans's attendance at Mallarmé's Tuesday gatherings on rue de Rome was deeper. Few would deny that Mallarmé hoped to do more than give a breath of fresh air to French poetry; he wanted to remake it. I have often wondered whether it was his inspiration that encouraged Huysmans to conduct his radical experiments with the novel. As said before, Huysmans was not the only innovator, he was but a part of a much larger movement. Nonetheless, for the present purposes, Huysmans provides an extremely important case. His departures from established practice were by no means limited to peripheral technique. His was a more basic temptation. It is almost as though he asked himself how far he could push the genre and still have a novel. In *En rade* (1887), which, though not his best known, is his most successful work, he provides the reader with a negative representation. This particular

approach has had profound repercussions. Especially since the
1950s, this variety of structure has been responsible for some of the
more startling effects. While most fiction gives us the positive
image, encouraging the reader to imagine events much as he might
see them on watching the people and activities of his world, *En rade*
proposes the negative. Readers must hold it up to the light, so to
speak, in order to project the negative and produce positive
representation. As is fairly common in works subsequent to 1950,
we are presented with a number of seemingly objective episodes
which make sense only when we understand that the author means
us to see them as indications of a character's state of mind. It uses an
external or objective reality to present the protagonist's psychological
state as the true center of interest. Only when the reader recognizes
that the "hero" alone holds the keys to all the disparate elements will
the text be unlocked and unified. *En rade* breaks with the past, and it
suggests the shape of fiction to come.

Proust's *A la recherche du temps perdu* (1913-27), the example
from which chapter 7 is drawn, constitutes a bigger work, for it
represents a *summum genus* of any number of nineteenth-century
currents and, as well, a work of breathtaking originality that not only
indicates but to a large degree forms the novel of the future. It serves
admirably to summarize the conclusions of previous chapters.
Critics have been quite right to see in it a particularly fine endomorphic
novel. I shall discuss the concepts of process, image, open, closed,
and negative structure, all in terms of the endomorphic novel, as
they are exemplified in *A la recherche*. There is, however, something
more radical taking place in Proust's masterpiece. Numerous critics
have mentioned the bothersome breaks in the novel's narrative
sequence. The temporal and causal gaps are particularly difficult to
understand, given the author's magnificently demonstrated skill. I
suggest that in contravening the normal conventions for chronological and causal motivation, Proust is forcing readers to seek other
organizational rules. I believe he has created a "paramorphic novel."
The term comes from mineralogy and refers to a structure created by
changing the physical characteristics without changing the chemical
composition. *A la recherche* is paramorphic to the degree that the
reader is encouraged to choose—consciously or unconsciously—
one of many possible systems laid out in the novel, any one of which
is capable of producing order and giving structure to the book.
Whether the reader seizes on the plot, on one or more characters or
objects, or on one of the many interweaving patterns of imagery

makes no significant difference to the novel's unity. The result will differ, but in unimportant ways.

The last half-century has produced legions of paramorphic works, particularly in the fine arts. Calder's mobiles perhaps come first to mind. In the final chapter, I shall refer to several modern novels which exploit the more significant patterns I have attempted to uncover in earlier chapters. There is no question that novelists continue to produce endomorphic fiction. Some of this work is very fine. But I wish to concentrate on the negative and paramorphic structures which make some modern works seem outrageous. *La Jalousie*'s negative representation is easily compared to *En rade*, and today's readers find few difficulties in understanding it. More problematic are those creations which seemingly allow readers unlimited freedom in the ways they organize the fictional text they read. In fact, as with *A la recherche* and Calder's creations, the apparent freedom is illusory. Each of the systems available to the reader or spectator is rigidly controlled and rigorously limited. Saporta's *Composition No. 1* (1962) offers an example of image structure in the paramorphic novel. It is unfortunately not a perfect example, but it is the best I have been able to discover. Process structures of the paramorphic variety occur in more abundance. I discuss both Julio Cortázar's *Rayuela* (*Hopscotch*—1963) and Jean Ricardou's *La Prise/Prose de Constantinople* (1965) as varying examples of seriality. Such instances serve both to suggest one direction the novel seems to have chosen and to summarize and thus conclude this volume. First, however, I must draw the broad, general outline of the endomorphic novel. It provides me with a conceptual background against which discussion of the paramorphic novel gains relief. As always, before arguing that something is changing, we have to establish what it is that is being changed.

## Chapter 2
## Process Structure in *La Chartreuse de Parme*

MUCH HAS BEEN MADE OF THE FEATURES distinguishing recent, French fiction from that of the nineteenth century. Stress on the differences occasionally leads New Novelists and their adherents to unjust condemnation of former masters and unjustifiable self-evaluation. While admitting that artistic excellence lies in the coherence of texts and in the ability to sustain vital relationships with readers,[1] the New Novelists' attacks on previous novels tend to center on aesthetic conventions and on the indisputable fact that, after all, times have changed. Does it really follow that "the character novel belongs entirely to the past, it characterizes an epoch: the one which marked the apex of the individual"?[2] Has nineteenth-century fiction been reduced to a "dead system" (ibid., p. 37) based on a "dead idea" (ibid., p. 29)? If it now provides nothing but sociological, psychological, theological testimony, nothing but historical monuments, it is indeed of little aesthetic interest. Robbe-Grillet, who clearly does not agree with Leo Spitzer that "the best document of the soul of a nation is its literature,"[3] would even deny it this small grace: "The person who is interested in these disciplines should read essays, it's safer."[4]

One gathers from what New Novelists say that the enlightened reader of today has no choice but to find the corpus of earlier prose fiction desiccated, dead, devoid of rejuvenating artistic waters. Robert Pinget is unequivocal: "For a French person of today, Balzac's novel [by which he means the nineteenth-century novel] is a form of art that is fitting for a period that believed in its perenniality and in particular in that of its scientific discoveries. This profession of faith can no longer be ours since we are discovering that everything has to be thought through again from new bases. I cannot risk myself in this domain—I am not a scientist. I simply wanted to focus my defiance of the traditional novel, which I admire as a witness of its day more than any other but which I reject as a model. Once again, to reveal the period when it appears, to be as it were the least contestable monument of its epoch is appropriate for art."[5] Certainly, if nineteenth-century literature no longer has value except as evidence of extraliterary realities, then Jean Alter is quite right to conclude, "The nineteenth [century] was a period when novelistic invention was impoverished, almost murdered."[6]

There are a number of possible responses to such claims. One could, for example, note with John Sturrock that the New Novelists' number includes many "alert publicists"[7] and dismiss their pronouncements as, at best, a demand for freedom to depart from the models of their ancestors. I believe this would be a mistake. No one can read the more adventuresome novels of the past quarter century without realizing that New Novelists have contributed extraordinarily interesting effects by their vision of the novel. It seems to me that a reconsideration of earlier fiction in the light of recent innovations results in a richer understanding of the past and, indeed, of the present. Though our ideas about the nature of action, character, description, and realism have changed considerably, one widely accepted touchstone of literary worth turns on whether or not the work can continue to sustain the "modern" readings of subsequent ages. Such an approach depends, not on stressing the differences— which has led to the regrettable condemnation of the past—rather on emphasizing those traits common to present and past art. Can "traditional" masterpieces like *La Chartreuse de Parme* satisfy us, in the light of what we have learned (or what currently interests us) about art and reading?

While developing effective ways of using phonic, morphological, and syntactical patterns to form structure, the New Novel has perhaps most notably led a concerted attack on worn-out conceptions of plot and character. It is not true that they have expunged the devices of "realistic" action, character, descriptive skill, and unambiguous narrations from their works, but they have come to view these conventions in different ways.

In the past, the conception of plot included the idea of a character doing something. One is then encouraged to ask, "What happens next?" (or "What happened before?") or, on a causal plane, "Why did it come about?" (or "What were the results?"). Both questions insist on the intimate relationship of the various events and on their distinction, but more importantly both stress the sequential change which plot requires. There are doubtless other questions readers might ask. Mukarovsky wonders "whether that which the speaker is saying actually happened, whether the details of those events were such as he describes"?[8] Such queries take us from the event-centered realm of plot, however, in this case to character (narrator's reliability) or, perhaps, to the problem of fictional truth.

Nonetheless, New Novelists have understood that there are principles other than causation or chronology that can and have ordered fictional events. They then view plot as the "dynamic, sequential element"[9] and use any number of elements to order the sequence. Allusion is a common, governing principle. When Camus implies that Meursault of *L'Etranger* (1942) represents a new Christ, we expect an execution before hate-filled bystanders, to cite but one example. Other sequences are equally possible. Michel Butor has experimented with the alphabet in *Mobile* (1962) and with numeration in *6 810 000 litres d'eau par seconde* (1966) (as has Philippe Sollers in his problematic *Nombres*, dating from 1968). One might also think of the potential of such natural orders as colors in the spectrum, degrees of stellar luminosity, or crystalline structures, though I know of no works of literature which have actually exploited them. Thomas Pynchon, however, uses "entropy" to good effect in *The Crying of Lot 49* (1966). Culturally, numerous systems have been used to order sequences. I think, for example, of Ovid's ages of man, the classical four elements, the Way of the Cross, the alchemical path to *aurum philosophicum*, various stages on the road to perfection as taught by certain eastern religions, and so on. Each of these systems could constitute a plot. (It is also worth mentioning that very few of them would require a character resembling a human being.) In short, in many recent novels, plot is the sequence or vector—a word that has the advantage of indicating both quantity and direction—of events. Its organizing principle may be chronology or causality, but it may be some other fundamental truth or conception.

One could easily make a great deal of the changes which have expanded plot to include sequences which have nothing to do with either time or cause. The difference is important. Still, I am not certain it would be appropriate to make too much of the innovation, for I do not believe it has altered either fiction's essence or the way it must be appreciated. I consequently group all novels that gain their organization from sequences or vectors, of whatever variety, in the category of "process novels."

One expects fictional texts to be constructed on some sort of an internal armature. If this structure were always a sequence or process, we could follow the lead of numerous critics and refer to such internally organized works as "vertebrate" and pass on. Unfortunately, not all fiction relies on process for its order. As the modern novel has demonstrated with some frequency, and as I shall point out in relation to Balzac's *Gobseck* in the next chapter, much fiction is organized around a static pattern or image. While I would distinguish such "image novels" from sequential varieties, it is worth noting that both are internally rather than externally shaped. Both are, then, *endo*-(within) *morphic* (form), a term which can subsume process and image novels and, in addition, prepare a helpful opposition to a new kind of structure that seems to be occurring more often in recent years.

Still, there is no question that most'novels depend upon action for their primary structuring element. This can perhaps be explained by the fact that readers must experience novels as process, at least on the first reading. Some might even say that the nature of novels is to be seriate. Perhaps that is why most—though not all—novelists exploit time, causal factors, or some other sequence. They then choose not to fly in the face of experiential reality but rather to bend to it, fashion it, and thus draw effects from enticing the reader towards an end he can at best vaguely perceive.

Stendhal's *La Chartreuse de Parme* (1839) provides an example of a "process novel" formed around a central plot. In addition, it opens perspectives on novelistic closure. Despite the praise surrounding it—praise which makes even Balzac seem restrained when he called it "the masterpiece of literature of ideas" or, elsewhere, "the most beautiful book which has been published in the last fifty years"[10]— a significant minority of critics and scholars view the novel with much less favor. They direct withering criticism toward *La Chartreuse*'s structure and conclusion. One recent writer, struck by what seems to him an arbitrary, ill-prepared ending, wonders rhetorically whether it is "a thrown-together novel?"[11] On reflection even such a strong supporter as Balzac viewed the last portion of the novel with reservation. Indeed, after surveying the secondary literature, one may observe that the way *La Chartreuse de Parme* concludes has generated a few unconvincing apologies and no enthusiasts.

No one doubts, of course, that *La Chartreuse de Parme* has a conclusion. The point of contention resides in whether or not the closure is well prepared and, thus, acceptable. I shall suggest that Stendhal thoroughly prepared it by means of such traditional narrative patterns as birth/death and by exploiting pietistic (sinner/ saint) and allusive (Petrarchan) models. I start, however, with the attempt to demonstrate that Stendhal's masterpiece is highly structured, for the preparation of closure is a function of structure.

Those who hold that *La Chartreuse* is a tightly constructed whole can scarcely be encouraged by what Stendhal revealed about his manner of composition. He insisted on his artlessness: "I had never thought about the *art* of making a novel. . . . When I lay things out ahead of time, I freeze. I compose 20 or 30 pages, then I need to be distracted; a little love when I can or a little drunken feasting; the next day I have forgotten everything. On reading the 3 or 4 last pages of the preceding day's chapter, the day's chapter comes to me."[12] Whatever dismay such comments have created in some, critics continue to seek the device or vehicle responsible for the order they sense in *La Chartreuse de Parme*. They may focus on one or more characters as technical means for narrative linking, on the ironic mode of the narration, on the setting, or on visual imagery, though perhaps most have been drawn to themes and thematic structure.[13]

F. W. J. Hemmings points, however, to the inadequacy of thematic rubrics like "Fear of the Counter-Revolution," "Eroticism and Machiavellianism," "Passion and Intelligence," or "Gaity Blended with Danger," in any attempt to categorize the novel. Believing that contrast and equilibrium are responsible for the artistic unity of *La Chartreuse,* he suggests that the novel should be seen as two conflicting tonalities, the first "lit by gaity, good humor, health and joy. The second plunges across deceptions, disillusionment, heart-break, and disappears in the shadow of the cloister and the darkness of the grave."[14] The problem with this notion becomes apparent on noting that Fabrice unequivocally preferred the supposedly unhappy portion of his life.

Nonetheless, Hemmings's view has the great virtue of insisting on the importance of Fabrice as the central organizing element in the changes that take place as the novel progresses. On reflection, those who believe that *La Chartreuse de Parme* concerns primarily the social backdrop, or la Sanseverina, or anything other than the hero, can scarcely fail to feel a certain dissatisfaction with the novel. As Stendhal gently queried, "Aren't I writing the life of Fabrice?"[15]

I want to take this rhetorical question in all seriousness, for, indeed, all the parts of the novel are subordinated to and highlight one interest alone—Fabrice and the pattern of his life. All the events and descriptions turn around Fabrice as we follow the narrative sequence of his progression from birth to death. Everything is oriented toward a conclusion. Fabrice, who begins by "giving and receiving numerous beatings,"[16] ends by joining the Carthusians. He becomes a contemplative devoted to achieving mystical union with a being outside himself. The pattern of the Carthusian's life serves very well, I shall suggest, as an image of the whole of Fabrice's life.

Still, readers are unquestionably drawn first of all to Fabrice's development as he engages in his various adventures. It is this side of the novel which recalls, as Georges Blin pointed out, a "chronicle, but tied together and centered better because of the concurrent use of another technique: sustained biography of the protagonist treated like a psychological monograph" (*Stendhal*, p. 62). In the early pages of our acquaintance with the protagonist, he combines many of the virtues, and a considerable number of the vices, of youth: "strange, amusing, very serious, but a handsome boy, and not too out of place in the salon of a fashionable woman, otherwise as ignorant as one could be" (p. 13). Add to this Fabrice's courage, enthusiasm, and naïveté (p. 17), and you have a thoroughly engaging creation. It was of course his naïveté which provided Stendhal with most of the occasions for his benevolent but ironic humor. The reality of Fabrice's life seldom quite measures up to what he wanted to be and do. "Is this a real battle?" he asks anxiously at Waterloo (p. 44). Finally, he is unable to avoid the hard truth that has brought many a boy to manhood: "So war was no longer this noble and shared élan of souls loving glory that he had imagined from Napoleon's proclamations!" (p. 49).

Given the widespread agreement on the importance of Fabrice, it is surprising that there has been so little recognition of the changes occurring in the hero himself. Many, for example, consider the portrayal of Fabrice at Waterloo one of the great moments of Western literature, but attention has focused on the realistic description to the virtual exclusion of the episode's function within *La Chartreuse*, that is, of the young hero's maturation. The changes in Fabrice are significant. After Waterloo, "The quantity of blood that he had lost had delivered him of the romantic side to his character" (p. 69). "Fabrice," the narrator says, "was as though another man. . . . He only remained a child on the following point: was what he had seen a battle, and secondly, was this battle Waterloo?" (p. 72). But it is his brother's betrayal that really affects him. As its most direct result, "He picked a fight . . . with a young man who was looking at him, he said, in a strange way. . . . In this moment of passion, Fabrice . . . once again became a creature of instinct, or, better, became the child of his memories" (p. 74). From this point on, we never again see him looking to someone else for an explanation of what he is. He becomes singularly self-contained.

The only striking break of his egotistical self-sufficiency and vanity comes during an hour in Bologna's San Petronio Cathedral. " 'How ungrateful I am,' he said suddenly, 'I go into a church to sit down, the way I go into a café! . . . Oh my God! I have so many things to thank you for. . . . My pride made me want to believe that it was my own human prudence that enabled me to escape the Spielberg prison' " (pp. 194-95). Fabrice's ingratitude is also sufficiently ample to include the human benefactors on whom he depends absolutely.

He makes almost no decisions regarding his present or his future; rather he follows the instructions of his adored and adoring Aunt Gina and her lover, Mosca. He is, however, strangely oblivious to the enormous debt he owes them. Apparently, he considers their devotion his due. Certainly, with rare exceptions (e.g., pp. 208-09), it escapes his notice for many years.

During this period prior to his first stay in the Farnese Tower, Fabrice has reverted to a second childhood, and Stendhal insists on his "childishness" (p. 210) and excessive vanity (pp. 206, 210, 215), Though basically well-meaning—"He thought it was loathsome to cause anyone at all, however unimportant he might be, to be unhappy" (p. 206), and he refuses to exercise his "right" to kill the young valet while stealing his horse (pp. 162-63)—his concern for others stops short of his mistresses. Both the narrator and Mosca agree that Fabrice is the kind of young man who loves his mistress less than his horse (pp. 87, 112), while Fabrice himself admits, "There is no doubt that I love, the way I have a good appetite at six o'clock!" (p. 208). The little Marietta's *mammacia* was quite right to be wary of Fabrice's reliability. When he sees Fausta F***, Marietta disappears from his life and from the novel without a trace.

Who knows where it would have ended had he been allowed to continue his egotistical frivolousness? The novelist-god is looking out for him, however, for Fabrice is literally caught up and constrained to enter the Farnese Tower, a concretization of what Petrarch called "la pregione ove Amor m'ebbe." Fabrice scarcely notices the prison; he can only think of Clélia's eyes. "Not once did he think, distinctly at least, of the big change that had taken place in his *sort*" (p. 253; my italics). On considering that *sort* can mean either "lot" or "fate," it is perhaps worth mentioning that, while his "lot" has changed, his "fate" has not. He is finally on the way to fulfilling his destiny.

Prison has enormous importance for the development of Fabrice. The narrator rather coyly predicts as much when he says, "[F]or the moment, we are obliged to leave Fabrice in his prison, up at the top of Parma's citadel; they are guarding him well, and we will find him again, perhaps somewhat changed" (p. 262). Prison itself seems to be responsible for some of the transformation. As Victor Brombert has recognized, "The most important function of the Stendhalian prison is that it restores his heroes to their own selves— or rather that it allows them to discover the self, and even to create it."[17] H. W. Wardman points out that Fabrice "is fitted only for the contemplative life."[18] Prison finally forces him to become the contemplative he is destined to be from the beginning.

Clélia is of course even more important in effecting the hero's conversion. The author went to considerable trouble to illuminate the degree to which the two lovers are made for each other. Stephen Gilman has indicated how Stendhal used even the smallest detail. The Governor's quarters, for example, which rise from the roof of the Citadel opposite Fabrice's cell, are always referred to as "pretty" and "little." They thus become the feminine counterpart of the masculine Farnese Tower. The image is later completed when Clélia uses her songs to warn Fabrice: She herself is a caged bird.[19] So we have two birds in neighboring cages.

The shape of the Farnese Tower itself has great significance. Gilman perceives it as a giant's body, whose head rises from its shoulders. The peep-holes which Fabrice cut in the wooden shutter become its eyes, while the resonant box designed to amplify sound, in which he is confined, serves as its ears (*Tower*, p. 53). The prison-body's "walls of flesh . . . condemn the soul to solitary confinement" (ibid.). This insight should be combined with Gilbert Chaitin's conviction that Fabrice's cell rather resembles a uterus, and others point with him to the important image of rebirth.[20] Chaitin correctly concludes that Stendhal could not have been unaware that the length of the hero's stay in the tower has considerable significance, for the author mentions the "nine months" of the incarceration on four different occasions.[21] I shall resist the temptation of proposing that Gina and Clélia function as midwives. There can however be no doubt that Stendhal meant to suggest a complete renewal by means of the nine-month gestation period. The narrator says so very plainly and repeatedly: "He was another man," he insists (p. 299); "Fabrice was entirely changed" (p. 373). Fabrice now agrees: "How different I am . . . from the frivolous, dissolute Fabrice who came in here nine months ago!" (p. 366).

The transformation goes deeper than the "anchorite's face" he sports (p. 444). The first indication of the new Fabrice occurs when he decides not to escape from prison. For the first time, he refuses to do his aunt Gina's will. "I see that I am about to give the duchess a serious reason for being discontented" (p. 325). Once out of prison and on the road to worldly, if ecclesiastical, success, he is completely uninterested in "all these honors, and much more unhappy in this magnificent apartment, with ten footmen bearing his livery, than he had been in his wooden room in the Farnese tower" (p. 435). After having chased Clélia from her garden and pursued her into a solitary street, Fabrice even shows his awareness of his beloved's feelings (p.

463). And he eventually recognizes all that he owes to his aunt and Mosca (pp. 456, 459).

Despite the two distinct parts of the book—the first presenting a free and the second an imprisoned Fabrice—the hero's character as it develops across the whole novel remains of the utmost significance. Hans Boll Johansen's insight into the women in Fabrice's life supports this view: "At the beginning of the novel, the women that he meets act maternally towards him: so it is with the beautiful jailer, the woman canteen-keeper . . . and the good mistress of the Etrille inn. . . . After Waterloo, the women who appear in Fabrice's life are sweethearts. At first, for Fabrice, it's a question of physical love, and then love that gratifies his vanity (with Fausta) . . . . The second part of the novel describes the passionate love that binds Fabrice and Clélia."[22] Fabrice moves, in short, from a self-centered or childlike to a progressively selfless love. Given his sincere piety, his withdrawal into a Charterhouse is perhaps to be expected. One might even note that Fabrice's development follows the traditional path from the love of his lady to a love of God. I shall return to this notion.

The pattern of Fabrice's existence is not completely clear until the novel's conclusion, however, and, as already indicated, the conclusion constitutes a serious problem. It is customary to bemoan the way *La Chartreuse de Parme* draws to a close. An implied curse on the remains of Stendhal's publisher is even *de mise,* if not *de rigueur.* The latter's greed was supposedly responsible for the telegraphic account of Sandrino's and Clélia's deaths and Fabrice's retreat to the Charterhouse of Parma. Henri Martineau states, for example, "One thing is certain, Dupont's greed was responsible for an epilogue which, we must admit, is to elliptical. Stendhal, fatigued by the creation of his book . . . did not dare resist his publisher. He awkwardly condensed the last pages of his novel. Later he would regret it."[23]

The evidence for this position is surprisingly scanty. In fact, we know very little about the few dozen lines which conclude the text as it now stands. We have no manuscripts whatsoever of the book. Though two of the three interleaved copies which Stendhal prepared for his revisions are now lost, none, apparently, did any more than demonstrate that he planned, for a while at least, to considerably expand the last 100 to 150 pages (chapters 23 through 28). Facing the last page of the novel in the Chaper edition, Stendhal wrote: "Read this volume by chance the evenings of November 10-17 [18]39. . . . Many words to be changed especially in the last hundred

pages [that is, from near the beginning of chapter 25 to the end]. Add
some bits of description. Make 3 volumes." He continues on the next
page, "all the more so since this was *hacked off* after about 300 [p. 300
is very near the end of ch. 23]. The bookseller Dupont thought the
volume enormous. 9<sup>b</sup> [er] 17, 1839." Then, on the recto side of the
next interleaf, he wrote, "Make 3 volumes by developing the ending
that M. Dupont strangled, then dividing the ms. into 3 equal
portions. Add some descriptions of the countryside. . . . July 27,
1840." Judging from the comments he scribbled elsewhere, his
major attention was directed toward passages describing Clélia's
and Fabrice's psychological states during periods of stress. Indeed,
Stendhal's most extensive rewriting for the second volume occurs
from approximately pp. 363 to 375 of the Chaper edition, covering
the period between Fabrice's release from prison to Clélia's marriage.[24]
The only indication that he would have changed any portion of the
telegraphic last few paragraphs occurs in the first draft of his bread and
butter letter to Balzac: "I wrote *la Chart[reuse]* with Sandrino's death in
mind, a fact which really touched me. . . . M. Dupont took the space to
paint it away from me."[25] There is no indication whatsoever that he
would have changed Fabrice's retreat and death. Indeed, the very
multiplication of deaths in a limited period of time is one of the more
"classic" means of inducing closure.

Presages, prophecies, and references to fate emphasize the
significance of what is to come. Like the vast majority of literary
dreams prior to Huysmans, the omens serve to suggest that there is
indeed some order to the rambling life of the hero. As Stephen
Gilman writes in an important excursus, "Fabrice's future is not self-
made through intellection, composition, or adaptation. Rather it is
discovered out there waiting for him. His is a path already determined,
a portion of which the novelist-god (for reasons of his own) decides
to reveal to him."[26] The supernatural hints of Fabrice's future also
whet the reader's desire to satisfy his curiosity by reading further.
The view of a Napoleonic eagle and budding leaves on his special
tree, planted by his mother during the winter of his birth, send him
off to Waterloo and provide rare examples of favorable omens. Most
are fearsome. He escapes from the prison of B . . . with the papers and
clothing of a Hussar who died behind bars. "Watch out for prison!. . .
The presage is clear, I will suffer a great deal from prison!" (p. 33).
This particular adumbration seems especially important in preparing
Father Blanès's prophecy: "Your soul may prepare itself for a much
more difficult prison, much more terrible! Probably you will get out
only by means of a crime, but, thanks be to God, you will not commit

this crime. . . . You will die like me, my son, seated on a wooden bench, far from luxury, undeceived by luxury, and like me not having to reproach yourself for anything serious" (p. 152). Fabrice has no respect for prophecy, but, on consideration, "Blanès's predictions . . . took on for him all the importance of veritable presages" (p. 169). And the reader is promised a happy ending, while being tantalized by an unclear oracle.

For novelistic purposes, the best omens lack clarity, though they draw the reader on into the adventure. They must also be appropriate to the character and situation. In this respect, no one could complain about either Father Blanès's predictions or Fabrice's acceptance of them as gospel. The astrologer-priest is carefully prepared, as is Fabrice's superstitious susceptibility to the occult. The final test of a good literary omen turns on whether it seems precisely accurate after the fact. Much if not most prophecy makes sense only after it has been fulfilled, but all elements of the prophetic utterance must be completely revealed or utilized in subsequent events.[27] That is the case with the predictions by Fabrice's priestly foster-father: "No matter how violently you may be tempted, never commit a crime; I think I see that it will be a question of killing an innocent, who, without realizing it, usurps your rights; if you resist the violent temptation which will seem to be justified by the laws of honor, your life will be very happy in the eyes of men. . . , and reasonably happy in the eyes of the wise" (p. 152). Fabrice is severely tempted very soon after being warned, but he resists and leaves the valet both twenty francs and his life, though without a horse. Likewise, he is not involved in the murder of the prince, which Gina arranged with Ferrante Palla, and, as a Carthusian, he does indeed die "on a wooden bench and dressed in white" (p. 153). It seems reasonable to assume that he also achieves "peace of soul" (ibid.). There are, in short, no loose ends, thus increasing the terminal sense of closure.

The exact identity of the "innocent," referred to in the passage just quoted, has aroused some perplexity. I take it to be the innocent valet, whom Fabrice unhorsed, while François Michel, F. W. J. Hemmings, and I. H. Smith conclude with varying assurance that it refers to Marquis Crescenzi.[28] In all three cases, they assume that the abbé here alludes to the same crime as the one mentioned several lines before: "Your soul may prepare itself for a much more difficult prison, much more terrible! Probably you will get out only by means of a crime, but, thanks be to God, you will not commit this crime. Never sink to crime. . ." A few lines farther on, the priest returns to the question of crime: "I saw . . . that after prison, but I don't know whether it is at the very moment of getting out, there will be what I call a crime, but happily I believe I may be sure that you will not commit it. If you are so weak that you become involved in this crime, all the rest of my calculations are nothing but one long error." If these three references refer to the same crime or if the crime against the "innocent" is dated by the other two references, then he can indeed only be Crescenzi.

I would propose, however, that the abbé refers to three separate crimes. It seems to me that the crime which permits Fabrice's escape is Clélia's betrayal of her father, as both Clélia (p. 341) and Gina (p. 375) term it. I would agree with Michel, Hemmings, and others that the crime "after prison" consists of the assassination of the prince. That leaves the "question of killing an innocent, who without realizing it, usurps your *rights*" (my italics). Only a very short time after the abbé's warning against succumbing to such a temptation, Fabrice considers killing the valet whose horse he needs. "If I were to reason like Mosca, Fabrice said to himself, when he repeats that the dangers a man runs are always the measure of his *rights* in regard to his neighbor, I would blow this valet's head off with my pistol" (pp. 162-63; my italics). Fabrice, of course, does not do so, much to Mosca's displeasure: "Since this valet held your life between his hands, you had the *right* to take his" (p. 167; my italics). Consequently, Mosca remonstrates: "Your excellency [i.e., Fabrice] acted frivolously in the affair of the horse, you were inches from perpetual imprisonment. This remark made Fabrice shiver; he remained profoundly astonished. Was that, he wondered, the prison I'm menaced with? Is that the crime that I was not supposed to commit? Blanés's predictions, which meant nothing to him as prophecies, took on all the importance of veritable presages" (p. 169).

With this interpretation pointing to the valet, there are no dangling modifiers in the good abbé's "prediction." The same cannot be said for Fabrice's chestnut tree, at least if we limit our reading of that omen to the interpretations provided by other critics. They stop with the broken limb, which has been viewed variously as "a castration symbol" (the tree then is phallic), as "the unusable portion of Fabrice's past; the cultivation and tree surgery, a preparation for the future to which he is now dedicated," and as "the death of Sandrino, his son, which will come in the last pages of this book."[29] Though each of these possibilities possesses a certain attractiveness, without exception they share the problem that all the elements of the tree mentioned are not later actualized in the fulfilled prophecy. In particular, Fabrice's efforts on two occasions to loosen the surrounding soil (pp. 28, 161) and the suggestion that the tree would be better for the pruning (p. 161) are ignored. If there be anything to the pattern of literary omens just proposed—1) they must be mysteriously and tantalizingly unclear, 2) appropriate to both characters and situations, and 3) *completely* explained after the fact—one might suggest that the tree either fails to pass muster or could bear further consideration.

If, as I have come to believe, the real ending of the book does not occur at the death of Sandrino, or of Clélia, rather when Fabrice withdraws to the Carthusian Charterhouse, prepares his soul and dies, it seems to me that one must take the religious theme of *La Chartreuse de Parme* in all seriousness. I am of course referring to the novel only; I am well aware of Stendhal's skepticism, but I treat the theme of religion as a literary rather than a biographical problem. Fabrice "was a believer" (p. 129); Stendhal was not.[30] It is perhaps worth pointing out that though the narrator is amused by the unthinking practices of Fabrice's faith, never does he mock the faith itself. The explanation is very simple. Fabrice's beliefs in God and especially in an afterlife are essential to the novel.

Given the fact that Fabrice's visit to his tree, just subsequent to hearing Father Blanès's prophecy, occurs after Fabrice has definitely committed himself to an ecclesiastical career and has received Gina's clear instructions for his behavior—"Be *apostolic!*" she tells him (p. 129—Fabrice's symbolic tree might make one sense biblical resonances. In regard to digging up the soil, Jesus's parable concerning the fruitless fig tree (Luke 13: 6-9) appears pertinent. When the owner tells the caretaker to cut it down, the latter responds, "Lord, let it alone this year also, till I shall dig about it, and dung it; and if it bear fruit, well; and if not, then after that thou shalt cut it down." Certainly, at the time Fabrice loosens the soil, even the most charitable assessment of his life could not deny the young man's fruitlessness, fruitlessness which, biblically, may also require pruning. "I am the true vine," Jesus said in John 15: 1-2, "and my Father is the husbandman. Every branch in me that beareth not fruit he taketh away: and every branch that beareth fruit, he purgeth it, that it may bring forth more fruit." Significantly, after the broken, desiccated branch has been cut away, "it is no longer injurious to the tree, and it would be even more tall" (p. 161). Fabrice, unfortunately, must wait until prison before his own purging and pruning begins. Still, in the end, one may confidently assume that he bears the fruit of eternal life. Such, at least, is the conclusion to be drawn from several systems of images.

The clearest support for this contention appears on reducing Fabrice's life to the barest of outlines: A young man falls in love, devotes his entire life to worshipful adoration of the lady, despairs at her death, and turns to God, knowing he will find his beloved in heaven. That is anything but an original story. One might think of Dante and Beatrice, for example, though by referring in an extremely pointed fashion to Petrarch on four occasions, Stendhal's novel directs the reader's mind toward the illustrious poet's *Canzoniere* celebrating Laura. On reflection, it is precisely Stendhal's lack of originality which makes his use of the Petrarchan model so interesting. His allusion to Petrarch's relationship with Laura is an important means of rendering a long, involved conclusion unnecessary. Incidently it contributes intensity, color, and nuance to Fabrice's story.

The first overt reference occurs when Fabrice sends Clélia a silk handkerchief on which has been printed one of Petrarch's sonnets (p. 382). Next, the young prince, Ranuce-Ernest V mentions the poet-laureate in a letter to Sanseverina. The prince's mother has decided to give her the little palace of San Giovanni, "which used to belong to Petrarch, at least people said so" (p. 393). Then "Clélia dared to repeat . . . two of Petrarch's verses to herself" (p. 450). The fact that the verses were actually written by Pietro Metastasio is of scholarly interest,[31] but does not diminish the emphasis on Petrarch. Repeatedly mentioning the great poet keeps his name in the mind of the reader, who may even sense that the following passage should be taken very seriously. Mosca offers Fabrice "Petrarch's former house on that beautiful hill in the middle of the forest near the Po river: if ever you become tired of the miserable little manoeuvres caused by envy, I thought *you might become Petrarch's successor. His fame will augment yours*" (p. 444; my italics).

At this point it is difficult not to recall that Fabrice is also a poet, a poet in the Petrarchan tradition. While in prison, Fabrice "had written a very exact diary of everything that was happening to him . . . in the margins [of a folio volume of Saint Jerome]; the big events were nothing but the ecstasy of 'divine' love (the word divine replaced another that he dared not write). Sometimes this divine love brought the prisoner to deep despair; at other times a voice heard in the distance gave him some hope and caused transports of happiness" (p. 376). The conceits are recognizable to anyone familiar with Petrarch. It is, however, worth remembering that though Stendhal mocks the use of the "divine" in the "divine love," in Petrarch's *Canzoniere* Laura is indeed responsible for leading the poet to the point where he finds the strength to turn his thoughts entirely toward God. The last *canzone* leaves no doubt of the spiritual revolution. At the time of Fabrice's first stay in the Farnese Tower, however, such a development is impossible. His sonnet says so clearly:

> What a wonderful idea: *dying near the person you love!* expressed in a hundred different ways, was followed by a sonnet where you saw that the soul which, after atrocious torments, was separated from the fragile body it had inhabited for twenty-three years, pushed by an instinctual desire for happiness which is natural for anything that has been given life, would not rise to heaven to join the chorus of angels as soon as it was free, and if the dreadful judgment would grant it pardon for its sins, but, happier after death than it had been during life, [it] would go a few steps from the prison where it had so long languished to join everything it had loved in the world. 'And so,' said the last line of the sonnet, 'I will have found my paradise on earth.'[32]

After an extensive search in Italian and French poetry, I have concluded that Stendhal himself authored this "sonnet." It is certain that Petrarch did not write the original. Nonetheless, it is clearly in the Petrarchan tradition, and most of the images were expressed by the Renaissance poet himself. Petrarch was, for example, fond of discussing the previously mentioned "prison of love." In one sonnet, to cite a further instance of the conceit, the poet concludes:

> Always in hate the window shall I bear,
> Whence Love has shot on me his shafts at will,
> Because not one of them sufficed to kill:
> For death is good when life is bright and fair,
> But in this earthly jail its term to outwear
> Is cause to me, alas! of infinite ill;
> And mine is worse because immortal still,
> Since from the heart the spirit may not tear.[33]

Although I can find nothing in Petrarch which suggests that he would refuse heaven to remain with his beloved, as the sonnet just quoted indicated, the thought is not far from his canon of tropes. Petrarch's *Secretum* develops the idea that his love of Laura separates him from God. The poet's St. Augustine is definite: "As for her having taught you to look upwards and separate yourself from the vulgar crowd, what else is it than to say by sitting at her feet you became so infatuated with the charm of her above as to studiously neglect everything else?"[34] Somewhat farther on, the saint expands on the reproof: "She has detached your mind from the love of heavenly things and has inclined your heart to love the creature more than the Creator: and that one path alone leads, sooner than any other, to death" (ibid., p. 124).

Elsewhere Fabrice's attention to Clélia's "celestial beauty" (p. 251), to her "gaze" (p. 253), "gaze which put [him] in ecstasy" (p. 447), and to her piousness (e.g., p. 375), is significant, as is the image of separating windows (pp. 249, 297-99, etc.) and, most of all, the image of a prison to which the "divine" beloved possesses the keys:

> By promise fair and artful flattery
> Me Love contrived in prison old to snare,
> And gave the keys to her my foe in care.   (Sonnet 56)

All this and much more recalls Petrarch. The great poet, for one further example, also hesitated to leave his prison. "I regain my freedom with a sigh," Petrarch says (ibid.).

The way religion becomes intertwined with Fabrice's and Clélia's love has drawn the interest of numerous critics.[35] Briefly, Fabrice uses the cross of his rosary to cut an opening in the shutter covering his window. Don Cesare, the prison priest, serves as the couple's intermediary. Fabrice's new breviary provides leaves for the alphabet that serves for direct communication. The copy of Saint Jerome's works becomes the hero's diary. And, finally, Clélia has the text of her vow, "*I will never look on him again*" (p. 420), burned on the altar where her uncle says Mass. Durand makes the additional point that the lovers go even further in their use of churches. They meet clandestinely in the prison chapel, and, after Clélia's marriage, they finally see each other again in the little church of Saint Mary of the Visitation. With this kind of preparation, how can any reader be astonished by the conclusion in which Fabrice makes use of God Himself to reach Clélia?

The Petrarchan allusion prepares Stendhal's conclusion, as well. After turning profane love into a religion, Petrarch does not hesitate to make God an accomplice. When his brother's mistress dies, the poet advises him to "Follow where she the safe short way has shown" (Sonnet, 70). Later, Petrarch takes his own advice. He prays,

If, to her eternal home to soar,
That heavenly spirit have left her earthly place.
Oh! then not distant may my last day be!   (Sonnet 213)

In part two, after Laura's death, he looks fervently to God, asking entrance to heaven (e.g., Sonnets 5, 11): "Now my whole thought, my wish to heaven I cast; / 'Tis Laura's voice I hear, and hence she bids me haste" (Sonnet 75). His thoughts turn less and less on his beloved, however, as he looks increasingly to God for his salvation (e.g., Sonnet 84). Confessing his sins (e.g., Sonnets 85, 86), he calls on the Virgin:

Virgin! to thy dear name
I consecrate and cleanse my thoughts, speech, pen,
My mind, and heart with all its tears and sighs;
Point then that better path,
And with complacence view my changed desires at least.
(Canzone 8)

Fabrice need not dwell on his similar aspirations. "He hoped to find Clélia again in a better world, but he was too intelligent not to sense that he had much to atone for" (p. 479). His illustrious predecessor, Petrarch, has given the reader all the detail necessary.

This allusion does not solve all the problems of the conclusion. I am not concerned with the fact that the Charterhouse of Parma has not been mentioned prior to the last page. Numerous critics have remarked that the previously mentioned Chartreuse de Velleja (pp. 186, 440, 443) prepares the final retreat, as does Fabrice's consideration, after Clélia's marriage, of the possibility of becoming a Carthusian (pp. 438, 443). I would also agree with other readers that, whether the Chartreuse de Parme appears early on in the text or not, it was present in Stendhal's mind as he wrote, and it is, because of the title, if nothing else, in the mind of the reader as he reads. The central difficulty seems somewhat different—why does Fabrice choose to withdraw into a *charterhouse*? Italy does not suffer from a dearth of orders offering retreats from the world and the opportunity to prepare one's soul for death. Why choose the Carthusians, one of the harshest of religious rules?

Luigi-Foscolo Benedetto was of the opinion that Stendhal uses the word "chartreuse" or "charterhouse" to refer to any enclosed convent or monastery.[36] I find no evidence to support this position. To the contrary, as Herbert Morris has shown, Stendhal's knowledge of the Carthusians was detailed, in general accurate, and possibly first hand.[37] I would make the further suggestion that the second portion of the novel consists of an extended allusion designed to intimate that Fabrice has entered the Carthusian novitiate. I already mentioned H. W. Wardman's belief that Fabrice is a failure as a man of action, for his talents lie primarily in the realm of contemplation. (One of Mosca's most important functions is to set off Fabrice's worldly incapacity by his own mundanity.[38]) The textual hint that Fabrice may be the bastard son of the French lieutenant Robert (pp. 9-11) and the repeated emphasis on how Fabrice differs from his father and brother mark the boy as what Martin Turnell has called an "outsider."[39] His aunt Gina's judgment—"Men will never like you, for you have too much fire for prosaic souls" (p. 29)—is but one more indication among many others that Fabrice is, in bibliical terms, separated or set apart.

Thanks to Rassi, Fabrice finds himself constrained to fast on Fridays and on the eves of major feast days (p. 242, 286). Though Carthusians did likewise, the practice was widespread, and this detail alone carries little weight. It is however not alone. The most striking aspect of the Carthusian rule is that they are permitted to join in conversation only once a week, during the *spatiementum* or weekly walk. In most Charterhouses it occurred on Mondays, though, as Morris says, Stendhal apparently believed it to fall on Thursdays (*Citadel*, p. 10). At other times, the monks were expected to maintain silence. Some writers erroneously believed that the monks communicated by signs; Stendhal may have shared this false impression (*Citadel*, pp. 15-17). In prison, Fabrice is surrounded by a "vast silence" (pp. 295-96). Neither the jailer, Grillo, nor the carpenter may speak to him (pp. 295, 297). He communicates, nonetheless, but by signs (pp. 301, 303-04, 309). Finally, "every Thursday, during the day, the excellent Father Don Cesare accorded Fabrice half an hour's walk on the terrace of the Farnese tower, but the other days of the week, this stroll, which could be seen by all the inhabitants of Parma and surrounding areas and [could] compromise the prison governor gravely, only took place at nightfall" (p. 328). Morris sees this arrangement for weekly exercise as an analogue of the Carthusians' *spatiementum* (*Citadel,* p. 17). I do not wish to force this parallel, but there is sufficient evidence to say that, just as the bell tower of Grianta introduces numerous objects, images, and sensations which will be repeated in respect to the citadel of Parma, so the Farnese Tower adumbrates the charterhouse to which Fabrice retires for good.

After the hero's second release he begins to dress in black (pp. 434, 444, 440). Carthusian novices wear black until their ordination, at which point they don the white robes that Father Blanès foresees. With Clélia's marriage, Fabrice orders his servant and the other employees of the archbishropic to refrain from speaking to him (p. 442). In short, Fabrice's withdrawal into the Charterhouse of Parma is to be expected. He has completed his novitiate and is ready to devote himself to silent contemplation of God. In no sense should this conclusion be considered tragic, for Fabrice, like Petrarch, has the encouraging hope of eternal life with his beloved.

I conclude that Stendhal not only did not plan to make any changes in the last five paragraphs of his novel, he would have been unwise to do so. It is hard to imagine a more adequately prepared conclusion. One expects a novel which begins with the birth of a hero to end in his death, as does *La Chartreuse*, a death that is multiplied, thus intensified, by those of Sandrino, Clélia, and Sanseverina. In addition, the most important omens are not fulfilled until the protagonist actually withdraws to his Charterhouse. Indeed, the pattern of his life suggests a Carthusian novitiate, symbolically marking the departure from a sinful world by shedding black robes for white. When so much is made of Fabrice as an outsider, separated unto the Church, if not God, one is surely encouraged to view his fleshly lusts as temporary hindrances (St. Augustine provides a well-known model). Lives of saints and the derivative pietistic fiction would in any case lead the reader to expect increasing dedication to God and the promise of heaven. And, of course, the Petrarchan allusion suggests a model which parallels Fabrice's path, presumably to heaven and the beloved. Whether or not one can place much credence in the pun noticed by Morris—*Chartreuse* and *chartre*, an obsolete French word for prison (*Citadel*, p. 21)—as an adumbration of the final retreat is an open question, but surely the possibility is not needed to conclude that Stendhal thoroughly prepared his conclusion. No lengthy coda was required to close this novel; more length, in the face of so many systems leading to this, the only possible end, could scarcely have avoided noticeable redundancy.

On viewing the evidence of the novel, it is difficult to understand
why the conclusion of *La Chartreuse* has sustained so much adverse
commentary. Could such criticism grow from excessive admiration
of Balzac and an overzealous willingness to adopt the master's belief
that Stendhal's novel dealt, not with Fabrice, but with the court, and
that it should then be concluded earlier? Balzac's pronouncement
has reverberated in the secondary literature for over a century: "In
spite of the title, the work ends when the count and countess Mosca
return to Parma and Fabrice is archbishop. The great comedy of the
court is finished."[40] Or could it be that some critics have been
inordinately influenced by the external, biographical evidence of
Stendhal's draft letter—a draft which was never sent, a passage which
Stendhal never allowed Balzac to read—striving to justify the
conclusion to his illustrious reviewer? There are no definitive
answers to these questions. The possibility of affirmative responses
does, however, indicate that one could perhaps add another argument
to those against the belief that omniscient readers are ideal readers.
However that may be, because of the narrative, thematic, and
allusive systems converging on the last few pages of Fabrice's life, *La
Chartreuse de Parme* may be said to have strong closure.

One of the most important effects available to process novels is
the sense of an ending. Frank Kermode has argued cogently that
human beings need finality or closure to balance their realization of
duration.[41] Conclusions communicate a sense of integrity to readers.
It is apparently important for the tensions aroused by a work to be
significantly abated and the reader's expectations fulfilled to some
degree, though, in fact, we understand very little about the psychological mechansims which cause readers to feel pleasure at the sense
of stability and finality, or closure, which brings works of art to an
end. Wallace Stevens puts it this way:

> Ramon Fernandez, tell me, if you know,
> Why, when the singing ended and we turned
> Toward the town, tell why the glassy lights,
> The lights in the fishing boats at anchor there,
> As the night descended, tilting in the air,
> Mastered the night and portioned out the sea,
> Fixing emblazoned Zones and Fiery poles,
> Arranging, deepening, enchanting night.
> Oh! Blessed rage for order, pale Ramon,
> The maker's rage to order words of the sea,
> Words of the fragrant portals, dimly-stared,

And of ourselves and of our origins,
In ghostlier demarcations, keener sounds.[42]

The need for closure has important ramifications in modern
art. Many artists have gone beyond Picasso's definition of a picture as
"a sum of destructions"[43] (which, of course, implies unity) to attempt
to reproduce and reflect their vision of a fragmented, dispersive
world. To their despair—though perhaps to their salvation, for, as
David Richter points out, the successful imitation of chaos is not
chaos... it is a lack of meaning[44]—readers seem to be so desirous of
closing the work and making a whole that, if they resist the
temptation to invent closure through misreading, they tend to
perform a similar function (whether disservice or no) by a facile,
unquestioning acceptance of the theme of disintegration, an
acceptance which, as Robin Wood points out, becomes a force
of integration.[45]

Much recent discussion about openness (defined as an opening
up, a refusal of closure or a denial of this particular kind of order)
grows either from an unwillingness to view an individual work of art
as distinct from the consuming, producing society or from the
realization that the author suggests the continuation of his fictional
life after the end of the book. While it is no doubt true that even
when all the major characters are dead, as for example at the end of
*King Lear*, "life goes on," such an insistence lacks good will, for it
ignores time-honored aesthetic markers of finality, substituting
instead an extra-textual truth that lacks internal support. Other
critics confuse resolution with finality. When confronted by one of
the legions of modern works that ends with the indication that the
characters will continue to drag on from day to day, as for example in
Gide's *Les Faux-Monnayeurs* (1925), insufficient attention is paid to
the well-established patterns of their lives that leave little room for
surprises. Certainly, both approaches have been responsible for
interesting, helpful work. It seems more useful, however, to define
closure as the resolution of the work's major conflicts. In such a case,
one may well doubt the possibility of art without closure, especially
when closure is coupled with completeness.[46] It can at least be said
with some assurance that most artistic works which have maintained
a consistant or recurring audience generally establish closure of one
kind or another (exceptions like Coleridge's "Kubla Khan"—
1816—lacking a conclusion and a substantial portion of the rest, are
far from uncommon; still, in these and other such instances, it seems
to me that we assume a conclusion which Coleridge would have

written had he not been interrupted). It is also clear that, while much
modern literature is claimed to create terminal "overture," in fact it
almost always establishes stable, though perhaps hidden, closure.
When the reader senses possible solutions to the mathematical
puzzles of Beckett's *Watt* (1953), or the central image of Saporta's
*Composition No. 1* (1962), or the shape of the paradigm in Borges's "La
Loteria en Babilonia" (1944), or the formula for the accelerating time
in Butor's *6 810 000 litres d'eau par seconde* (1966), or the pattern of
recurring behavior at the end of *Les Faux-Monnayeurs*, the closure is
complete, whether the reader explicitly grasps the reasons for it or
not. Another kind of closure is experiential. In chapter 7, I shall
argue that *A la recherche du temps perdu* was designed to cause the reader
to experience a "blessed moment." Once experienced, the novel
closes. These types of closure are typical of those modern novels in
which one is less interested in the extremities or the pattern itself
than in the principle or parameters responsible for the process of the
work. At the point of apprehension of whatever completes the
system, the work closes.

It is perhaps easier to recognize more traditional devices which
depend on sensitivity to how the pattern terminates. Though in
Brecht and Balzac such closure can be used to stimulate opening
through revolt and the construction of new structures, in general,
endomorphic novels imply a lack of continuation or seriation.
Certainly, as Edith Wharton, I. A. Richards, Edward W. Said, and
others have indicated, the strategy of the work's initial overture
usually implies termination.[47] This closure may be brought about
through many vehicles. David H. Richter's *Fable's End: Completeness
and Closure in Rhetorical Fiction* emphasizes the importance of thematic
development. Barbara Herrnstein Smith's *Poetic Closure: A Study of
How Poems End* stresses linguistic, prosodic, and rhetorical devices
like verbal repetitions, monosyllabic diction, metrical regularity,
alliteration, assonance, internal rhyme, and balanced antithesis,
which, though they make significant appearances in novels by
Flaubert, Gide, and Pinget, among others, are less important in
prose than poetry. It is true that recent novelists are exploiting such
possibilities more frequently, and we may learn to be more sensitive
to them. Nevertheless, novels most commonly make use of frames
(as in the reference to the Grandlieus at the beginning and end of
*Gobseck*) or references to various natural patterns: birth and death
(e.g., *The Golovlyovs*—1876[48]), departure and return (e.g., *Adventures
of Huckleberry Finn*—1884), arrival and departure (e.g., *La Princesse de
Clèves*—1678).

Plots which utilize cultural patterns of metamorphosis are also common. The *Bildungsroman* is, of course, familiar, as is "rags to riches," the "Sleeping Beauty" pattern of young love to happy marriage (or its reverse, in *La Chartreuse* or, for another instance, in *Madame Bovary*), or the pietistic "sinner to saint" found, for example, in Huysman's *Là-Bas* (1891). Each of these narrative patterns suggests the appropriate endings: Don Juans go to hell, but shoeshine boys finally roll in riches. Such plot patterns as these are frequently enriched by complex thematic structures, designed to aid closure. Writers often reinforce termination with references to death, sleep, winter.

Genres themselves carry the implication of closure; the Russian Formalists had much to say about such literary expectations. We count on tragedies ending in death, for example, and Broadway musicals concluding at the pot of gold. An exception to this latter pattern, *West Side Story* (1957), draws attention to another, extremely important means of closure: allusion.[49] Though the original Broadway audiences surely looked forward to a happy ending, the concluding, tragic deaths were not disappointing, because so well prepared by the allusion to *Romeo and Juliet*. All of these patterns bring a well-integrated conclusion, which may be strong, as in the allusion to Christ in *Light in August* (1932), or weak, as in the protagonist's return to bestial "normalcy" at the end of Anthony Burgess's *A Clockwork Orange* (1962). Closure need not be prepared, however, and poorly prepared conclusions need not ruin the work (*Tartuffe*'s contrived, *deus ex machina* ending of 1664 is certainly not irremissible). Nonetheless, either through the recognition of a structuring pattern or principle or through some other means (a simple announcement can do the trick—e.g., "Here our play has ending" in Shakespeare's *Pericles*), readers expect the "payoff" of closure.

Still, despite the unquestioned importance of the conclusion, *La Chartreuse* is primarily important to this study because it offers an excellent example of process structure in the endomorphic novel. Every aspect of the work, whether event or image, functions to highlight the changes that take place in the main character. As he changes from an uncaring, selfish child to someone capable of sacrificial love, and finally to a religious devoted to meditation, one could compare the sequences of episodes, themes, allusions, images, motifs to a fluvial map of the Mississippi basin. After having read the book, one might view it as a static whole, an immobile map hung on the walls of one's mind, but, in fact, to do so is to distort. Just as the water flows from snow or rain to trickle, creek, stream, river until it joins the Mississippi and enters the Gulf of Mexico, so the essential quality of Stendhal's novel remains change, transformation, the process of Fabrice's development. One may rightly talk of a developmental action consisting of Fabrice's life, which serves as the novel's backbone. Not all process novels are so dependent on the vehicle of plot and character, though that is surely the most common and consequently the easiest to perceive. In the next chapter, I turn to another variety of the endomorphic novel, one where process is subsumed to a static image of a character and a society.

## Chapter 3
## Balzac's *Gobseck* and Image Structure

ONE COULD ARGUE, I SUPPOSE, that every successful novel creates an image in the mind of the reader, since after it is understood our minds tend to simplify radically for the purposes of classification and storage. Even in the case of novels where there exists a decided change in characters—take George Eliot's *Middlemarch: A Study of Provincial Life* (1871-72), for example—readers might pick one scene or make a composite of several episodes involving Dorothea, though it appears more likely that they will retain a complex image having to do with the feelings one has before the heroine's lusterless existence. Certainly, such a reduction falsifies the essential development of the novel. Still, on reading Eliot's "Prelude," it seems at least possible that the author sought to elicit something of the sort. She says, "Here and there a cygnet is reared uneasily among the ducklings in the brown pond, and never finds the living stream in fellowship with its own oary-footed kind. Here and there is born a Saint Theresa, foundress of nothing, whose loving heartbeats and sobs after an unattained goodness tremble off and are dispersed among hindrances, instead of centering in some long-recognizable deed."[1]

Of course, most readers would willingly admit that *Middlemarch* concerns the changes that take place in Dorothea's life, changes that may have been caused by her naive and stubborn idealism but which are no less plural and long-lived for the unitary cause. Without a novel's length, it would have been impossible to communicate the essential feeling of duration. One image of Dorothea will simply not do. We must have a sequence of them, for only then can we share the experience of the process.

Some writers never stop yearning for a means of overcoming the novel's seriate nature. It is as though there were something especially effective about image structure, something denied the novel. Jean Giono writes, for instance:

Writing is not a particularly docile instrument. Musicians can make us hear a very great number of timbres simultaneously. Obviously, there is a limit they cannot go beyond, but we, with writing, would be quite satisfied to reach this limit. For we are obliged to tell in Indian file; words are written one after another, and all one can do with stories is tie them together. As for Breughel, he kills a

pig in the left corner, he plucks a goose a little higher up,
he slips a rascally hand down to cup the breasts of a woman
in red and, up there to the right, he sits on a barrel
brandishing a skewer passing through a row of six beautiful,
blue blackbirds. And no matter how hard you try to pay
attention only to the pink pig and the steel of the knife
cutting his throat, at the same time your eye picks up the
white of the feathers, the red of the bodice (and the
fullness of the red breasts), the brown of the barrel and the
blue of the blackbirds. For me to tell the same thing, I
have nothing but words that people read one after
another (and they skip some).[2]

The prognosis is far from hopeless, as Giono well knew. . . . The
passage is taken from *Noé* (1947), his fine example of a novel which
encourages the creation of an image and allows inaction to dominate.
Regardless of the sequential way readers first experience novels,
novelists have been very successful at subsequently inciting them to
view their works as atemporal wholes.

By image I do not refer to a figure of speech or even what
Northrop Frye defines as "a unit of verbal structure seen as part of a
total pattern of rhythm,"[3] though these are possible usages. I mean
rather something which, because of a text's stimulation, occurs in a
reader's mind: a mental complex, pattern, or organization of
interdependent or interacting parts which, like a connoisseur before
a masterful painting, can profitably be studied over a period of time
but which is, most importantly, subject to instantaneous comprehension.[4] "Image structure" is simply a pattern that subordinates
chronological experience to a momentary comprehension of the
whole.

I turn to *Gobseck* (1830-35) because it offers an excellent
example of this sort of static structuring. In addition, it provides an
opportunity to review the recent theory concerning "openness,"
which I believe constitutes an important and valid entrance to new
readings of traditional masterworks. Central to New Novelists'
objections to nineteenth-century fiction is the assertion that, while
the preceding novel was "closed," the new is "open," allowing
readers virtually free creation.[5] Unfortunately, assertions of unfettered
opening in modern works are generally found without specific
examples subjected to rigorous analysis. They occur in imprecise
discussions of recent novels or as an unspecific opposition to
nineteenth-century prose fiction. When, however, a Barthes or a

Ricardou concentrates on a particular modern text, it rapidly becomes clear that not just the linguistic elements but the connoted themes as well converge to create rigorous structures.[6] With some relief, we may conclude that readers are not being invited to a Kabbalistic *Gematria,* which Harold Bloom defines as "interpretative freedom gone mad, in which any text can be made to mean anything."[7] I know of no New or, for that matter, no Former Novel composed of what Umberto Eco describes as "an agglomerate of chance elements, ready to emerge from chaos to take any form at all." Of course, as Eco goes on to point out, the dictionary represents an example of such a work. Anyone is free to use its thousands of words to make poems, treatises, "or anonymous letters. It is in this sense 'open' to all possible compositions of the material it proposes. But it is clearly not a *work*. The 'overture' and the dynamism of a work are very different things. They depend on a work's aptitude for integrating diverse objects by making them enter into the play of its organic vitality."[8] One can nonetheless not dismiss the concept of openness.

Eco's use of overture is worth some comment. Although, in English, the term means the prelude or introductory part, he uses it in a different sense, for the activity incited by an entire work which then seems like an introduction to the activity including the creation and continuing beyond it. I believe a satisfactory conception of overture may be found on further consideration of Eco's study, *L'Oeuvre ouverte*. His base definition concerns the possibility of the reader's creation: "From Baroque to Symbolism, it is always a question of 'overture' based on the *theoretical, mental* collaboration of the reader who must freely interpret an aesthetic fact which has *already* been organized and gifted with a given structure (even if this structure must permit an infinity of interpretations)" (ibid., p. 25). The reader creates the closure according to implicit ordering factors. Unfortunately, Eco believes his formulation inappropriate for more recent artistic creations which allow the reader or performer to manipulate some, but not all, of the components physically. I disagree. Marc Saporta's deck-book, *Composition No. 1,*[9] and Calder's most successful mobiles, to cite just two examples, suggest, on the one hand, that the possible rearrangements make little significant difference or, on the other, that the possible movements constitute rigorously integrated systems.

Eco is particularly interested in the overture that ambiguity offers. Given his clear understanding that this ambiguity, in and for itself, becomes a subject, indicates meaning, and provides closure, one wonders why he refuses himself the use of his helpful definition. In fact, it continues to function satisfactorily. The reader's inability to construct a system from the language of *Finnegans Wake* which will subordinate all others indicates modern man's similar incapacity before the world (*Oeuvre ouverte*, p. 292). When the reader reaches this understanding, the work "closes." Using the definition of overture, which Eco wishes to restrict to earlier periods, I would say it is precisely this created "closure" that guarantees *Finnegans Wake* its aesthetic "overture."

There is another type of opening which Eco finds implicit in the Joycean universe and clearly present in Brecht. The latter "is content to present the spectator, with detachment and as though from the outside, the facts to observe—[he] proposes no solutions. It is for the spectator to draw the critical conclusions from what he has seen. . . . Consequently, the work is 'open' in the sense of a debate: we wait, we wish for a solution but it must be born from the public's realization. The 'opening' becomes an instrument for revolutionary pedagogy" (ibid., pp. 24-25). I shall propose that this constitutes the finale in a series of overtures provided by *Gobseck*. Without question, Balzac would have preferred the revolution reactionary. Nonetheless, the societal construct he describes demands a response, an opening into our world, which, of course, is Balzac's.

The essential first step in this sequence of open structures requires the acceptance of Balzac's conventions. From the beginning the reader must recognize the potential of words to have symbolic and mythic meaning. Given Robbe-Grillet's celebrated condemnation of novels where, "at every moment, cultural fringes (psychology, ethics, metaphysics, etc.) come to join things,"[10] this may be difficult for some. As I argued previously, however, this kind of connotation is in essence no different from any other semantic or linguistic significance.[11] Without exception, they are referents. In all cases, the reader attributes the cultural meaning, whether uni- or polivalent and whatever it may be, to the printed sign. After the reader has learned the requisite codes and can thus understand Balzac's language, after he has accepted the text's conventions, after he has actively collaborated with the author and created the necessary images— when he finally arrives at the point where the various levels of *signifiers* converge into a system of the *signified*—it is essential to consider carefully the ramifications of the relationship established between the textual image or process and its isomorphe, whether subjective, societal, or universal. Though there may be tentative efforts along this line throughout the reading, the final overture cannot take place until the initial series have been completed. Despite different conventions or codes, precisely the same steps must be followed with modern texts. The ability of a text, *nouveau* or *ancien,* to elicit this ultimate opening determines whether or not it lives in its own and in each succeeding age. If Leonard B. Meyer is correct in addressing himself to "the pluralism of the present," in his *Music, the Arts and Ideas,* the ability and willingness to accept Balzac's conventions (that is, his referential systems) is to be expected. The possibility of a final Diechtian overture, however, remains to be demonstrated.

Though few would consider Balzac an "avant-garde" writer distinguished by esoteric linguistic games, the wider significance and the aesthetic attractions which draw today's readers depend upon his patterns of meaning which are beyond the scope of most dictionaries. He creates his own language, which, as Martin Kanes suggests pertinently in his *Balzac's Comedy of Words,*[12] constantly strives to overcome the limitations of this most imperfect tool. I believe this true of all Balzac's best work; here, however, I shall limit myself to his masterful *Gobseck.* For the sake of convenience, I abide by the convention of referring to Gobseck as "him"; still, I consider him less a "character" than a figure or image, that is, a complex of interrelated, interdependent, interacting elements. The personage is then subordinated to his ramifications, a procedure that received some support from Balzac. As he said in "Lettres sur la littérature... I," "Whatever may be the number of accessories and the multiplicity of figures, a modern novelist must... group them according to their importance, subordinating them to the sun of his system, an interest, or a hero, and lead them like a brilliant constellation in an orderly fashion."[13] Gobseck, then, is part of a constellation. This is not so far removed from recent conceptions of character, where the being or agent may be nothing but a consciousness, and it corresponds to Henry Céard's recognition back in 1885 that novels could dispense with individualized personages.[14] Julia Kristeva goes even further to propose a novel without any governing consciousness.[15]

My point of departure resides in some of the usurer's attributes, in his association with several mythic personae, and in his name. Some might consider this "mere" detail, though I take courage in the fact that Balzac stated in 1830: "Detail alone will henceforth constitute the merit of works improperly called *Novels* [*Romans*]."[16]

Certainly, little else would at first glance recommend *Gobseck* or explain why, with *Père Goriot* and *Eugénie Grandet*, it remains among the best known of Balzac's creations. The story and the main character are typical of the Romantics and resemble all too closely other efforts of the day. Like many nineteenth-century prose works, it is "framed"—not by the railway carriage so dear to Maupassant, rather by the similarly well-worn gathering in a salon. Derville, Balzac's successful attorney, has noticed Camille de Grandlieu's interest in Ernest de Restaud. So has Camille's mother, "one of the most remarkable women of the Saint-Germain quarter,"[17] who heartily disapproves of the attraction. Derville takes advantage of his favored position as an intimate friend, responsible for restoring the family fortune after the Revolution, and explains why Ernest constitutes an acceptable match. Derville knows the story because Gobseck facilitated and thus profited from Mme de Restaud's illicit obsession with the wastrel, Maxine de Trailles. At one point, Ernest's mother had pledged the Restaud diamonds in order to pay Maxine's gambling debts. She was well on the road to ruining the whole family, when M. de Restaud concocted a plan. While pretending to imitate his extravagantly frivolous wife, he secretly transferred the family fortune to Gobseck for safekeeping. Then he took sick and died.

Gobseck is the very rich, though miserly, usurer whom Derville met as a struggling clerk in Paris. The miser, we gradually learn, was responsible for Derville meeting his beloved wife, for loaning him the money to buy his practice (at onerous interest), for facilitating and thus profiting from Mme de Restaud's irresponsibility, and, finally, for preserving the Restaud fortune. All would have been well, if Derville could have reached M. de Restaud before his death, but Anastasie's nose for money made her realize that her husband had come up with a way to cheat her of what she thought her due. Consequently, the countess established an impenetrable barrier around her dying husband. Almost immediately after the latter died, his wife tore through the room, dumped the count's body into the space between the bed and wall, and, on locating the papers which she thought deprived her of a fortune, burned them as Derville entered the room. This rash and selfish act received poetic justice. All proof of the real owner had gone up in smoke. Before the law, Gobseck was master. He instituted his reign by throwing Mme de Restaud and her children into the street. Fortunately for everyone, however, the usurer has just died, and, because Derville serves as executor, all will be righted. The boy will receive his fortune, and Camille will be able to marry as her heart desires.

Clearly, the story has everything a Romantic could wish: romance, a mysterious, fabulously wealthy, and monstrous miser, and a surprise ending which will allow the innocent young lovers to marry and live happily ever after. By the same token, however skillful the narration, and indeed it is masterful, little would distinguish it from reams of melodramatic drivel that have drifted into well-deserved oblivion. But *Gobseck* offers considerably more.

I would suggest that a simple adjective, "lunar," provides a key to Gobseck's most important attributes and to those of the novella. Others have been attracted by the word. For B. Lalande it provides an example of Balzac's "fund of expressions, of rhythmo, and ideas which easily come to his pen."[18] The novelist's Gobseck *and* Goriot have "a *lunar* face." Émile Faguet saw in it the opportunity for the traditional disquisition on Balzac's stylistic inadequacies, on his inability to attain the heights of the *mot juste*: "Wrong note. Balzac calls it *lunar* because it is pale and wan, I know, but 'lunar face' will always suggest in the mind of everyone the idea of a round, blossoming countenance, and the countenance of a miser is always (and right here that of Balzac's is) the exact converse."[19] On considering Balzac's passage itself—"Do you clearly grasp this pale, wan countenance, which I would like the Academy to give me permission to call a *lunar* face? It resembled vermeil with the gilt rubbed off" (p. 377)—and on noting that the adjective is marked by its parenthetical position, by italics, and by the ironic wish for permission to use the malapropism, *lunar*, further reflection seems in order.

Within the tradition of Occidental symbolism, the moon may perhaps be best understood in relation to the sun. The latter is, of course, the source of light, heat, and life. Because it has been seen as celestial influence, the sun has been related to the divine, to the manifestation of God, and to spirituality. It represents authority and is then considered masculine or paternal. Paul Diel has pointed to its important implications in respect to the mystery of the conscious intellect. The moon, on the other hand, though queen of the night, of water and humidity and, thus, of the unconscious, has only reflected light or life. It is passive and feminine. Diel says that it symbolizes an unhealthy, exalting imagination growing from the subconscious. However the case may be, it is generally considered the source of second sight or clairvoyance. Because of its periodic renewal, tradition relates it to passing time, to transition, and to fecundity in the plant and animal kingdoms. In general, it is associated with animals and animal life. In particular, as Mircea Eliade points out, it is coupled with owls, oysters, snails, and seashells. Eliade also dwells on the moon as representative of an elementary form of psychic existence, a place of transition where the

animal soul of man goes and is trapped in the physical substance of
the moon until freed, either to return to earth or to be absorbed by
the sun. According to some, the eighteenth key of the Tarot's Major
Arcana likewise uses lunar symbolism to signify submersion in
matter. In short, where the sun refers to light, heat, and to the
intellect and spirituality, the moon connotes darkness, cold, the
unconscious, and the material world. The moon is the place of
reflection and appearance; it is *not* reality.[20]

Artemidorus Daldianus provides one possible transition back
to Gobseck on noting that dreaming of the moon is propitious for
usurers.[21] But there are many others. Gobseck is compared to such
animals as a deer (p. 379) and to a boa (p. 419). Perhaps the narrator's
exclamation on considering the miser and the latter's humid, dark
house holds even more interest, given Eliade's already mentioned
comments on the lunar shell-fish: "He and his house resembled
each other. You would have said the oyster and its rock" (p. 378).
Like other nocturnal creatures, moreover, "His little eyes had
almost no lashes and feared light" (p. 377). Passive, he avoids strong
emotions (p. 382). "He economized the vital processes" (p. 378).
Nonetheless, the text calls attention repeatedly to his occult
powers. Derville suspects the old man may be clairvoyant (p. 390);
Gobseck declares that he can see into the very hearts of people (p.
388). He is one of the twelve "silent, unknown kings, arbitrators of
your destinies," who penetrate financial mysteries and know the
secrets of all families (p. 388). It may also be important to mention
that he is Jewish, since the Hebrews traditionally associated themselves
with the moon, perhaps because of their nomadic existence. As
Hutton Webster points out, "To the Israelites . . . the moon was pre-
eminently the 'wanderer.' "[22] Gobseck's previous life, we remember,
had been that of a nomad (pp. 379-80).

I suspect, however, that the usurer's most important lunar
qualities have to do with his lack of what are normally called
"spiritual values." Derville remarks, "If humanity, if sociability are a
religion, he could be considered an atheist" (p. 380). This deficiency
receives emphasis in several ways: by the previously cited animal
comparisons—which may also derive from Balzac's scientific pretentions—but especially by the insistence on the mechanistic pattern of
the miser's life. For Gobseck, "Happiness consists . . . in regulated
occupations which turn it into an English mechanism functioning to
a regular beat" (p. 382). Indeed, "His actions from rising in the
morning to his attacks of coughing in the evening were as regular as a
pendulum" (p. 378), so much so that the doorkeeper compares him

to "the bird in my big clock" (p. 419). When the dying Gobseck observes, "I have carphology" (p. 420), this mechanical movement of the hands, pulling and pushing the covers, seemingly grasping for objects that are not there, is the image of the man. The movement is contained in embryo in Derville's comment: "He was something of a *model man* [*homme-modèle*] that sleep wound up again" (p. 378). I take the italicized "*homme-modèle*" to mean, not an exemplary person, which would have no hyphen, rather the representation of a man, a mechanical man. Gobseck, whom Derville calls a neuter (p. 380), is not whole. Though he boasts of having learned to control his sensibilities, of his nerves of steel (p. 407), he thereby provides but another indication that he is not a human being.

On remembering that the moon is the place of appearance, as opposed to reality, that the unconscious, lunar influence on the imagination is frequently unhealthy and certainly untrustworthy, one is reminded of Gobseck's disdain for reality. As he says, "I have traveled, I've seen that there are plains or mountains everywhere. The plains are boring and the mountains tiring; places then signify nothing" (p. 382). His experience with man in society across the world convinces him that there are no worthwhile values save one: "As for manners, man is everywhere the same: everywhere the combat between rich and poor is established, everywhere it is inevitable; it is then better to exploit than be exploited; everywhere . . . pleasures are the same, for everywhere the senses exhaust themselves, and only one sentiment survives them: that is vanity! Vanity! It is always the self. Vanity is not satisfied by anything but floods of gold" (p. 382). At first, this one value was twofold, the ego and gold, but Gobseck believed so strongly in the dependence of the self on gold that he subordinated the former to the latter. Gobseck "had turned himself into gold" (p. 380). He makes of the metal, gold, the only value and his only religion: "Gold," he says, "is the spiritualism of your present societies" (p. 388).

Alchemists and cabalists from the brilliant Paracelsus to the limited, though earnest, Eliphas Lévi of Balzac's day might have been encouraged by the statement. For them, gold was *aurum philosophicum* and represented wisdom, unity in the spirit, truth. Of course, they recognized that the other kind of gold existed as well, but that was vulgar, if not evil. As Paul Diel put it, fiduciary gold is the symbol of perversion and the impure exaltation of desires.[23] And Gobseck leaves no doubt about which kind of gold he worships. He wants no truck with the solar, philosopher's gold; he demands what he would call the real thing, the only real thing: the base metal

from the earth. "If you had lived as much as I have, you would know
that there is only one material thing whose value is sufficiently
certain to occupy a man. This thing. . . is GOLD" (pp. 381-82).

The fundamental misconception on which Gobseck bases his
faith provides an indication of why Marxists like Lukács are so
attracted to Balzac. Gobseck makes what is for such critics the
seminal mistake of capitalistic societies: he confuses the means for
the end. Gold in itself has little real worth. One cannot eat it, and it is
too soft to make an effective building material. Its value exists for
the most part by convention, as a *means* of exchange. According to
Gobseck, "Means are always confused with results" (p. 388). In fact,
he has taken what gold can buy for gold itself. "According to him,
money is a commodity" (p. 405). The means becomes the end.
"Gold represents all human force. Gold contains everything in
principle, and gives everything in reality" (p. 382).

At the thought of gold, his imagination is inflamed, and his
eloquence proves without a doubt that he is correct in claiming to be
a poet (p. 381). His muse, however, is the moon. Because of gold, "I
possess the world without fatigue, and the world has not the slightest
claim on me" (p. 383). "I am rich enough to purchase the consciences
of those who move ministers, from their office boys to their mistresses.
Isn't that Power? I can have the most beautiful women and their
tenderest caresses. Isn't that Pleasure? Don't Power and Pleasure
sum up your whole social order?" (p. 388). True, it is unthinkable
that he would actually succumb to one of these women. He remains
content with the knowledge that his gold would allow him the
pleasure, should he wish it. He and his eleven colleagues "are sated
with everything and have reached the point of loving power and
money for nothing but power and money alone" (p. 389). His
pleasure remains abstract. Similarly, though there can be no doubting
his power—he is "a fantastic image where the power of gold was
personified" (p. 389)—this quality as well has no physical existence.
And because the metal is material and durable, if not permanent,
Gobseck believes *his* spiritual values are as well. A few minutes
before his death, Derville finds him out of bed. Gobseck explains, "I
thought I saw my room full of living gold, and I got up to get some"
(p. 420). Even at his death, he has not learned that there is no such
thing as "living gold." He had spent his life in a love affair with
things, cold things which lacked the warmth of living beings. By
turning himself into gold, an effort highlighted by his yellow skin,[24]
"this man who had turned himself into gold" aspires likewise to
permanence or, put another way, to complete identification with his

beloved metal. "He abhorred his heirs and could not conceive of his fortune ever belonging to anyone but himself, even after his death" (p. 379).

The confusion of Gobseck's beliefs is emphasized by the addition Balzac made in 1835. There we find the dying Gobseck cloistered in his rooms. He has become involved in indemnifying the former Haitian colonials and, for his trouble, has received gifts of all sorts. "Gobseck took everything from the poor devil's hamper to pounds' weight of candlewax from frugal people" (p. 419). Because such goods can be converted into money, and because Gobseck's passion has been "converted into a sort of madness" (p. 418), the miser attributes the permanence of gold to the merchandise he has received, whether silverware or food. Overcome by greed, he quibbles about the exchange value, refuses to part with the tribute, and he dies surrounded by spoilage. "In the room next door to where Gobseck had died were rotten pâtés, a mass of all kinds of edibles, even shell-fish and fish with barbels whose differing vile odors almost asphyxiated me" (p. 421). Perhaps the best image of Gobseck's mistake appears in his fireplace. After his death, Derville's "eyes . . . rested on the pile of ashes whose bulk struck me. I took the pincers, and when I plunged them in it, I struck a heap of gold and silver" (p. 420). The gold remains, but Gobseck's "spiritual" values are reduced to ashes.

Ideally, the reader will have formed a mental image of this lunar, golden Gobseck. If this image has not been limited to the figure of a mere man, the framework will rapidly open and extend over the whole of society. Despite the ridiculousness, the comedy even, of the miser's death, the societal implications of his life remain. Neither gold, the fiduciary medium of exchange, nor the lunar Gobseck himself have any value or power except insofar as society accords it. Just as Mme de Restaud was a "bad daughter" (p. 416) who "behaved badly toward her father" (p. 375), all for the purpose of pandering to her frivolous passion for Maxime de Trailles (who represents "vanity, pleasure, the allurement of society"—p. 398), so Paris is abandoning true values in its frantic quest for power and pleasure, in short, for self-satisfaction. Gobseck lists the most common Parisian activities: gambling, gossip, adultery, politics, ostentatious display. . . "Isn't that the life of your Parisians translated into a few sentences?" (p. 382). All of these vain dissipations require gold and, inevitably, Gobseck. "Without dissipaters what would become of you?" M. de Trailles asks rhetorically. "The two of us are like body and soul." The usurer agrees (p. 397). Like Mme de

Restaud, Paris has committed patricide and chosen a new, unnatural father: *Papa Gobseck*. "*Ego sum papa!*" he says emphatically (p. 402). With this statement, Gobseck takes his most presumptuous step. The lunar figure attempts to usurp the paternal sun's place. In addition, as David Lee Rubin pointed out to me, Gobseck thus insists on his importance as a religious leader. "*Ego sum papa!*" may be translated, "*I am the pope!*"

Gobseck's reflected power is in fact so great that he has become a god. This significant morsel of information appears in the novella's title and, in addition, each time the usurer's name occurs in the narration. A philologically oriented critic will recognize that the *Gob* of Gobseck is one of the variants deriving from the etymon of "God" (the possibility is also evoked through paronomasia), while the *sec* of *-seck* suggests the French word *sac* or "purse" through paronomasia. Here, I wish to dispute neither H. U. Forest's suggestion that *Gob-* brings *gober* (gulp) to mind, nor the obvious connection between *-seck* and *sec* (dry) for such associations clearly highlight the avariciousness of this desiccated old usurer.[25] Nonetheless, as J. Wayne Conner has showed in series of excellent articles, the genius of Balzac's names grows from the fact that they frequently bear several pertinent meanings and consequently work on several levels to support important themes. Conner also makes Balzac's extensive philological knowledge clear.[26] It was then for good reason that the novelist had his narrator draw attention to the name: "By a singularity that Sterne would call predestination, this man was named Gobseck" (p. 379).

Whether or not the reader recognizes that the name proclaims Gobseck "god of the purse," the story stresses the point in other ways. Gobseck, for example, states, "My eyes are like God's, I see into hearts. Nothing is hidden from me. People refuse nothing to the one *who ties and unties the purse* [sac] *strings*" (p. 388; my italics). Gobseck is, however, a cruel god who entraps and destroys all who stumble while in his way. Naturally, he looks upon himself as a just instrument of revenge. He and his kingly friends meet at the Themis Café, named after the Greek goddess of justice (p. 388). One is then not surprised to see Gobseck touching his forehead and saying, "Here, finally, . . . is a balance in which the inheritances and concerns of the whole of Paris are weighed" (p. 389). Still, the usurer seems to feel an even stronger identification with Themis's sisters, the Furies. According to Derville, "Shame, Remorse, and Poverty are three Furies into whose hands women must inevitably fall as soon as they cross the boundaries" (p. 407). When Mme de Restaud succumbs to

Maxime de Trailles and thus lays herself open to Gobseck, she believes she is confronting an ogre (p. 409)—the flesh-eating giant deriving from the Roman Orcus—but Gobseck prefers to think of himself as one of the three sisters with a similar predilection for flesh. The Furies, after all, particularly punished those who sinned against the family, and Mme de Restaud was at least partially responsible for her father's miserable death. Gobseck remarks, "For you who go to bed on and under silk, beneath your smiles there is remorse, grinding teeth, and the maws of fantastic lions that bite into your hearts" (p. 385). He makes the rich feel "Necessity's claw" (p. 384). In short, "I am there as an avenger, I appear like a remorse" (p. 383).

For all his mythological associations, Gobseck does not reside off in some mythic realm where he can be comfortably forgotten. He embodies the new faith in the here and now, while serving as its priest. That he lives in a "house [which] once was a part of a convent"[27] stresses the degree to which, as already mentioned, the usurer's materialistic love of gold has become spiritualized into a true religion. The institutionalized quality of the faith is later highlighted when he compares himself and his friends to "a Holy Office [of the Inquisition] where the least important actions of anyone having any fortune at all are judged" (pp. 388-89). Derville returns to the image farther on to describe Maxime de Trailles and Mme de Restaud as they stand before Gobseck, hoping for a loan: "At this moment, the two of them were before their judge, who examined them as an old sixteenth-century Dominican must have watched two Moors being tortured in the subterranean depths of the Holy Office" (p. 399). If gold has become god, power and pleasure the spirit, then Gobseck is the earthly incarnation. The three have once again become one. But because man is no longer God's creation, one need no longer treat one's brother as one's self. On consideration, there might be a certain comfort in the thought that Gobseck only destroys the faithless Mme de Restaud. She is, appropriately enough, compared to Herodias (p. 385), the Biblical adulteress vilified by John the Baptist. However that may be, the image of the divine priest, Gobseck, should be firmly integrated into that of the lunar complex mentioned before.

At this point, one might say that *Gobseck* is a better than average story. The characters seem well delineated, and we know that Gobseck has risen above the ordinary to enter that rarified realm of beings who live beyond the pages which created them. I think, for example, of Molière's Alceste or Proust's Charlus. It is, however, in response to the application of such aesthetic criteria of judgment as economy and coherence that one begins to perceive a deeper and more interesting interpretation. Do all the elements of *Gobseck* cohere? Is every part essential to the story? At first glance, the answer in both cases is no. The fact that the Grandlieu salon serves as a frame finds little internal justification, for example. Mme de Grandlieu herself suggests as much when she interjects: "But I don't see anything in all that which concerns us."[28] Her brother, the Count de Born, dozes. And Derville swears impatiently. "I'm certainly going to wake Mademoiselle Camille up when I tell her that her happiness once depended on Papa Gobseck," he says (ibid.).

On realizing that Derville here emphasizes the extent of Gobseck's power, we not only understand that the frame both coheres and is essential to the story, but we are led into what seems to me its essence. While the *dissipator*, Maxime de Trailles, confronts the *conservator*, Derville, while the dissipated Mme de Restaud is balanced by the virtuous Fanny Malvaut, now Derville's wife,"[29] and are thus maintained in a kind of precarious equilibrium, the apparent balance is revealed as meaningless on recognizing that Gobseck stands above them all. Without the usurer, Derville would perhaps never have discovered Fanny, and the marriage might not have occurred. Papa Gobseck, priestly father god of Paris, blesses the union. Without Gobseck, Derville might never have purchased the law firm and could not have subsequently saved the Grandlieu's fortune.

In addition, it is well known that Balzac considered such great families as the Grandlieus essential to the preservation of civilization. His monarchism can to some degree be explained by his belief that the old aristocratic families joined the institutions of church and state to maintain the traditions and the structures which resist anarchy and chaos. If Gobseck can reach into the hearth of a Grandlieu, if Gobseck can decide whether a Grandlieu can marry Ernest de Restaud, conditions are in dire need of correction. That, of course, is the case. Had Gobseck not died, the young count Ernest would probably not have received his rightful fortune in time to marry Camille. From all indications, the obsessed Gobseck is unwilling to give up anything at all, and Derville shows himself helpless to affect the miser's decisions. On further considering the Grandlieus, one notices that had Gobseck not staked Derville to his practice, the latter could not have aided the Grandlieus to regain their fortune, and the great family might well have been condemned to more or less discreet poverty. The Restauds repeat the pattern,

for, despite the tragic mismatch which introduced Anastasie Goriot
to their midst, it remains a fine old family. The arms, of course, prove
the family's distinction in Balzac's curious world. What Albert
Béguin has termed an "occult power [which] reigns from the depths
of his miserable lodging . . . disdaining the visible attributes of his
monarchy that he wants to remain solitary and hidden"[30] has
influence which reaches into one of those rich and powerful aristocratic families that Balzac considered veritable pillars of society,
forces of order and stability, bulwarks against anarchy and chaos.

It is surely purposeful that the story of *Gobseck* was framed by
the Grandlieu family's salon, for the work's significance grows from
this setting. When money, when the god of the purse can become so
powerful as to touch the very foundations of society, the whole of
civilization is in danger. One can sense Balzac's horror when Mme de
Grandlieu fails to perceive how the story of Gobseck affects her
family. The novelist appears to be sounding the alarm, attempting to
awaken his fellow citizens to the danger that threatens them. It is but
one more indication of Balzac's genius to note that he was able to
take the "frame" and turn it into a means, not of limitation and
closure, rather of overture. It is perhaps the clearest indication that
the image of Gobseck is permutable into its isomorph, society.

It seems to me that the reasons for the effectiveness of this
work come within our grasp when we weigh its use of symbols and,
especially, both its exploitation of myth—those tales from Greece
and Rome—and its role as myth—an archetype. The fact that the
story refers to Themis and the Furies is important, because it sets the
stage for the story's larger function. On considering the widely
accepted assertions that myths as wholes overcome diachronicity,
even though they unfold in time,[31] one might further suggest that
passing indications of myths, at least, have the same end result. Such
a possibility not only points to the importance of what might be
called synoptic allusions (as opposed to the extended allusions I
treated previously[32]), it also recognizes that brief references largely
by-pass myth's need for narration in a temporal frame. Synoptic
allusions to myth can in certain instances call up the entire mythic
complex.

In the midst of realistic detail informing the reader of the
period's interest rates, the dress of the day, the objects decorating
the rooms of the poor and the rich, the allusions to Greco-Roman
mythology introduce a timeless element into the fictional chronology.
And as we more fully perceive the all-pervading power of this
heartless, golden "banknote-man" (p. 378), as we understand that

society's vices have created him, as we fully grasp the mortal danger Gobseck incarnates, the novella itself rises above the realistic setting, above its time and day. Balzac has given concrete form to an archetypal pattern, a truly modern myth. Taylor Caldwell's depiction, in *Captains and the Kings* (1972), of European bankers making and unmaking political leaders, deluding public opinion, toying with the world's economy, all for their own private benefit, provides proof of the myth's continuing attraction. Realistically, we believe that no man or group of men could have this power, but deep within ourselves we apparently suspect that very possibility. Though Godot never comes, Gobseck may be sitting today with his eleven colleagues deciding our destiny. And in some fifty pages, Balzac has animated an archetype still capable of awakening secret nightmares, a coherent myth that leaves mere realism far behind to become an aesthetic reality.[33]

For all this, *Gobseck* is not a New Novel. It is no shorter than many recent prose creations published separately, but its subject concerns neither the act of writing nor the nature of language, and it makes little use of phonic, syntactical, or morphological patterns in establishing its structure. Still, as said at the outset, I am less interested here in the differences between new and old novels than in perceiving those qualities which modern art has taught us to seek, which are frequently ignored, and which exist in great works of the past. The interpretation I propose would be impossible if the reading were restricted, as is often the case in criticism of nineteenth-century fiction, to explicit discourse. None of the narrator's explanations, for example, go beyond the fictional motivation for the story, beyond, that is, Derville's desire to change Mme de Grandlieu's opposition to her daughter's interest in the Restaud boy. Nor can one rely heavily on a naïve optic, where character is perceived as a pseudo-human being or an imagined "everyday being of flesh and bone which could . . . serve as a referent"[34] and plot as the prosaic sequence of pseudo-real events. If one refuses to allow the connotations of the text's language to form systems of meaning, the more or less complete study of Gobseck and his personality as it exists and develops leaves the character as little more than an improbable neurotic. And Gobseck's little speeches come off as poorly disguised justifications for his own obsessions. Just as an isolated and limited conception of character provides little of significance, so the plot or, better, the plots. They suggest in fact a lack of unity. If Gobseck's activity was supposed to be the center of the work, one must notice that he does very little. Furthermore, his relationship with the other plots remains tangential. In no literal sense could one consider him the *causa causans* of the sequence of episodes concerning Camille and Ernest, Mme de Restaud and Maxime de Trailles, or M. and Mme de Restaud, for example. Gobseck touches each of these plots, but only in passing, as they rise or fall.

It is rather the detail that indicates the substantial unity and significance of Balzac's Gobseck, for it binds the usurer firmly to the physical and intellectual surroundings of the textual universe in which he lives. Such supposedly gratuitous elements furthermore establish relationships joining him to Balzac's world. Gobseck's every act is both influenced by and influences the same web of interrelated bonds that continue to constitute our civilization and our universe. Though the miser has no real import in and for himself, his importance rises from the subtle indications of what he means: he is the egotistical and destructive product of a sick society. Balzac wrote in the early years of the industrial revolution and during the youth of our modern capitalistic society. It seemed to him that in the stead of the age-old humanistic values, protected and advanced by the institutions of family, church, and motherland, man was raising a golden idol to his own ego. To the insatiable hunger of capital for more capital for the sake of capital was joined individuals' frenetic need for pleasure and power, all for the further glorification of the self. Money became necessary to satisfy egotistical needs and, inevitably, was becoming the ultimate perversion—a value in itself. Gobseck, the god of the purse, was created because church, family, and state were losing the loyalties of the citizenry. Only money could buy what they wanted. But the price was Gobseck.

Balzac returned over and over again to the theme. In another story of the same period, "La Fille aux yeux d'or" (1835), the narrator summarizes the drama of Paris's slavery: "What, then, rules in this country without morals, without beliefs, without any sentiment whatsoever; what is the beginning and end of such sentiments, beliefs, and morals as they have? Gold and pleasure. Take these two words for illumination."[35] Perhaps the most explicit version appears in the late *Splendeurs et misères des courtisanes* (1838-47) where the archcriminal Vautrin blackmails himself into a position of governmental importance. Repeatedly, Balzac painted the predators, the sick, and the depraved as they came into the sun and power, all because the preservative institutions had lost their support and thus their ability to repress such nocturnal creatures. Under the influence of the moon's unhealthy emanations, they created values out of the unsubstantial. At the same time they sowed the seeds of civilization's death; with the benign approval of Themis, they gave birth to avenging Furies.

This, I suggest, is the thrust of *Gobseck*. Though nothing of any significance happens, though narrative itself cannot account for the structure of the whole, though Gobseck considered as a character in the traditional sense has little import, the work succeeds admirably, and this because the entire text functions to create in the reader's mind the image of an unacceptable society (whether it be Balzac's or ours makes no difference; in this respect we remain in the novelist's world). *Gobseck* uses narration to form description. By making use of all the characters, all the plots, all the symbols and allusions, it becomes an image of society.

Balzac was not basically a storyteller, though his talents as a raconteur stand well against those of such masters as Maupassant. He was, in truth, exactly what he claimed: a historian, a "creative historian," perhaps, but a historian nevertheless. Balzac's goal was to provide the people of his day with an image which would make them more able to see and understand their world. No aesthete he. Huysmans's "Literature has only one reason for being: to save the one who creates it from an aversion for living!"[36] suggests a completely different creed. The thought of withdrawing from the world to such solitary pleasures never occurred to Balzac. Nor, at another extreme, does he become a Bouvard or Pécuchet *avant l'heure*, faithfully and happily taking dictation. The artist as "recording instrument," praised by William S. Burroughs in *Naked Lunch* (1959)[37] could never satisfy the great nineteenth-century novelist. Balzac took huge handfuls of life and transformed them into an image which was true to his vision.

Perhaps this explains Balzac's sovereign disdain for plot. In a note appended to *Scènes de la vie privée*, he declares: "Amusing oneself with looking for new plots is putting more importance on the frame than on the picture."[38] It is true that he was responding to the accusation of plagiarism; still, the statement construes rather well with what we know of his work. I need not dwell on the long descriptions which introduce many of his novels. In recent years, we have learned that they are not mere adjuncts; they are analogues, the place where those who savor Balzacian prose in depth find the story played out figuratively and in advance. It is for good reason that Balzac's primary justification for *La Comédie humaine*, as seen in the "Forward" of 1842, concerns a description of man in his society.

*Gobseck*, then, provides an excellent example of "image structure." It should be contrasted with "process structure," which, as previously argued, constitutes an organization that must be appreciated as a development over time, for it consists of a succession or series of some sort. Without question, when one thinks of the novel, one thinks first of sequential ordering. We expect novels to be in the business of telling about some kind of change. It may be an infinitesimal change, a mere "movement between two states of equilibrium" (Todorov's definition of narrative),[39] but we expect something to happen and thus vary the introductory condition for better or worse. Indeed, that is the predominant pattern, and I shall return to it in the next chapter. It is not, however, the only structure to be found in the novel, as *Gobseck* demonstrates.

"Image" and "process" account for the structure of all novels, and of much else besides. Psychologists for example, tell us that the human mind normally categorizes information according to sequence, which is handled by the left hemisphere of the brain, and shape, form, texture, which are processed by the right cerebrial hemisphere.[40] When the right side of a person's brain does not function properly, he tends to have trouble fitting the various parts of, say, a friend's face into a recognizable pattern, while a person suffering from dysfunction of the left cerebral hemisphere will normally recognize the whole of a friend's face but be unable to connect it with a name. The creation and recognition of structures which can be related to concepts of either image (static) or process (sequence) appear to be basic to human consciousness.

Such concepts have also had considerable importance to criticism.[41] The literary terms of "narration" and "description" correspond to the mental schemata just discussed. While narration communicates a sense of action, movement, change, development for better or worse, description seems quite different. It causes Frederic Thomas Blanchard to wax poetic and, in the process, to make several points that represent the traditional position on this mode of writing. "Though queen of lyric poetry," he says, "description has often been the Cinderella of prose fiction, the unconsidered servant who, except for infrequent but exquisite triumphs in portraiture or landscape painting, has merely kept the narrative house in order."[42] Description—the representation of a static (rather than dynamic) image or impression of something, whether character, object, or state—has indeed been a second-class citizen in prose fiction. Gérard Genette provides a case in point when he explains that, though description was "a major element in the exposition" of works in the Balzacian tradition, narration nevertheless "constantly plays the most important role" in all traditions. "Description is quite naturally an *ancilla narrationis,* a slave which, while always necessary, is always submissive, never emancipated."[43] Jean Ricardou uses a similar understanding to condemn a predecessor: "In reducing description to an ornament of no use to the understanding of the text, Balzac reinforced the wretched prejudice assuring that all descriptive pages are to be skipped in a novel.[44] And Roland Barthes, in a discussion which is informed by his belief in the primary importance of plot, equates description with "useless details."[45]

Barthes's (and, I suspect, the others') preference of plot, to the detriment of description, grows from two fundamental positions: first, that the description which indicates character or atmosphere indirectly will, through repetition, become a part of the structure (what Barthes calls "the main articulations of the narrative") and is thus redundant, and, second, that description does not motivate action, or, as Barthes puts it, "It is justified by no finality of action or communication."[46] In fact, however, as Mieke Bal has shown in reference to *Madame Bovary* (1857), description can motivate action.[47]

The action of *Gobseck* becomes description, in much the same way as in Robbe-Grillet's "La Plage," a lovely *Instantané* (1962), in which three children walk along a beach. There is no question that the children move, and that the eye of the narrator follows them. Nonetheless, the piece remains a description. If anything, the children's progression reinforces the quality of timelessness and stasis. Perhaps the determining factor is the significance of time and change, for here, though the children move and though the beach changes momentarily to reflect their passage, the impression grows that neither time nor change affects anything at all; the events are ephemeral. Rather like Jakobson's paradigm falling onto the syntagma, the narration slides into description, or, more precisely, it fades into an over-riding descriptive structure which motivates the action. Narration then becomes, not even the handmaiden of description, it is one of the constituent parts, one of the building blocks, a mere element in the image portrayed.

Balzac's refusal of narration provided him with a wonderful opportunity to incite overture of the kind Eco terms Brechtian. Only when the mental complex created by Balzac's work opens and the reader establishes a relationship with the isomorph of society does the possibility of disequilibrium, thus of narration, occur. Plot, however, takes place outside the text, in the real world, when the reader revolts against the society that Balzac has pictured so well.

However different the goals of his revolution be from those of Marx, Balzac constitutes a profoundly revolutionary writer. More important for my purposes, by presenting the problem in astonishingly vivid terms, the novelist provides the opportunity for overture, and the reader discovers that, by accepting the author's conventions and cooperating with him in the process of creation, he has ultimately created his own life. The same thing is true, in one way or another, with all great texts. Of course, if I am correct in believing that *Gobseck* still has social and aesthetic significance, it is only because of the entire, coherent vision; if it confronts readers with a "modern" *and* "traditional" reality, it does so only because it is a whole in which all elements—plot, character, explicit discourse and descriptive detail— work together to make a total image with still vital overture. And, while action is deactivated, description quivers with a life of its own.

In a way, *Gobseck* and *La Chartreuse de Parme* do their job too well. While they admirably exemplify novels which, on the one hand, create an image that rises above various actions to represent the whole of a society in a particular period, and, on the other, organize all their material around a mainstream story of a character who is shaped and formed in the flow of the fiction, they seem too pat. The next chapter turns to a far more complex, and controversial, work. Despite almost universal agreement that Zola's *Germinal* is a masterpiece, critics diverge on its thrust. It then offers an opportunity to test the vocabulary developed in the last two chapters and, finally, to speculate on subordinate forms, as they occur in the endomorphic novel.

## Chapter 4

## *Germinal* and the Endomorphic Novel

IN STUDYING *GOBSECK*, I INSISTED that it was necessary to view the miser as a figure or image rather than as what is generally known as a "character." Writers have long been conscious of the fact that fictional personages are not people. Proust, for example, pointed out that "the ingenuity of the first novelist consisted in understanding that within the apparatus of our emotions, because the image is the only essential element, the simplification which would consist of purely and simply suppressing real personages would be a decisive improvement."[1] It is true that very few authors carry this so far as to suppress all or even most of the human traits of their characters. In recent novels, however, it happens occasionally. Jean Ricardou, for example, concludes his *La Prise de Constantinople* (1965) with the following passage: "A certain kind of conscientious reading now suffices for the irradiation of the whole figure to elaborate who I AM, and by a not too unexpected, reflective phenomenon, in a flash, to deliver it to me, THE BOOK," and, on closing the novel, the reader discovers that what read *La Prise de Constantinople* [*The Capture of Constantinople*] on the front cover now reads *La Prose de Constantinople* [*The Prose of Constantinople*] on the back. It is far more common for novelists to weight their characters with significance that perhaps only popes or kings and queens have in real life. Almost no critics would follow Juan Ignacio Ferraras and explicitly deny that novelistic personages have connotations,[2] but any extensive reading of criticism dealing with specific novels makes it clear that such is the common practice. Most professional readers look at characters as though they were real people. I suspect it is an important cause of difficulty in respect to *Germinal*.

The secondary literature reveals a significant problem in our understanding of Zola's masterpiece. Although it is generally assumed that *Germinal* (1885) constitutes a prophetic novel, it is anything but certain what it prophesies. René Ternois, for example, states:

> The end of the novel leaves no hope. The revolts of wretched people are fatal, and in addition, aggravate their suffering. Accumulated defeats, hatred prepare the final "catastrophy," where the old world will collapse. Beyond this destruction, Zola sees nothing. . . .

Spring, light, growing wheat must not lead us astray.
Zola is one of whose middle-class people whom the law of
1884 and the organization of unions terrified. The danger
of a revolution seems more menacing to him than it was
during the period of violence and disorder [a few years
before]. He sees nothing but a catastrophy in the future.
He would like to give the illusion of hope, but he does not
find any words except "the future century germinating in
the furrow," words which have no sense either for him or
anyone else.[3]

The categorical tone of Ternois's judgment would make one believe
that there can be no question about interpretation, and his reading
does indeed find support in the novel. Still, we know that Elliott M.
Grant, another widely respected Zola scholar, had but a few years
earlier come to quite a different conclusion. He points out that not
only he but many other students of *Germinal* consider the book a
"work of indignation, compassion, and, in the last analysis, hope."[4]
Clearly, Ternois's Armageddon differs significantly from Grant's
reading, which stresses the germination imagery of the conclusion.
This understanding, like that of Ternois, is also well supported
elsewhere in Zola's novel.

Neither Ternois's nor Grant's arguments provide a basis either
for choosing between them or for resolving their differences (the
same may be said for other similar conclusions). Not surprisingly,
several critics have mentioned *Germinal's* ambiguity and contradictions.[5] The very fact that the critical literature reveals widespread
inability to agree, despite similar presuppositions and methodology
drawn from literary history, suggests that another critical optic is
perhaps appropriate.

As should be clear by this point, I expect novels to incorporate
a predominant principle, system, or pattern of relationships, which
organizes the constituent parts. Henry James uses different vocabulary
to say the same thing: "It is a familiar truth to the novelist, at the
strenuous hour, that, as certain elements in any work are of the
essence, so others are only of the form; that as this or that character,
this or that disposition of the material, belongs to the subject
directly, so to speak, so this or that other belongs to it but
indirectly—belongs intimately to the treatment."[6] There is something central, essential, fundamental to every novel, to which
everything else is subordinated. James calls it the "subject." It may
be a character, as it was in *Gobseck*, while in *La Chartreuse de Parme,* the

central system was the plot of Fabrice as he progressed from birth to his Carthusian vocation and, one assumes, to a better life by far. All the other elements are subsumed under this overriding development. Though such a system permits of the differing interpretations that arise from differing methodologies, whenever critics using a similar approach come to irreconcilably different conclusions about a particular novel, the explanations for the disagreement are limited: either the novel is flawed or the readings fall short of adequacy. (I speak here only of interpretations which attempt to come to terms with a text's entirety.)

In respect to *Germinal*, it seems to me that more attention should be paid to the connotations of the main character. I would suggest, furthermore, that the central, organizing sequence is not what Etienne actually does, rather the complex of allusions which he keys—including a number of Greek myths and the story of the New Testament Church. That the significant plot does not consist of Etienne's activities in the mining region where the novel is set, but in the sequence of allusions, does not prevent *Germinal* from exemplifying an endomorphic novel. As mentioned before, endomorphic novels are constructed on clearly delimited armatures, whether plot, character, or theme. Endomorphic novels may be of either the image (*Gobseck*) or the sequential (*La Chartreuse*) variety, and numerous examples of both exist. In addition, as I shall point out in more detail farther on, the endomorphic novel may be broken down into trajectory, bead, serial, and mirror structures.

When I turn to the nonmimetic levels of Zola's *Germinal*, I follow the pioneering lead of Marcel Girard and Philip Walker.[7] The former is doubtless responsible for the most convincing demonstration of the personification of the Voreux and surrounding countryside as a giant. According to him, Zola saw the Voreux as a gigantic, monstrous animal. Girard notes its horn, its eyes, its mouth that breathes, eats men, and, when mortally wounded, emits a death rattle. As the human nourishment descends into the subterranean galleries it arrives in the voracious ogre's bowels, capable of digesting a multitude. Then Girard concludes by speculating on the mine's back entrance: "And one easily imagines what function Zola assigns—whether consciously or not—to the other entrance of the mine, 'the grassy, hairy entrance,' the Réquillart hole, a haven of warmth and comfort for Jeanlin, then for Étienne, around which the boys and girls freely possess one another."[8] Girard is of the opinion that "this anxiety about anthropomorphic details is sometimes even injurious to the grandeur of Émile Zola's myths" (ibid., p. 67). It seems to me, however, that when regarded as an integral part of the rest of Zola's mythopoeic system, the giant, from mouth to groin, is essential to the conveyance of *Germinal*'s meaning and an understanding of its structure.

As has frequently been pointed out, *Germinal* sets off the Voreux-Réquillart giant against a god residing in a tabernacle located someplace in the mysterious distance. It is perhaps equally important to note that the mine represents man's incursion into nature, a force that seems malevolent, perhaps only because it is mindless. (In some respects, it resembles Capital, the soulless and distant "squatting god," likewise a force, at the other end of the book's mythic spectrum.) Zola was far more precise about the true character of the earth in his later (1887) *La Terre* [*The Earth*]—Fouan "had loved the earth like a woman who kills and for whom people murder. Not a wife, or children, or anybody at all, nothing human. . . the earth!"—but in both *La Terre* and *Germinal*, whether human or not, the earth comes alive. One could think that the miners would be more aware of nature's power, for they live in the very grip of her four elements: air (pit-gas), earth (cave-ins), water (the Torrent), and fire (Tartaret). Interestingly enough, they only notice the danger when nature kills or injures someone by breaking through the guard the company has obliged them to raise. Indeed, not only do the workers live in such unceasing contact with the mine that they ignore its menace, but they feel at home there. The confirmation, for instance, that Etienne is truly a miner comes when we read that "the more he descended into the darkness the more he felt at home."9

In some respects, there is no distinction between man and nature, of which, after all, man is but a part. One thinks for example of Zola's well-known letter to Jules Lemaître on March 14, 1885: "The soul which you enclose within a being, I sense it spread everywhere, in human beings and outside of them, in animals whose brother man is, in plants, in pebbles." Still, one should not fail to note that in *Germinal* Zola builds a hierarchy into nature. At the bottom of the scale is the earth, for, as suggested before, it is mindless. Animals do have a mind. They love (pp. 1499-1550), pity (p. 1295), suffer (p. 1500), and remember (p. 1182), to such a degree, in fact, that Trompette seemingly dies of homesickness (p. 1499). As Jean-Pierre Davoine has pointed out, the frequent comparisons of animals and miners intensify the terrible conditions and suffering of both. "The men and the animals live the same adventure: companions and victims of work (Trompette, Bataille), brought to death by cruelty or economic necessity (Pologne), the animals resemble the miners whose lot they share."[10] Such explicit and implied comparisons also serve to highlight a difference of great importance. Animals can only dream of what they have already experienced, whereas, although the men of the mining village are treated like animals, although the only morality they experience—either from the company or from the menacing forces of nature—is *might is right,* they dream of something beyond their experience: absolute justice.[11] "When you live like animals with your nose to the ground, you have to have a secret place inside you where you amuse yourself enjoying things you'll never have. And what excited her, what made her agree with the young man was the idea of justice" (p. 1279).

This is not to say that men are by nature preserved from descending Zola's scale of being, for that is far from the truth of the matter. Zola considered humanness a goal toward which one struggles. Consequently, given the pitiable abjectness of most of the characters in this book, one is almost amazed to hear, for example, Maheu's insistence on justice when he realizes that only he has had pork brawn: "You know, I don't like these injustices" (p. 1229), or to find Catherine hanging desperately, albeit from fear, to her standard of fidelity (e.g., p. 1490). Either from overcrowding, which encourages promiscuity and drunkenness (p. 1275), or from example, as seems to be the case with Chaval who strong-arms Catherine into compliance (p. 1331), or because of a combination of heredity and a terrible accident, the apparent causes of Jeanlin's turning from a vicious child into a predatory, kill-crazy animal, or because of the inhuman conditions of the mine that make an imbecile and a dangerous brute of Bonnemort, the sum total of the miners' world tends to brutalize—and that in the most literal sense of the word. Even their glorious dreams rapidly become just another variation of the only morality they experience: *Might is right*—"What a dream! to be the masters, to stop suffering, to enjoy finally!—That's it, by God! It's our turn now!... Death to the exploiters!" (p. 1380). These characters live in a jungle. Because they only rarely see beyond its law, the novel insists over and over again on the need for education.[12] Indeed, when Étienne is at the apogee of his revolutionary fervor ("Souvarine, if he had deigned to come, would have applauded his ideas"—p. 1381), he retains "the article on education" (ibid.). The conditions at Montsou make it seem only natural that, harnessed "like horses" (p. 1517), the workers should slip down the scale of being, feel "the assault of bestiality" (p. 1169), act "under the impulsion of instinct's whip" (p. 1240), "necessarily grow rotten together" (p. 1275),

engage in "the rut of people" (p. 1380), and become at first "like
wolves"[13] and then, very simply, "the beast" (p. 1442).

We are now well into an important metaphor of *Germinal*, the
key to which appears in the following passage: "Your Karl Marx is
still at the point of wanting to let natural forces act." Souvarine, who
speaks here, is of course opposed to such a laissez-faire attitude, and
he commands, "Set the four corners of cities on fire, mow the people
down, raze everything, and when nothing remains of this rotten
world, perhaps a better one will grow back" (p. 1255). But as Zola
apparently understood, direct action was and is not necessary.
Ignorance and misery are by themselves enough to turn human
beings into brutes (v., p. 1416) and finally into "a force of nature"
(p. 1437).

The predominant images describing the mob's rampage across
the countryside turn around water and wind. "The band flowed" (p.
1437) "like overflowing water that follows the slopes" (p. 1410)
"with the accrued force of a rolling, mountain stream" (p. 1425).
While Mme Hennebeau and her terrified guests watch, "on the
empty road a tempest wind seemed to blow, similar to those sudden
squalls that proceed big storms" (p. 1435). They hear "the roll of
thunder" approaching (ibid.), and their very words are drowned out
"in the hurricane of gestures and cries" (ibid.). The workers, having
lost all semblance of human beings, pass, and the bourgeois
"received their terrible wind in the face" (p. 1437). The wind
imagery is the seemingly natural outcome of a phenomenon begun
much earlier. With the outrage over the threat of lower pay, "a
rebellion germinated in this narrow corner, about six hundred
meters beneath the ground" (p. 1184). It very quickly becomes "a
wind of revolt, which came from the Voreux" (p. 1193).

What could be more natural than this wind which builds to
hurricane force? What could seem more natural than these men,
who live most of their waking lives in the earth, buffeted by wind,
tortured by insufferable heat, and drenched by water,[14] who not
only take on the qualities of their constant neighbor, the earth, but
who actually become forces of nature? There is, however, a curious
development that should be noted. Of the four elements available to
the miners, they only assume two: wind and water. Doubtless, these
forces are very destructive. By the time they destroy the pump at
Gaston-Marie (p. 1425) and thus flood Jean-Bart (p. 1418), Deneulin,
the energetic representative of private rather than corporate enterprise, is a ruined man. But the most destructive element remains.
Although Brulé wants to turn loose fire (p. 1413), the others clearly

hesitate to do so. " 'That's enough!' " Maheude yells. " 'The storeroom is on fire' " (ibid.). And, before leaving Jean-Bart, the strikers extinguish the last flames with buckets of water (p. 1414). It is almost as though the workers believe that only the company has the right to fire. The mine authorities, in their role as Providence, have long dominated fire by distributing or withholding coal.[15] Still, the workers are beginning to question the company's claim to exclusive control. Étienne asks that it stop playing "the role of providence" (p. 1322), and Maheude asserts her right to glean coal (p. 1357). The potential exists, then, that the miners will assume the power of fire, especially after the other elements have failed. They became wind, and they accomplished nothing. They turned water loose in Jean-Bart, with equal lack of success. When this latter movement is continued to little avail by Souvarine, who floods the Voreux and simultaneously sets off a series of cave-ins, thus releasing earth, only one elemental force remains to be exploited. Fire.

From the beginning Souvarine has proclaimed the efficacy of fire,[16] and when he leaves Montsou, "He was going with his tranquil air to the extermination, wherever there would be dynamite, to blow up cities and men" (p. 1548). Once again, however, Zola proceeds to indicate that anarchists are not the only danger. In the end, with the sullen miners reduced anew to subhuman life, like the earth, available for the exploitation of the company, it is surely not accidental that Maheude is positioned beneath Tartaret, working her fan in the infernal heat. "For ten hours, with aching back, she turned her wheel at the bottom of a burning flue" (p. 1584). Zola makes masterful use of this metaphorical progression from wind, to water, to earth, for he implies that the movement may be completed. When men are brutalized and, thus, forced to the bottom of the scale of being, it is only a matter of time before they turn to fire, the most destructive of the four elements. Partially because of this imagery, "the feverish hope of revenge" (ibid.) seems more than an idle threat.

But the author's allusion to myth is perhaps more important. Philip Walker was, to the best of my knowledge, the first to have the perceptive insight that Zola alluded to "not just any Greco-Roman myths but particularly stories of the Creation and the War of the Gods: the primordial cosmic struggles between Uranus and Cronus, Cronus and Jupiter.[17] His argument is necessarily brief, for it is only part of a much larger subject. Perhaps for this reason he has not found universal acceptance.[18] Nonetheless, if for no other reason than that Zola's references to Furies, Tartarus, and Ceres, to mention only three, are too clear to be ignored, Walker's insight seems worthy of further consideration.

A rereading of Hesiod's *Theogony* reinforces the impression that Zola made expert use of mythic parallels. Hesiod, of course, begins with the creation and the birth of the gods, among whom should be mentioned those monstrous brothers, the Titans, Cyclopes, and Hecatonchires, who represent the unruly forces of nature. Zola incorporates them into his account of the Titanomachy. The Olympian gods, against whom the Titans revolted, were the "givers of good,"[19] which immediately distinguishes Hesiod's story from Zola's, for the Montsou Mining company, though providential, scarcely qualifies among "givers of good things" (v. 664). Zola has then reversed the roles of good and evil. Otherwise, however, the similarities are suggestive. Hesiod breaks the War of the Titans into two sequences for the purposes of narration. During the first, "the issue of the war hung evenly balanced" (vv. 635-38). And this despite the fact that the grateful Cyclopes had already taken thunder, thunderbolt, and lightning from Earth's hiding place and given them to Zeus (vv. 503-06). During the second sequence, Hesiod tells us that "Zeus no longer held back his might" (v. 687), so for some reason or other he did not take full advantage of the Cyclopes' gift at the outset of the war. The Cyclopes, as previous owners of lightning, should not be passed over, especially on noting that Zola, temporarily at least, encloses fire within the earth when he places it in a Tartaret.

But Zeus's next ploy is even more important than the weapons which he turned against the Titans. The father-god enlists the aid of another set of the Titans' brothers, the Hundred-Handed, also called the Hecatonchires. The great Olympian fully commits himself and, with the aid of the three Hundred-Handed, the tide turns. In the second war sequence, the Titans are vanquished and shut away in Tartarus, largely because of their brothers—the Cyclopes' gift of lightning and the Hecatonchires' active support of Zeus.

In *Germinal*, the events of the strike follow a similar pattern. The first phase, up through the mutilation of Maigrat, ends pretty much in a draw. Both the miners and company are hurt; neither is ready to give in. The situation changes when the soldiers arrive and take an active part. Zola insists that the soldiers are fellow workers "taken from the people, and who were armed against the people" (p. 1464); indeed, "They were all brothers, they should get along with each other" (p. 1501). Étienne reminds the soldiers "that they were common people too, that they ought to be with common people, against the exploiters of poverty" (p. 1502), but in vain. Where Zeus succeeds by using his lightning bolt and turning the Hecatonchires against their own brothers, the company succeeds with rifle *fire* loosed by workers in the guise of soldiers. "The squad's fire [*feu*] swept the piece of ground" (p. 1510) and the strike is broken. Finally, just as the Titans were shut away in Tartarus, so the workers continue "all the gloomy work of the subterranean jail, so crushed by the enormous mass of rocks that, in order to distinguish the big painful sigh, you had to know it was there" (p. 1590). The defeated workers are like "wild animals in a cage" (p. 1457).

The myth, however, continues. Apollodorus tells us that Earth was vexed on account of the Titans.[20] She turned to other sons of hers, the Giants, whom she had borne when blood, resulting from Uranus's emasculation, had dropped to the ground. (At the same time and in the same way, the Furies were produced. Considering that Zola compares the furious women in *Germinal* to Furies after they have mutilated Maigrat—p. 1454—it seems at least possible that this series of myths was in Zola's mind.) At Earth's bidding, the Giants attacked Olympus, where the gods were helpless. "Now the gods had an oracle that none of the giants could perish at the hand of gods, but that with the help of a mortal they would be made an end of" (I, vi, 1). Zeus rounded up Heracles. Working together, Zeus, the other Olympians, and Heracles defeat the Giants. In *Germinal*, the Giants have not yet been born, but, as Étienne walks off into the distance, they are certainly in the making.

> Now, the April sun was gloriously shining in a clear sky, warming the childbearing earth. Life was springing from the nutritious flanks, buds were bursting into green leaves, the fields were quivering from the growth of the grass. On every side, seed-grain was swelling, stretching out, cracking the plain, tormented with a need for heat and light. An overflowing of sap mixed with whispering voices, the noise of sprouting germs expanded in a big kiss. Again and again, more and more distinctly, as though they were approaching the ground, the camrades were hammering. In the enflamed rays of the sun on this youthful morning, the countryside seemed pregnant with that sound. Men were burgeoning, a black, avenging army, which was slowly germinating in the furrows, growing for the harvests of the next century, and this germination would soon split the earth wide open. (p. 1591)

This passage concludes *Germinal.* Not only do we remember both the implicit menace of Maheude's busy fan "beneath Tartaret" (p. 1584) and the fiery annihilation that is to come after the Biblical Deluge, but the last few lines strongly suggest the coming Gigantomachy, the mythic sequel to the Titanomachy. I quoted more than the last few lines of *Germinal*'s conclusion, however, for the passage is far from unequivocal. The implicit hope of this joyous, life-filled spring day clashes strangely with the terminal promise of a new and terrible war. Given the fact that the bloodless company and the spineless bourgeois have already shown their weakness, that the Empire itself is wounded, there would seem to be only one possible justification for this hope: that Heracles, the sole protection against the revolt of Earth's giant children, has been born.

Indeed, at least one such mortal hero has appeared, and the reader watches him walk toward the mysterious tabernacle of the "sated, squatting god" (p. 1591). At this point, Étienne Lantier is reborn a new man. He sees beyond the workers' unrealistic dreams and unreasoning rage, and he simultaneously recognizes the inhumanity of the bourgeoisie and Capital. The means and the event of this birth are clarified by a combination of remarkable insights by Marcel Girard, who, as already mentioned, points to the existence of the Voreux giant's groin at the Réquillart opening, and by Philip Walker who, in a footnote to "The *Ébauche* of *Germinal*," calls attention to a parallel suggested by a reading of Eliade's *Myth and Reality*:

> A large number of myths feature . . . initiatory passage through a *vagina dentata*, or the dangerous descent into a cave or crevice assimilated to the mouth or uterus of Mother Earth. All these adventures are in fact initiatory ordeals, after accomplishing which the victorious hero acquires a new mode of being.[21]

To this could perhaps be added another insight, also from Eliade:

> Flood corresponds to the three days of darkness, or "death," of the moon. It is a cataclysm, but never a final one, for it takes place under the seal of the moon and the waters, which are pre-eminently the sign of growth and regeneration. A flood destroys simply because the "forms" are old and worn out, but it is always followed by a new humanity and a new history. The vast majority of deluge

myths tell how a single individual survived, and how the new race was descended from him.[22]

These passages add another dimension to certain events in *Germinal*. After the deluge of the mine, Étienne reverts to a primitive, subhuman state, symbolized by the brutal murder of Chaval: "Despite the revolt which came from his upbringing, a sort of gladness made his heart beat, the animal joy of an appetite finally satisfied. Then he felt pride, the pride of the mightiest" (p. 1572). The water continues to rise, slowly enveloping them, and the lamp dies. "Death blows out the lamp," says Catherine (p. 1573). "Back bent" (p. 1573), head down (ibid.), occasionally in a fetal position (p. 1575), they await the seemingly inevitable end. They hear the signal announcing a rescue attempt. "[T]hey were evidently coming through Réquillart. The gallery descended into the bed. . . .[A]nd their legs seemed to melt in this bath of ice" (pp. 1574-75). Like the most primitive forms of life, they eat wood (p. 1575), drink water, perhaps even blood (p. 1576). Étienne's punishment for his murder of Chaval is truly terrible, but the water eventually carries off the body, and Étienne's "hebetude" spares him further suffering. The initiation nears its end when Étienne and Catherine make love. She dies, and for two days, Étienne holds her gently and lovingly.[23]

Finally, thanks to the joint labor of miners and the bourgeois Négrel, Étienne is delivered, torn rather from the bowels of the giant, Earth. Then "the rebellious worker and the skeptical boss throw themselves into each others' arms, sobbing loudly in the deep upheaval of all the humanity that was in them. It was an immense sadness, the misery of generations, the excessive grief into which life can fall" (p. 1580). The new Étienne's hair is white (ibid.), and, as the narrator states explicitly, he is finally ready: "His formation was finished, he left armed, as a rational soldier of the revolution, having declared war on society as he saw it and as he condemned it" (p. 1588). No longer fired by personal ambition, as was previously the case (e.g., p. 1329), no longer counted among the "detested bourgeoisie with its comfort and intellectual satisfactions,"[24] neither bourgeois nor worker (pp. 1588-89), he is perhaps capable of providing the means for the workers to rise and receive justice. The means is important. Always before, this was precisely where his thinking became fuzzy.[25] Freed of the personal ambition that caused the International to fail, he wishes to turn the workers into heroes, "the unique force in which humanity could be renewed" (p. 1589),

even though they might well devour him in the process (ibid.). As his
means, he will use the human force of law and justice, rather than the
mindless force of nature: "He now thought that perhaps violence
didn't speed things up. . . . Vaguely, he guessed that one day legality
could be more terrible. His reasoning powers were maturing; he had
sown the wild oats of his rancor" (p. 1590).

When Philip Walker considers the final pages of the novel, he
concludes "that Zola presents a vision of nature as earth-mother
bringing forth, as in the myth of Deucalion and Pyrrha, a new and
hardier race of men springing up from under the growing wheat—an
autochthonous race well adapted to labor and the struggles that will
result in the return of paradise."[26] There is in fact very little evidence
of an allusion to the myth of Deucalion and Pyrrha, the only survivers
of the terrible flood that came upon the earth after Jove visited earth
and discovered man's evil. Ovid tells us that Jove, looking forward to
what he would do after the deluge, planned to create a better
humanity, "unlike the first, created / Out of a miracle."[27] After the
waters receded, the only survivors, Deucalion and Pyrrha, beg
Themis to repopulate the world. The goddess instructs them to
"scatter your mother's bones" (ibid., p. 41), a shocking suggestion,
until the mortals realize that Themis wants them to scatter the
stones of Mother Earth. Then, following directions,

> They descended,
> Covered their heads, loosened their garments, threw
> The stones behind them as the goddess ordered.
> The stones—who would believe it, had we not
> The unimpeachable witness of Tradition?—
> Began to lose their hardness, to soften, slowly,
> To take on form, to grow in size, a little,
> Become less rough, to look like human beings,
> Or anyway as much like human beings
> As statues do, when the sculptor is only starting,
> Images half blocked out. The earthy portion,
> Damp with some moisture, turned to flesh, the solid
> Was bone, the veins were as they always had been.
> The stones the man had thrown turned into men,
> The stones the woman threw turned into women,
> Such being the will of God. Hence we derive
> The hardness that we have, and our endurance
> Gives proof of what we have come from. (Bk. I, p. 15)

And a new world springs into being.

> So when earth,
> After that flood, still muddy, took the heat,
> Felt the warm fire of sunlight, she conceived,
> Brought forth, after their fashion, all the creatures,
> Some old, some strange and monstrous. (Bk. I, p. 16)

In *Germinal*, "The sun appeared at the glorious horizon; it was a joyous awakening across the entire countryside. . . . This living warmth was winning, spreading out in a youthful thrill" (p. 1588). And I have already quoted *Germinal's* concluding passage, where "the April sun gloriously shining in a clear sky, warming the childbearing earth. . . .An overflowing of sap mixed with whispering voices, the noise of sprouting germs expanded in a big kiss. Again and again, more and more distinctly, as though they were aproaching the ground, the camrades were hammering" (p. 1591). Still, as said before, however suggestive these parallels may be, they are very few: the flood, followed by a sunny day, the knowledge that the earth has swallowed many bones (e.g., p. 1140), and the possibility that men are rising from the soil. There is no specific, unequivocal reference to the myth.

I believe, however, that Walker is correct to think of Deucalion. We have to remember that the nineteenth-century Frenchman had an excellent grasp of classical mythology—Zola's many references to the subject in his letters, journalistic writings, and novels prove that he was no exception—both because of schooling and because of the newspapers which were reporting the century's many archaeological discoveries. Considerable attention was also paid to the subsequent speculations by specialists in comparative religions. In short, neither Zola nor his readers needed to have every jot and tittle included for them to sense an allusion to Greek and Roman mythology.[28]

Still, if one may legitimately infer an allusion to the Deucalion myth in *Germinal's* conclusion, it is just as possible that Zola was implying an analogy with the myth of Cadmus. This Greek hero, the founder of Thebes, had the ill luck to have all (or almost all, depending on the version) his men slain by Mars' enormous serpent. When Ovid's Cadmus

> saw the bodies,
> He saw the great victorious serpent, gloating,
> Licking the wounds with bloody tongue.[29]

He is filled with a furious desire for vengeance. Cadmus attacks and destroys the beast. Minerva, knowing that he needs help to establish the new city, "gave him orders / To plow the earth, to sow the teeth of the serpent / Which would become the seed of future people" (Bk. III, p. 60). This he did.

> The covered earth broke open, and the clods
> Began to stir, and first the points of spears
> Rose from the ground, then colored plumes, and helmets,
> Shoulders of men, and chests, arms full of weapons,
> A very harvest of the shields of warriors,
> The opposite of the way a curtain rises,
> Showing the feet first, then knees, and waists, and bodies
> And faces last of all. (Bk. III, p. 60)

They warn Cadmus to stay out of their "civil war" and fall on each other.

>                    And that madness
> Raged through them all; the sudden brothers perished
> By wounds they gave each other, and the earth,
> Their mother, felt their short-lived blood upon her,
> Warm from their brief existence. Only five
> Were left at last, and one of these, Echion,
> Let fall his weapons, as Minerva ordered,
> Asked peace, and won it, from the other brothers,
> And Cadmus found them helpers and companions
> In the building of the town Apollo promised.
>                    (Bk. III, pp. 60-61)

No one, to the best of my knowledge, has mentioned Cadmus in reference to *Germinal*. Philip Walker, however, points to a metaphorical development concerning serpents which, though not predominant, is certainly noticeable. "[W]ith only one exception," he says, "[Zola] always evokes the image of the serpent in passages consecrated to descriptions of the miners' lives in the galleries, . . . so that one is led to conclude that the idea of serpents joins with the imagistic conception that he had of this life. And, in fact, one senses that he needed the image to obtain all the symbolic power and nightmarish effect he purposely gave to these descriptions of the subterranean world."[30] When the Voreux collapses and sinks into the water-filled grave, there is an explicit reference to the way one portion of it, at least, resembles the "powerful knee of a giant" (p. 1546). But Zola was never hesitant to make his central symbols do double, triple, or even quadruple duty. In this case, he seems to have wanted to broaden the connotations beyond that of the important giant, perhaps because of Ovid's previous vision of the dying serpent:

> The throat is swollen, veins stand out, the jaws
> Froth with white poison, and the sound of metal
> Clangs from the ground as the great scales rasp across it.
> The smell of his breath infects the noisome air.
> He coils, he writhes, he straightens, like a beam
> Or battering-ram, comes on, like a flooding river
> Sweeping the trees before it. (Bk. III, p. 59)

Cadmus forced "the beast" back

> And Cadmus, following hard, keeps pointing, pressing,
> Backing the serpent up against an oak-tree,
> Pinning him there, and the oak-tree bends, protesting
> Under that weight and all that furious lashing. (Bk. III, p. 60)

The monstrous Voreux makes a similar commotion as it succumbs. "It was finished; the evil beast, squatting in this hollow, gorged with human flesh, was no longer breathing with its long, coarse respiration" (p. 1547). Cadmus sows the monster's teeth and watches in horror as the resultant *Spartoi* (Greek for "sown men") rise out of the ground and destroy each other. In *Germinal*, the workers have already killed many of their own, and Étienne knows very well that they might destroy him as well (p. 1589). As he leaves, "Men were burgeoning, a black avenging army, which was slowly germinating in the furrows" (p. 1591).

There are simply not enough significant indicators to advance either of these possible allusions with any assurance. Nonetheless, especially since when taken together they highlight the two potentials of the conclusion, it is appropriate to mention them. The myth of Deucalion implies the possibility of a better future. That of Cadmus suggests the very real menace of wholesale self-destruction which would bring civilization tumbling down. Whether one grants the presence of allusions to Deucalion and Cadmus or not, however, there can be no question that the conclusion of *Germinal* is ambiguous. This is what makes it a truly prophetic novel. Where the Biblical prophets ordered compliance with God's will, under pain of prophesied death, Zola, likewise a prophet, announces similar alternatives. Either the workers will through education and law form a revitalizing humanity ruled by justice and reason *or* the forces of nature will be turned loose in a terrible holocaust.[31] Only Étienne or someone like him can avoid Souvarine's "somber dream of this extermination of the world, mowed level with the ground like a field of rye" (p. 1343). On this point, and on this point only, Souvarine, Rasseneur, and Étienne are agreed: present conditions must end—"[I]n one way or another, it was time to be done with it, whether nicely, by laws, by a friendly understanding, or like savages by burning everything and devouring each other" (p. 1256). The message comes through on every level of the text.

Zola's avowed purpose in writing *Germinal* was to frighten his middle-class readers. "[T]he bourgeois reader must shiver with terror," he said in the dossier of his preliminary notes.[32] At least one critic still found it alarming in the mid-twentieth century. "Even today," Erich Auerbach said in *Mimesis,* "after half a century the last decades of which have brought us experiences such as Zola never dreamed of, *Germinal* is still a terrifying book. And even today it has lost none of its significance and indeed none of its timeliness."[33] On reviewing the interpretation I have proposed, however, it is difficult to understand why anyone would be terrified. It is easy to imagine a detached reader saying, "Justice or holocaust? Nonsense! The workers will tire of this business, and we shall return to the good old ways, without all this socialistic disruption."

As though Zola sensed the possibility in advance, he developed an allusion to the New Testament which must surely rank among the most curious in literature. Taking a pattern that Christians understand to signify comfort and hope, the author of *Les Rougon-Macquart* used it to arouse terror in the hearts of his bourgeois readers.

In the very beginning of *Germinal*, Zola inserted a brief formula, repeated half a dozen times with but slight variations, that characterizes the "old" religion of capitalism. When Étienne asks Bonnemort who owns the mining complex, the latter's voice takes on "a sort of religious fear as though he were talking about an inaccessible tabernacle in which there hid the sated, squatting god to whom they all gave their flesh and whom they had never seen" (p. 1141). During Étienne's oration in the forest, he emphasizes the vileness of "this impersonal god, unknown to the worker, squatting someplace in the mystery of his tabernacle from where he sucked the life from these starvelings who nourished him! They would go there; they would finally see his face in the light of the fires; they would drown this unspeakable foul swine, this monstrous idol gorged with human flesh, in blood!" (p. 1384), but it remains the same basic image, as it is in the conclusion of the novel, where Étienne foresees that with the awakening of truth and justice: "The sated, squatting god, the monstrous idol hidden in the back of his tabernacle in that unknown distance where the wretched people nourished him with their flesh would immediately die" (p. 1591). The figure served Zola well in characterizing the dreadful, old gods against whom the children of the earth revolt (in a rewriting of the mythic reality). At some point, it occurred to the novelist that it could also serve to suggest a new faith, which could be brilliantly illuminated by alluding to the birth and spread of Christianity. After all, what Jesus had said about the scribes and Pharisees could be said of the bourgeoisie of Zola's day: "[T]hey bind heavy burdens and grievous to be borne, and lay them on men's shoulders, but they themselves will not move them with one of their fingers" (Matt. 23: 4).

Perhaps while reading Paul Leroy-Beaulieu's *La Question ouvrière au XIX^e siècle* of 1872, Zola recognized the degree to which the labor movement constituted a religion, for in summarizing this book, the novelist wrote, "No more religious belief, no more life after death, and consequently the need to possess and enjoy during this life. The idea of justice is then put on this earth in an ideal society. . . .The religious character of socialist ideas."[34] In the novel, the established religion is dismissed in a few words. Not only do the workers laugh at the priests' stories of a life after this one (p. 1277), the Church has become the vile handmaiden of Capital. A priest like Father Joire, whose major effort consists of angering neither miner nor boss, is promoted,[35] while the bishop accedes to a company request and transfers Father Ranvier, who takes the side of the downtrodden (p. 1522).

But Étienne wonders, "Do you need God and his heaven to be happy?" (p. 1278). He then proceeds to construct a new religion on the Christian pattern: "[I]n a fairytale burst of light, justice was coming down from heaven. Since God was dead, justice was going to assure the happiness of men by making equality and brotherhood reign. A new society grew in a day, as in dreams, an enormous city with mirage-like splendor. . . . The old, rotten world had fallen to dust. . . . And, continually, this dream grew" (ibid.). In the New Testament, Jesus prophesied the destruction of Jerusalem (Luke 19: 44) and, before His coming in judgment and the advent of the New Jerusalem, the "abomination of desolation, spoken of by Daniel the

prophet" standing in the holy place (Matt. 24: 15). Later, John saw
the Heavenly City "coming down from God out of heaven, prepared
as a bride adorned for her husband" (Rev. 21:2). *Germinal* likewise
alludes to damned cities,[36] reports that there is an "unspeakably
foul swine" in the temple (p. 1384), and follows the miners' "religious
expectation of a miracle, the ideal manifested, the sudden entry into
the city of justice that [Étienne] had promised to them" (p. 1474).
Étienne and his companions keep many of the Christian images,
though they empty them of the message of Christ's resurrection and
redemption.

   While reading E. de Laveleye's *Le Socialisme contemporain* (1881),
Zola noted that the International Workmen's Association had had
"the same expansion as Christianity"; this may have given him the
idea to insist on the qualities which make these miners resemble the
first Christians.[37] The Maheus have "the blind faith of new believers,
similar to those Christians of the first years of the Church who awaited
the coming of a perfect society on the dung-heap of the ancient
world" (p. 1279). When food runs out and the strikers face hunger,
they feel "absolute confidence, a religious faith, the blind gift of a
believing populace. Since they had been promised an era of justice,
they were ready to suffer for the conquest of universal happiness. . . .
When the Maheus and others had digested their soup of clear water
too rapidly, they thus rose into a state of semi-giddiness, the ecstasy
of a better life which once threw martyrs to the beasts" (pp. 1327-
38). "Never had an aborning religion made so many faithful" (p.
1348). And when they arrive in the clearing for the mass meeting, the
women are "as serious as at church" (p. 1376). They are "catechumens"
ready to return to the "early commune" (p. 1379). As Étienne talks,
they are moved by "religious exaltation . . . the hope-filled fever of
the first Christians of the Church" (p. 1380). Given the fact that
Jesus insisted that a grain of wheat must fall to the ground and die,
before bearing fruit (John 12: 24), it is perhaps not surprising that
"the miner was awakening in the depths, germinating in the earth
like a true grain" (p. 1277), an image picked up again in the
conclusion: "On every side, seed-grain was swelling, stretching out,
cracking the plain, tormented with a need for heat and light."[38]

   Étienne bears an appropriate name for a religious leader, since
"Étienne" is the French version of "Stephen," the name of the first
Christian martyr. Although St. Stephen was only a deacon, while
Étienne is an "apostle bearing truth" (p. 1378), they have a number
of qualities in common. As deacon, St. Stephen was charged with
looking after the food and other physical needs of the early church

(Acts 6: 3); Zola's Étienne, "a sort of business agent, charged with correspondence, consulted by the households about delicate problems," is responsible for the strike fund (tactfully called the "precautionary fund" [*caisse de prévoyance*] —p. 1280), which was supposed to preserve the strikers from starvation. When St. Stephen spoke, those opposing him "were not able to resist the wisdom and the Spirit by which he spoke" (Acts 6: 10), and we remember Étienne's control over the crowd in the forest. Rasseneur was no match for him. Stephen gained his power from the Pentacostal wind; Étienne "had arrived in the big wind" (p. 1246). Like St. Stephen, Étienne wishes to raise "the enormous cathedral of the future world" (p. 1347), and similar to St. Stephen, who was a Grecian Jew stoned by his fellow Jews, Étienne is stoned by his fellow workers (pp. 1519-20). The Bible says that St. Stephen "fell asleep" (Acts 7: 60). Étienne, as pointed out previously, is buried alive, only to be reborn. Neither the fact that Étienne leaves the area to go to Paris, nor, indeed, the later information from *Le Docteur Pascal* that he was exiled to New Caledonia is designed to promote restful slumber in the bourgeoisie. To the contrary, it reminds us that even though the early Christians suffered and died, they spread their message across the whole world. So, we infer, it will be with the miners and their new faith. Socialism cannot be stopped. The middle class is then able to avoid the terrible effects of its greed only if it institutes a new reign of justice, equality, and education for the oppressed working class.

In a recognizable analogue of many Biblical passages—for example Revelation 14: 19: "And the angel thrust in his sickle into the earth, and gathered the vine of the earth, and cast it into the great winepress of the wrath of God"—Zola illuminates Étienne who, while orating, "threw down the iniquitous monument of dead centuries with a large gesture, always the same, the gesture of a mower who cuts the ripe harvest."[39] And Souvarine, in one of his "religious rages," further announces that *his* Messiah is coming: "[T]he one who will annihilate your race of cowards and sensualists will come" (p. 1482). The "abomination," we remember, already stands "in the holy place" (Matt. 24: 15). As the workers suffer and die, the seed-grain prepares a terrible harvest: "An army was growing from the depths of the pits, a harvest of citizens whose seed was germinating and would burst the earth wide open one bright and sunny day" (p. 1383). The image is repeated almost word for word in the last paragraph of the novel. Maheu's calm constitutes perhaps the most frightening aspect of the final warning: " 'It won't bring the bourgeois luck to have killed so many poor people. Of course they'll be punished one day, because you pay for everything. We won't even have to get mixed up in it; the joint will blow up all by itself; the soldiers will shoot the bosses, the way they shot the workers.' And, in her secular resignation . . . a work had been done: the certainty that injustice could not last any longer and that if there were no longer a God, another would grow to avenge the wretched" (p. 1586).

Despite the forcefulness of the allusion to God's terrible punishment, which will be inflicted on the iniquitous, we must not lose sight of the accompanying promise of salvation for the righteous. *Germinal* gives no decisive indication of a bias toward one or the other of the alternatives proposed. Will the future hold holocaust or justice? The choice is with the novel's readers and what they do to rectify the social evils that debase human beings. As a result, *Germinal* constitutes a truly open novel, not in the sense that Roger Ripoll uses the term, though it is true that *Germinal* suggests that its action continues into the future,[40] but in the sense of a lack of resolution between two possible futures. This ambiguity, of course, does not mean a lack of unity. *Germinal* remains one of the great novels of the western world precisely because Zola succeeded in structuring the novel around the prophetic message, "Repent, and turn away from your evil, or be destroyed." Nor does the novel lack sufficient closure to satisfy our aesthetic demands for some sort of stability and finality. For that, Zola used a simple plot device. The hero who arrives departs, or, as Zola put it in his preliminary notes, "I show Étienne leaving one evening in the rain, as he arrived one frosty morning."[41] Zola changed his mind, to some degree, about the weather, but the essential pattern remains.

Étienne is the vehicle for *Germinal*'s prophetic message. As Henri Mitterand has seen, however, Etienne and his activities are not limited to the mining country: "[H]is passage through Montsou is only a stopping-place in a much more extensive itinerary, which he will take up again at the end of the novel. That comes through in the reading, and it is what assures, in part, the novel its dynamism. The action is born beneath the feet of Étienne."[42] As I have attempted to show, Étienne and what he does must be seen in the full context of the metaphorical significance. Étienne is the key, for he serves as the focal point of the miners' identification with the four classical elements, as the miners descend the scale of being to become something even more frightening than brutish beings: forces of nature. He is also central to the earth children's revolt against the corrupt, sated god, Capital, which crouches in a distant tabernacle, and, though the many allusions to the New Testament Church make it clear that the new socialistic religion cannot fail to win its place in the sun, the fact that Étienne leaves believing in the potential of law offers hope to counterbalance the awesome threat of a vengeful army rising from the soil.

*Germinal* is, then, constructed on an armature the shape and limits of which are clear and to which all elements of the novel are subordinated. We begin as Étienne arrives; we follow him as he progresses from beast to nature, to saint and, finally, to reborn Heraclean hero who will see that justice prevails, whatever the cost. The novel has been fleshed out in such a way that we are seldom conscious of the skeletal structure, but there can be no doubt that *Germinal* is vertebrate, thus, an endomorphic novel.

One could further characterize the novel's armature as a trajectory, the most common of the varieties in the process novel. It begins in "normalcy" or relative peace, rises to a climax of tension, and suggests that there will one day be a resolution, though the particular novel may not describe the exact shape of that conclusion. The narration of trajectory novels may begin at any point. It is common for adventure stories to initiate the narrative at a point of climax, depending on flashbacks to fill out the pattern. Though mystery novels usually reverse the process, that is, they begin with the crime, working backwards in time and from effect to cause (what Barthes calls "hermeneutic structure"[43]), the variance remains insignificant. I say this despite the fascinating work of Victor Shklovsky and Boris Tomashevsky, who distinguish between "story" (events in their "natural," chronological and causal order) and "plot" (the artistic arrangement),[44] for it seems to me that readers relatively quickly and perhaps automatically translate the "plot" into "story." At the level of generalization where I am currently operating, such distinctions are simply not as important as "sequence" or "trajectory." Both *Germinal* and *La Chartreuse de Parme* provide relatively simple examples of the schema of the trajectory novel, as do all *Bildings-romane*. Some would have us believe that true novels without exception can be put under the rubric of "Bildungsroman,"[45] but that is surely not the case. Such an artificial limitation has the serious disadvantage of attempting to define a genre according to its subject matter, which, of course, has been done and will be done again. Still, just as claiming that only Holsteins are cows will not convince anyone who has seen Herefords, so such restrictive definitions will not satisfy anyone who has read widely in the recent or past novel.

Many endomorphic novels written prior to 1800 have what might be called bead structure. In such fictional works there is little, if any, development from one episode to another. Rather frequently, only the linking element of a common protagonist keeps them from exemplifying extreme forms of parataxis. I think, for example, of Lesage's *Gil Blas de Santillane* (1715-35). And just as most trajectory novels are sequential, so most bead novels are of the image variety. Lessage's *Gil Blas*, for example, has as its clear purpose throughout to present a portrait of society.

In some endomorphic novels, it may be difficult to ascertain the variety of structure, for, as with all attempts to categorize or codify, there always exist hybrid varieties which require careful evaluation. (To continue my previous analogy: some might mistakenly classify brahmans with camels.) The change in Manon, which eventually produces what the novel terms a "preference for a virtuous love," is, I think, sufficiently important to indicate that Abbé Prévost's *Manon Lescaut* (1731) constitutes a trajectory novel. Voltaire's *Candide* (1759), however, provides another problematic example which, it appears to me, should be grouped with "bead" novels. When Candide says early in chapter 13 that, had Pangloss lived, Candide would have dared to object to the master's continual insistence that all is for the best in this best of all possible worlds, we know something has taken place. This is the first of several indications that Candide has begun a process of development that will leave him considerably less naïve. Nonetheless, the change affects very little in the novel (while that in *Manon* brings about the heroine's flight and death), though it does allow Candide to withdraw from the world and "cultivate [his] garden." The primary thrust of Voltaire's most famous philosophic novel appears in every chapter (many of which could have changed their position without affecting the work in any important way) as the author weaves together the rich network of themes, mostly an ironic commentary on Leibnitzian optimism, and less important motifs, like the reappearance of minor characters or Candide's continuing desire to find his beloved Cunégonde. The themes and motifs are strands in the string of episodes or beads.

In addition to the observation that it may be difficult to distinguish one variety of endomorphic novel from another, one might remark as well that novels constructed like a string of beads can be extended almost indefinitely. *Candide*, for example, has nothing which truly requires the conclusion. This, indeed, points to the main difficulty with "bead" structure—how does one bring such

novels to an end? If the main character develops little or not at all and
if there is no significant crescendo, there is no natural stopping
place. Mark Twain humorously calls attention to the problem in the
conclusion of *The Adventures of Tom Sawyer* (1876). "So endeth this
chronicle. It being strictly a history of a *boy*, it must stop here; the
story could not go much further without becoming the history of a
*man*. When one writes a novel about grown people, he knows exactly
where to stop—that is, with a marriage; but when he writes of
juveniles, he must stop where he best can."

Serial structure, which has been called "circular" or "spiral,"
occurs when novels are organized around the suggestion that the
essence of one dominant pattern is or will be repeated over and over
again. Flaubert's *L'Education sentimentale* (1869) provides an example.
Frédéric Moreau and his friend Deslauriers repeatedly show their
inability to bring anything to fruitful conclusion as they stumble
after their dreams of love and power. The novel ends as they
recognize that their lives were failures, that they have missed life. In
the last hundred years, it has been common to use the entire novel to
establish one single pattern and to conclude with the indication that
the pattern will be continued with few, if any, variations. Zola's *La
Terre* (1887) emphasizes the importance of the "eternal return" of the
earth's seasons and the insignificance of the precise identities of the
human creatures that attempt to tear a livelihood from it.[46] Similarly,
at the end of Gide's *Les Faux-Monnayeurs*, we know Edouard will repeat
the sterile pattern which the novel outlines, just as the anonymous
narrator in Robbe-Grillet's *La Jalousie* (1957) will relive the terrible
rise and fall of his obsession.[47] After completing such novels, the
reader is left with the sense of an interminable recurrance of similar
events stretching out into the future.

Perhaps least common are endomorphic novels that exploit
mirror structure, where everything is subordinated to the establish-
ment of a positive or negative reflection. Unfortunately, I know of
no "pure" forms. Even in the classic case of André Maurois's *Climats*
(1928), there are two trajectories, though both are definitely
subsumed beneath the overall reflective pattern. The first half,
supposedly written by Philippe, tells of his great love for his wife,
Odile, who fell in love with François. This prepares the second,
concluding panel, written by Philippe's second wife, Isabelle, who
loves him and watches as he becomes passionately enamored of
Solange.

Frances McNeely Leonard points to a considerably more
intricate example of mirror structure in Zola's *Nana* (1880). The

book is laid out in two distinct portions, like *Climats*, the first seven
chapters recounting Nana's rise as an actress and the second seven
her ascension as a courtisane. More remarkably, however, each of
the chapters has its mirror image in the other half of the novel.

> Chapter Seven, in which Nana sends the cuckold Muffat
> to walk the streets, has as its companion Chapter Eight, in
> which Fontan and his new mistress expel Nana, once
> again a street-walker, from the love nest. Chapter Six,
> where Nana, after upsetting the demeanor of Mme Hugon's
> house party, finally takes Muffat as a lover, is balanced
> against Chapter Nine, where Nana in her foolish desire to
> play a 'respectable woman' usurps Rose Mignon's role and
> resumes Muffat as lover. Chapters Three and Twelve, each
> two from the beginning and end of the novel, concern
> parties at the home of Countess Sabine. And certainly
> Chapter Fourteen is a repetition of Chapter One. As Paris
> awaited the revelation of Nana at the *théâtre des Variétés*, so
> do the *demi-monde* and the reader await the final unveiling
> of Nana destroyed by small-pox.[48]

This kind of reflection is much more complicated, not to mention
significant, than simple repetitions—like Nemour's theft of the
Princess of Clève's portrait, followed by the latter's theft of the
duke's cane. But whether as a major or minor device, oppositions
and thus true mirror images frequently entice novelists. Which is
not to say that parallels no longer occur. Frames similar to that
of *Gobseck* are important because they provide direct analogues of
the rest of the novel. The same should also be said of the device
of *mise en abyme* or interior duplication—for example the performance
of *As You Like It* in chapter eleven of Théophile Gautier's *Mademoiselle
de Maupin* (1835).

Mirror structure need not be limited to image novels. Though
Father Docre's obscene crucifix, which constituted the negative
reflection of the Grunewald crucifixion, with which J.-K. Huysmans's
*Là-Bas* (1891) begins, resembles the examples just discussed, the
novel as a whole exemplifies mirror structure in the sequential novel.
Durtal's dabbling in the occult is recounted little by little across the
novel and is interspersed with chapters from Durtal's biography of
Gilles de Rais (Bluebeard). As the baron de Rais descends to the
depths of evil, Durtal follows. Huysmans's nineteenth-century
protagonist does not sink as low as his famous predecessor, or,

perhaps, rise as high subsequently; nevertheless, the account of Gilles de Rais's confession and reintegration into the Christian faith leaves little doubt that Durtal's conversion is not far behind. This then is not a static mirror, rather "a mirror taken for a walk along the road," if I may be forgiven for quoting Stendhal out of context.[49]

With mirror structure, I complete the tour of the endomorphic novel, by far the most common variety. Certainly, popular fiction almost always falls into this category (I know of no exceptions, but I lack the courage to leave "always" unmodified). Examples of this type of novel abound, whether it makes use of trajectory, bead, serial, or mirror structure and whether, over all, the particular novel composes a sequence or an image in the reader's mind. Some works cross over and blur the edges of the categories I propose. It would be nice if all fiction fell into the rather neat classifications I have outlined in this chapter, though life and art are seldom so amenable to reason. I could go on and give more examples, attempting to catch every variation within my net, but in the end that would be a fruitless, idle effort. The pattern is clear enough. Readers will have hundreds of their own examples in mind, and with the outlines of the endomorphic novel established as the prevailing model, divergences should be highlighted. And there were divergences. As the Russian Formalists argued, any time an aesthetic practice becomes the general mode, an artist inevitably comes along who will attempt to subvert the pattern more or less overtly. In this case, it was a series of late nineteenth- and early twentieth-century writers who left few established canons unshaken.

## Chapter 5
## Subversive Structure in Gide's *L'Immoraliste*

IN THE ARTS, A CLEAR UNDERSTANDING of the prevailing paradigm—that is, of the accepted set of beliefs, values, techniques and models—seems to signal its demise. Effective aesthetic procedures apparently require the ability to surprise or to shock, however mildly. When devices and models become commonplace and thus lose the vigor of novelty, it is only a matter of time until they are relegated to escapist art, become objects of ridicule, or are subjected to new pressures that often make them unrecognizable. One of the signs of the banalization of a technique consists of readers' ability to recognize it for what it is. What was form becomes formula. No longer "taken in," the old ways neither convince nor astonish. That, of course, requires insight into the art form in question. A large degree of such awareness appears typical of those periods when artists are in the process of rejecting the established paradigm, while seeking something new and more challenging.

Without question, one would have difficulty faulting Gide's understanding of the accomplishments and potential of the novel as it had been exploited up to his day. Albert Sonnenfeld even concludes that "Gide loved the calculated effect," that "he was obsessed with technique, preferred himself to all other readers of his work (their interpretations might not be sufficiently complex)."[1] Gide was indeed obsessed with his art. But, then, perhaps that explains why the self-conscious *Immoraliste* (1902) represents an outstanding precursor of the recent novel. Gide put the language and structure of his novel[2] under extreme pressure by making each technique or pattern bear an inordinate weight of significance. At that point, he placed it in opposition to some other meaningful unit. The resultant network of tensions puts extraordinary demands on readers, who must participate actively.

Gide was not optimistic about discovering the audience *L'Immoraliste* requires. As Justin O'Brien pointed out, *L'Immoraliste* was "published in May 1902 in an edition of 300 copies, the number at which the young author then estimated [his] potential public."[3] Gide was writing for a very specific kind of reader, a reader he did not expect to find, and he was thus forced to become his own reader. In the significant "De l'importance du public" (1903) he says, "The artist cannot get by without a public. And when the public is absent, what does he do? He invents one, and, turning his back on his own period, he expects what the present denies him from the future."[4] He had already said something similar in the preface to *L'Immoraliste*: "I believe one may without too much complacency prefer the risk of failing to interest when a work first appears, with interesting things—rather than arousing a short-lived passion in a public that is fond of twaddle."[5] Journal entries dating from 1902 provide some indications of the kind of reader he sought: "I read the way I would like people to read me: that is to say, very slowly. For me, to read a book is to absent myself for two whole weeks with the author," and "That a young man of my age and of my *value* would one day be moved in reading me and *remade* as I still am at thirty years of age in reading Stendhal's *Souvenirs d'Egotisme*, I have no other ambition. At least it seems that way to me while reading it."[6] At the epoch of *L'Immoraliste,* Gide was writing for a future reader whom he wished to affect, who would live the experience of reading—but not just any reader, he wanted one who would be as sensitive and cultivated as himself.

On the most accessible level, *L'Immoraliste* is just a good story, resembling many nineteenth-century works which the reader may enjoy passively or accept as a realistic portrayal of a possible adventure. He may act as a distant observer, or join Michel's friends while they listen to the account, or even to some degree identify with Michel. Gide's fictional audience did the latter: "We also fell silent, each of us caught up in a strange indisposition. It seemed to us, alas, that in telling it to us, Michel had rendered his action more legitimate. Not knowing where to disapprove of it . . . made us almost accomplices. It was as though we were a part of it" (p. 470). Some readers have been similarly affected. François Porché, for example, wrote to Gide, "The *Immoraliste* does not transpose anything. It does not say, it allows us to understand, but, whether it is a novel or a lyrical confession, the completely modern work addresses us directly in a whispering voice. The *Immoraliste* can disturb us. *Saül* cannot."[7] For Porché, the work was a tempting, convincing defense of irresponsible egotism and sensualism.

However common this reading may be, it is nonetheless unacceptable, for irony undermines it on every level of the text. To feel complicity is to have abandoned a rational, critical sense of reality and to have committed Michel's crime, that is, to have given in to instinct and sensation. Hytier reminds us of what *L'Immoraliste* says clearly: "For Gide, intelligence is an essential value; the critical mind is at the base of true progress and doubtless also of true love."[8] Gide was not at all reticent about calling attention to this irony. In one widely quoted passage, for example, he says, "With the single exception of my *Nourritures,* all my books are ironic books; they are critical books. . . . The *Immoraliste* [critical] of a form of individualism. (This put summarily.)"[9] But, as Gide suggests parenthetically, neither this statement, nor others,[10] do justice to the depth and implications of his irony.

Doubtless there is validity in the suggestion that, because Michel was shaped to a degree in Gide's own image, his condemnation implies authorial self-irony. Far more important, however, are those devices that undermine the protagonist and, as well, the naive reader. Of course, as Grahame C. Jones pointed out, any irony presupposes an ironic attack against one of two assumed types of readers: not against those who understand the deeper significance that the more accessible levels of the text belie, but against those who are oblivious to anything but the surface, thus falling victim, in a sense, to the author. Because of the subtlety of the ironic processes, "It is . . . especially for knowing readers that the ironist destines his work. They constitute a refined public to whom he addresses winks that others do not notice."[11] Those devices which undermine Michel and reveal his unreliability join with others to destroy the verisimilitude of *L'Immoraliste.* The "reality" of "art" is called into question. By assuring that this work would not be taken either as "life" or as idealistic abstractions removed from reality,[12] Gide affirmed the reality of *L'Immoraliste* as art, that is, as a "compromise" between the two opposing poles.[13]

Lack of verisimilitude seems to me to be the primary thrust of both Michel's style and the structure of his story. J. C. Davis puts it this way: "If we demanded strict authenticity, we might ask Gide how it is that an archaeologist without especial literary pretensions, however brilliant he might be, could relate his story in a style so rich in literary merit, so full of excellent lyrical and dramatic qualities and containing such a wealth of suggestive images. Or we might wonder how a man so disillusioned and broken in spirit as Michel appears to be, could rise at times to such lyrical heights as does the narrator in telling his story to the friends who have come to rescue him. Michel's tone is not always strictly in harmony either with his professional interests or with the mood of extreme dejection in which he appears before his friends."[14]

Michel, in short, is unrealistic, and because of this fact, the work is as well. Today, applying the criterion of verisimilitude to a work of art may seem both out-of-date and naive. As Ullmann suggests, "It could of course be argued that the novelist . . . could legitimately aim at a . . . style which would correspond to the narrator's character but would be transposed into a purer and more artistic key."[15] Since we present-day readers know that no work can ever be truly realistic, that a certain amount of artifice is unavoidable, we tend to accept artificialities without question. It is worth recalling, however, that whenever an artist pushes the style of his characters beyond credence, "such a solution, whatever its advantages, is bound to affect verisimilitude, 'that willing suspension of disbelief for the moment, which constitutes poetic faith ' " (ibid.). Furthermore, when Gide was working on L'Immoraliste, the canon of realism was very much alive, though not universally adhered to. Gide could not have failed to know of the dangers of Michel's style. Why did he nonetheless allow his character to speak in a fashion that would not only undermine the speaker, but the work as well? I would hesitate to put it down to inexperience or bad judgment, for Gide was in no sense a beginner. By the time of L'Immoraliste, he had already authored a considerable body of work which shows a mastery of the writer's trade. Furthermore, because he elsewhere suggested that such artificiality was inherent, indeed, essential to art and because the artificiality extends beyond the portions for which Michel is putatively responsible, one begins to suspect that Gide intended his récit to be unrealistic.

Even the introductory letter swarms with clichéd devices, any one of which would increase a reader's distance. As Germaine Brée has suggested, the letter presenting Michel's account is "artificial." It relies "on the conventional and rather awkward narrative device by which the story purports to be told by a witness. . . . [and] as a way of setting his story in motion, Gide uses another well-worn device, the adolescent pact."[16] Although less-knowing readers might not go so far, surely even the most susceptible, trained by nineteenth-century fiction and ready to experience the illusion of "real life" while reading, must find it at least somewhat difficult to believe in the introductory letter to the scribe's brother, the Premier. The letter appears to guarantee the reliability of Michel's story, which is to follow. But it is an ironic document where style joins with the worn-out devices noted by Brée to vitiate any verisimilitude it may have. The only indication that the scribe destines the letter for a close relative appears in the familiar address and in the colloquial turn of a very few sentences, for example, the first which begins in medias res: (here and in a few other instances where style is important, I give the French) "Oui, tu le pensais bien: Michel nous a parlé, mon cher frère" ("Yes, you were right, my dear brother, Michel talked to us"—p. 369). Otherwise, an author of a handbook of rhetoric could well mine it for a multitude of examples. The style is periodic and polished. It makes frequent use of antitheses, binary and ternary constructions, and repetitive sounds, words, and phrases. "Le récit qu'il nous fit, le voici. Tu l'avais demandé; je te l'avais promis" ("Here is the story he told us. You asked for it; I promised it to you"—ibid.). This compar, the first of several alexandrines, leads directly into another equally artificial clause marked by anaphora: "Mais à l'instant de l'envoyer, j'hésite encore, et plus je le relis et plus il me paraît affreux" ("But at the moment of sending it off, I still hesitate, and the more I reread it, the more awful it seems to me"— ibid.). The two binary constructions are then followed by three rhetorical questions, and the paragraph ends with a summary alloiosis: "Will someone be able to invent a way of using so much intelligence and force—or will we keep all that outside the city gates?"—ibid.). The letter subsequently tells the Premier what he already knows: "You know about the friendship that ties Michel to Denis, to Daniel, to me. It was already strong in high school, but it has grown each year." It further introduces the major images and sets the scene. Then, without further ado, the scribe turns the podium over to Michel. Should the reader still be willing to suspend his disbelief (as was the judge at the obscenity trial of *Jurgen*, after having read James Branch Cabell's similarly artificial introduction), Michel's highly polished presentation and unbelievably stylized account should at the very least impede involvement with the characters and events.

If the first level of *L'Immoraliste* consists of the straightforward account of a moral crisis, the second is the realization of the unreliability of the narrator.[17] Not only does Michel not tell the truth, he uses his listeners in the same way he used Marceline—to prove his freedom. The text does not provide sufficient evidence for affirming his awareness of what he is doing. One should perhaps not make too much of his inadvertent admission when he talks of his right to do as he has done (p. 471). His choices may be unconscious. We know only that he is unreliable, that both he and his philosophy must be rejected.

Through an ironic device common to farce, Michel gives himself away. Like Jérôme in *La Porte étroite*, like Gérard in *Isabelle*, and like the somewhat too obvious pastor in *La Symphonie pastorale*, he unwittingly lets slip the truth he elsewhere denies. After having said, "I want no other help than that: to talk to you"(p. 372), he gives a skillful exposition that succeeds in making his companions feel the already mentioned guilty complicity. Only then does Michel finally reveal his true reasons for telling the story: he wants them to take him away, and he feels the necessity of proving "to himself" that he has not exceeded his rights (p. 471). It is left for us to see that this self-justification consists partly, perhaps wholly, perhaps unconsciously, in swaying his friends.

Earlier, at the beginning of his account, Michel tells his friends that he will tell his story simply (p. 372). This claim of simplicity is essential, for simplicity has long been considered the guarantee of sincerity. Roy Pascal goes so far as to maintain that excessive rhetoric warns readers to suspect the sincerity of autobiographers.[18] One could argue that Pascal makes a mistake in using a stylistic convention of autobiographies as a means of judging truth. We know, for example, that Rousseau labored over at least three, and possibly four, versions and an unknown number of drafts to give *Les Confessions* an air of spontaneity and artlessness.[19] Of course, whether or not Rousseau was sincere is beside the point. It is pertinent, however, to point to his cognizance of the need to adhere to a convention of simplicity if his readers were to believe in his sincerity. By Gide's time, the convention was firmly established, and it becomes increasingly important to note that while Michel is well aware of the need to convince his listeners of his artlessness and, thus, insists that he is going to "tell my life, simply," his style gives him the lie.[20] People simply do not talk the way he does, unless they have carefully prepared. In fact, if the works of such contemporary, established novelists as Barrès, Bourget, Zola, Anatole France, or Huysmans are any indication, neither do literary creations. Michel's speech is overly artificial and unrealistic.

This hyperstylization is most pronounced in Michel's opening words:

> Mes chers amis, je vous savais fidèles. A mon appel vous êtes accourus, tout comme j'eusse fait au vôtre. Pourtant voici trois ans que vous ne m'aviez vu. Puisse votre amitié qui résiste si bien à l'absence, résister aussi bien au récit que je veux vous faire. Car si je vous appelai brusquement, et vous fis voyager jusqu'à ma demeure lointaine, c'est pour vous voir, uniquement, et pour que vous puissiez m'entendre. Je ne veux pas d'autre secours que celui-là: vous parler. —Car je suis à tel point de ma vie que je ne peux plus dépasser. Pourtant ce n'est pas lassitude. Mais je ne comprends plus. J'ai besoin... J'ai besoin de parler,

vous dis-je. Savoir se libérer n'est rien; l'ardu, c'est savoir
être libre. —Souffrez que je parle de moi; je vais vous
raconter ma vie, simplement, sans modestie et sans
orgueil, plus simplement que si je parlais à moi-même.
Ecoutez-moi. (p. 372)

(My dear friends, I knew you were faithful. At my call,
you came running, just as I would have done at yours. And
yet, here it is three years that you have not seen me. May
your friendship which resists absence so well also resist
the story I want to tell you. For if I called you suddenly,
and had you travel all the way to my distant home, it is in
order to see you, uniquely, and so that you could hear me.
I want no other help than that: to talk to you. For I have
reached a point in my life that I cannot go beyond. And yet
it is not lassitude. But I no longer understand. I need... I
need to talk, I tell you. Knowing how to free oneself is
nothing; what is arduous is knowing how to be free. Let
me talk about myself; I am going to tell you my life story,
simply, without modesty and without pride, more simply
than if I were talking to myself. Listen to me.—p. 372).

What Michel says in this exordium of the *insinuatio* type is contradicted
by the way he says it. The insistent alliteration of *s* in the first four
lines may even add a strange element of ominousness to Michel's
honeyed words. The repetitive *vous* and *je* prepares Michel's synthesis
where he tells them that he will talk as though to himself, a
movement that ends with the scribe feeling guilty complicity (p.
470). One is reminded of Jean-Baptiste Clamence's later trick in
Camus's *La Chute* (1956): "Then I pass imperceptibly from 'I' to 'us'
in my talk. When I arrive at 'That's where we are,' the trick is
played."

The *p* alliterated throughout the passage leads to the verb, *parler*,
repeated four times. Not only does Michel use the pluperfect
subjunctive and the past definite, but his periods use syntax which, if
not convoluted, is scarcely common. They lead inexorably to the end
of the paragraph and on into the narration. After the apothegm—
"Savoir se libérer..."—which is preceded and highlighted by three
successive negative clauses, two "j'ai besoin"s, and the single
"parler," Michel says, "Souffrez que je parle de moi; je vais vous
raconter ma vie, simplement, sans modestie et sans orgueil, plus
simplement que si je parlais à moi-même." Aside from continuing
the already noted alliteration, the sentence forcefully contradicts

the claimed simplicity through the smooth, carefully modulated members, the amplification, the conduplicatio of *simplement*. It thus emphasizes the ironical nature of the introduction.

Although such extended and dense clusters of rhetorical devices do not occur from this point on, the narrator's style continues to be of sufficient quality to cause considerable doubt about its "simplicity," hence about Michel's reliability. The strange conflicts within Michel's discourse have been recognized by a number of critics.[21] Rather than duplicate the excellent, existent work, let me end this portion of my discussion by citing one of the most amusing of Michel's ironically revealing statements: "Ma négligence, en ce récit, est volontaire" ("My negligence, in this story, is on purpose"—p. 386). The claim of heedlessness lacks force for it is expressed in a perfectly balanced, Romantic alexandrine. Though the verse form may have seemed disorderly when introduced in Victor Hugo's revolt against classical canons, such knowing integration of context, content, and structure indicates very firm control. Deliberate negligence, indeed![22]

Style is, of course, not the only indication that Michel's story lacks the unstudied, unaffected, guileless qualities he claims for it. Considering that organization requires planning, if not art, as in the case of his highly polished, rhetorical style, the presence of excessively rigorous composition serves to sound the alarm. And when Gide has Michel obliquely admit the structure of his story, the irony becomes even more piquant. Michel's statement: "It would be in vain for me to seek to impose more order on my story than there was in my life" (p. 464), is particularly damaging when seen in conjunction with his claim of simplicity, for he implicitly admits to having previously "imposed order." Furthermore, at this point in the account, the "disorder" to which he calls attention is already both well established and necessary to communicate the feeling that the narrator was unable to control himself. As town after town flashes precipitously by, the impression arises that Michel is driven, that he cannot make rational decisions, that he is, therefore, not responsible. Because one can scarcely fail to perceive the artificially rigid structure of Michel's story and to note the discrepancy between it and his pretensions to simplicity, the structure becomes an ironic device for betraying the untrustworthiness of this most unreliable narrator.

Even without the Roman numerals marking the various divisions in the book, the structure of *L'Immoraliste* is nothing if not obvious. Michel implicitly admits his share in the effort when he says at the end of part I, "What would the story of happiness be? Nothing but what prepares it, then what destroys it, can be told. And I have now told you everything that had prepared it" (p. 408). Formally, the book breaks into three main divisions: a rise, a leveling, a fall.[23] The first major part has nine chapters, the second three, and the third only one. The movement from nine to one supports Michel's growing isolation and finds further support in the motifs of travel and time.[24] In part I, concerned with Michel's spiritual embarkation, both the marriage and the voyage highlight the importance of his rebirth and renewal after the incidents of coughing blood. The phrase "new being" (p. 403) further suggests the importance of time to Michel's quest. Time is equally important to Ménalque, the goal of whose life is to enjoy the present—"For each action, the pleasure that I gain is a sign that I was to do it" (p. 431)—but he realizes that to achieve this pleasure, he must "turn the page" (ibid.). The past must be forgotten; for full life in the present, one must orient oneself toward the future. " 'I do not wish to remember,' [Ménalque] responded. Doing that would make me think I was keeping the future from arriving and causing the past to encroach [on the future]. I create the novelty of each hour from the complete oblivion of yesterday. . . . I do not believe in dead things" (p. 436).

In part II, despite the move to Paris and back to La Morinière, the emphasis rests on immobility since Michel seems primarily concerned with putting down roots. While attempting to come to terms with his life, he struggles to integrate an aspiration for "the authentic being" (p. 398) with the claims of his past. The study of Athalaric apparently represents an attempt to make his background serve the new inclinations. Whereas part I centers on aspiration for the being he wishes to become, part II recounts the effort to synthesize past, present, and future, although it gradually narrows to Michel's dissatisfaction with the present. Unfortunately, he forgets Ménalque's warnings: "The most delicate [memories] are cast off, the most voluptuous rot, the most delicious are the most dangerous later on" (p. 436), for in part III, Michel attempts to retrieve his past, perhaps because he seeks the "*old* man" (p. 398; my italics). After having asked, "What more can man do?" (p. 457), he scurries to Biskra, the scene of former joys, and finds that the children "have grown horribly. . . . What fatigues, what laziness, what vices have already placed so much ugliness on these faces, where so much youth used to shine? . . . Ménalque was right. Memory is an ill-starred invention" (p. 466). As Davis points out, the symmetry of parts I and III emphasizes the change from joyous discovery to despair and dispersion.[25] Only Moktir leads him on. At the conclusion of the book, the future has ceased to exist; Michel is enslaved to present sensation; and the past lives on through his need to tell: "I have reached a point in my life that I cannot go beyond. . . . I need... I need to talk, I tell you."

Another motif, as Roy Jay Nelson suggested to me, turns the work into a quinquepartite structure. Part I takes place primarily in the *untamed countries*: "This land of voluptuousness [which] satisfies but does not appease desire" (p. 464). Of part II's three chapters, the first is situated in Normandy, the land of "this ordered abundance, of this joyous submission" (p. 410). The second, the formal center of the book in which Ménalque appears, is located in Paris, the land of the dead and of masks where people only seem to live. The third takes the reader back to the *land of ordered abundance*. In part III, the concluding section of the book, the "order" of La Morinière finds an echo in Switzerland, but for the most part, the activity takes place once again in Italy and the *untamed countries* of North Africa.

Statements about the tripartite and quinquepartite structure of *L'Immoraliste* must not obscure the more forceful movement that appears to change direction in part II. Where in part I, Michel seems to be ascending hesitantly towards self-integration, later, at La Morinière in part II, he begins to take advantage of his wife's generosity and pays less attention to her. Soon, he finds himself with "more than a hundred hectares on his hands" (p. 419). His life has begun to disintegrate. Then, in the second chapter of part II, after leaving his seriously ill wife to visit Ménalque, after the miscarriage, after angrily giving Marceline the requested rosary and storming from the room, the disintregration becomes so pronounced that even Michel recognizes it. He speaks of his "unsettled life" (pp. 441, 453). Where Ménalque knew that "You have to choose" (p. 435), Michel tries to live with opposites. When Charles says, "You cannot protect the guard and the poacher at the same time," Michel responds, "Why?" (p. 452). Not even his decision to sell La Morinière reflects an attempt to unify his life, rather a desire for more dispersion. The will power that drew him from his sick bed and created his healthy body gradually gives way, and, as Marceline weakens physically, he loses self-control to those dark forces of the "old [Adamic] man" he has sought and found.

Because the formal structure emphasizes external factors over which Michel would appear to have little control, it stresses his lack of responsibility. It gives the impression that as he moves north he gains control, confidence, and happiness. After North Africa, Italy, and La Morinière produce the desired self-integration, Paris seemingly destroys that fine balance. The capital city appears to be the fulcrum for the lever of Ménalque and the miscarriage to reverse Michel's direction. Paris seems responsible. Even a return to La Morinière has no effect, and the voyage south causes him to revert to his original state of helplessness. The clearly tendentious structure functions in conjunction with Michel's style to undermine the narrator. As has become more and more apparent during this section, the structure of *L'Immoraliste* is too perfect, too well balanced. Neither Michel's background, nor his activities during the period he recounts, nor his current apathetic mood would permit us to believe that he is capable of such a finely wrought construction. It is unrealistic and, consequently, joins the style of his account as an ironic device which encourages the suspicion that he has carefully planned and rehearsed, that his discourse is therefore tendentious, and that we must consequently stay on our guard.

"If we demand strict authenticity," says J. C. Davies in the previously quoted passage, and that, it seems to me, is precisely what we must do. The text leaves little choice. To become so deeply involved in Michel's story that one consistently accepts him at face value is not only to ignore but to deny the obvious. Gide, of course, pointed to *L'Immoraliste*'s lack of verisimilitude in a widely quoted letter: "No, I do not think Michel could ever write. . . Believe me, dear Scheffer, it is only because I am not Michel that I was able to tell his story so 'remarkably well,' as you put it."[26] I would go further and suggest that the reader must recognize the structural and rhetorical games in the work; he must sense that these devices, developed long ago by other writers to increase verisimilitude, function ironically in *L'Immoraliste* to achieve the opposite result. At the same time that the text explicitly promises to give us the exact words that were spoken by Michel, implicitly it says the contrary, "I, the text, am not real; I am not even lifelike; I am art." Of course, not every reader would sense this ironic message, nor, as previously noted, did Gide expect them to.

I do not wish to overemphasize the irony, however, for it is not sufficiently strong to negate the undeniable attraction the work exerts. Even when an expert reader like Martin Turnell has recognized the artificiality, he nonetheless admits to being under the sway of *L'Immoraliste*'s insidious enchantment.[27] For such people a particular kind of reading results: "The pleasure of art alternates with the shock of truth. This is one of the sources for the special enjoyment—this spiritual trouble, this bewitchment, this state of objective life and artistic irreality—that the Gidian tale procures. The reader occasionally experiences the need to take stock of his own position and that of his characters. Where are we? Who is talking? What are they doing with me? These are the questions that are most often thrust upon us during the account where truth at its most naked alternates with literary artifice and hors d'oeuvres."[28] The reader participates on two levels. While subjectifying the account, thus "living" it, he objectifies it, thus judging it. This kind of a reading correlates exactly with the first two steps of Gide's description of creation and art, as expounded during the summer of 1901 while he was working on *L'Immoraliste*.

> We have been told, "Man proposes and God disposes." This is true in nature, but . . . in works of art, *God proposes and man disposes*, and anyone who claims to produce works of art who is not conscious of this is anything you like, except an artist.
>
> Cut the phrase in two; take only one of the two parts of the formula as your credo, and you will have the two major artistic heresies which, always anew, struggle against each other because of a failure to understand that it is from their very union and from their compromise that the birth of art is possible.
>
> *God proposes* is naturalism, objectivism, or whatever you want to call it.
>
> *Man disposes* is a priorism, idealism...
>
> *God proposes and man disposes* is the work of art.
>
> . . . . . . . . . . . . . . . . . . . . . . . . . . . . . . . . . . . . . . . . . . . . . . . .
>
> Art is a tempered thing. I certainly do not wish to say . . . that the most accomplished work of art would be the one which stands at an equal distance from idealism and realism. Certainly not! Indeed, the artist may approach one of the two poles, but only if he keeps his foot on the other. One step further and he will lose his balance.[29]

Gide had previously produced works that conform to the first two categories. For what he calls naturalism or objectivism, *God proposes,* there is *Les Nourritures terrestres*—a strange sort of naturalism, perhaps, but, as he points out elsewhere, the work satisfies his definitions: "When my *Nourritures* appeared, we were right in the midst of symbolism. It seemed to me that art was running a serious risk in being separated from life and what is natural. But my book was much too natural for it not to seem facticious to those who no longer had a taste for anything but the artificial. And precisely because it escaped the bounds of literature, at first people saw nothing but the quintessence of literature in it."[30] For a prioristic idealism or *man disposes*, perhaps the best example is *Le Prométhée mal enchaîné*, excellently studied by Holdheim.[31] In neither case, however, do we find the "compromise" he mentions in 1901. *Les Nourritures terrestres* leans too much toward an indiscriminant recording of impressions to satisfy the category of "man disposes," and *Le Prométhée* tends in the other direction toward a contortionist's mannered, though amusing, *tour de force*. An early attempt at concession might be found in *Paludes*. Nonetheless, one must wait until *L'Immoraliste* to find a clear, and successful, example of all three levels. There, while suggesting life (a point I shall make in more detail), he simultaneously undermines it with irony and prepares the third level—art.

After having noticed the function of the letter-document, the style and structure of Michel's account and having, as well, grown distrustful of what Albert J. Guérard has aptly called the "deceptive simplicity of surface [that] invites casual and very literal reading,"[32] numerous unanswered questions remain. If, for example, Michel was progressing toward spiritual and physical regeneration in North Africa, how did he go wrong? Perhaps this question will incite the reader to go beyond the stage of alternating participation and judgment to find the final stage: *God proposes and man disposes*. It seems to me that this marrow is in the subsurface structure of coherent imagery Gide employed as a major conveyor of *L'Immoraliste*'s meaning. A system of images metaphorically climbing from darkness through various levels of water to light highlights the protagonist's struggle toward spiritual and physical health; whereas his subsequent psychic disintergration reverses the symbolic movement and descends to darkness.

Although Robert Goodhand has argued convincingly that Gide employed allusions to the New Testament story of Peter, suggesting that images of light and darkness symbolize Christian and non-Christian elements respectively,[33] it seems to me that allusions to the Bible and to Christian practice appear as only one part of the complex of imagery serving to highlight the conflict between Michel's conscious, rational mind and his unconscious.[34] No one would deny that Gide's Protestant heritage was important both to him and to *L'Immoraliste,*[35] but it is far from being the only influence or his only preoccupation.[36] I would prefer to say that the chiaroscuro represents the forces of Apollo (representative of light, integration, heroism, activity, góod judgment, and will power) and Dionysus (associated with the infernal, a lack of control, the unleasing of desire, chaos, dissolution, passivity, and the unconscious). This opposition between the conscious and unconscious mind, which provides the nucleus of the story Michel tells, occurs very early in the narrative sequence. The introductory letter names the listeners: "Denis, Daniel and I." Lest the reader make the mistake of ignoring them, the names are repeated five times in thirty-three lines (pp. 369-70). The attitude required in confronting the story is partially defined with the recognition that Denis derives from Dionysus, and Daniel from the Hebrew Dan for judge, thus related to the qualities of Apollo. Within these same lines, other names—Silas and Will— reiterate the theme. "Will" comes from a Teutonic word meaning "resolute," and "Silas" derives from Silvanus, the Latin sylvan deity (traditionally related to the dark forces, hence the unconscious and Dionysus). These names join the light and darkness imagery in suggesting the major conflict in *L'Immoraliste* between Apollo and Dionysus.[37]

No reader of Gide's early work can seriously doubt that the author had a wide knowledge of traditional symbols. Although he no longer adhered to the narrow Symbolist doctrine by the time of *L'Immoraliste*, he continued to use symbols, both private and traditional, throughout his literary career. He did mock the device in *Paludes* and *Les Caves du Vatican*,[38] but the counterfeit coin of *Les Faux-Monnayeurs* and the precious stones in *Thésée*, for example, show that he was not denying the effectiveness of symbols in literature. The difference between the symbolism of *Le Traité du Narcisse* or *El Hadj* and that of *L'Immoraliste* resides in degree of subtlety. In *L'Immoraliste* the symbols are attributes inherent to the fictional world; they are neither incongruous nor exotic and, thus, do not call attention to themselves. The realistic objects gradually take on symbolic significance by reason of context and repetition.[39]

Even if the reader were not aware that the night traditionally represents the demonic, *L'Immoraliste* emphasizes its fearsome nature through insistent association with destruction. It is at night that Michel begins coughing blood, that Marceline miscarries, that the phlebitis occurs, that the embolism strikes, that Marceline begins to cough and finally that she dies. When Michel begins to open his windows (in contrast to the narrator of *Paludes*, who spends his time closing them), it is to the night. "I don't know how I had managed sleeping until then with my windows closed. So, on the advice of T... I tried opening them at night, a little at first; soon I pushed them wide open; soon it was a habit, a need so strong that as soon as the window was closed I began to suffocate. Later, it was pure joy to feel the night wind blowing in toward me, the moonlight..." (p. 387). Windows traditionally represent penetration, transcendence. It seems significant that with a few notable exceptions the windows of *L'Immoraliste* open wide to the night and to the moon.[40] After two such instances, Michel quotes portions of the Biblical passage: "Now thou girdest thyself and walkest whither thou wouldst; but when thou shalt be old, thou shalt stretch forth thy hands..."[41] which ends: "and another shall gird thee, and carry *thee* whither thou wouldest not" (John 21: 18). Only once does the text explicitly state that the sun entered his window—the morning after his marriage was finally consummated (p. 406). By the time of the second visit to La Morinière, Michel has come under the domination of the night. Although the alluring daytime sounds enter through his open window, he resists the temptation to go out until nightfall. And in the little house at Sidi b.M., his absolute freedom finds support through the "vast holes in the walls" (p. 370) instead of windows, and his incapacity to make use of this freedom through the low wall surrounding the property. He is a night creature when his friends arrive. Appropriately, Michel begins his story only when "it was night."[42] The importance of this statement becomes clear when the reader notes that in the first half of the book after the couple's arrival in Biskra, images of light predominate, even in the shadow: "I moved into its shadow with delight. The air was luminous... The shadow was mobile and quick; it didn't fall to the ground, it seemed barely to land on it. Oh light!" (p. 390). Twice as many references to the night occur in the second half of the novel as in the first. At the end of *L'Immoraliste*, although there is sunlight in the desert, Michel only comes alive at night.

Michel's room in Biskra provides a related, supporting image which Gide exploited more fully in *La Porte étroite*. "A small door led to Marceline's room; a big, windowed door opened onto the terrace" (p. 381). Michel chooses the large door and penetrates farther and farther into the world, to the terrace (p. 383), to the public garden (p. 387), to the "marvelous orchards of the oasis" (p. 391), and "farther on" (p. 393).

As Michel moves from his room and from the garden, he and Marceline follow the river. The river may be a reference to time, for when the couple pause beneath some palm trees, Michel says, "It was a place... which seemed as though sheltered from time" (p. 392). At this point in the narrative sequence, his need for water has already been emphasized: "There was a bottle of mineral water; I drank a glass, two glasses; the third time, I put the bottle to my lips and finished it without pausing" (p. 385). Michel's health improves, and they leave Biskra and the river for Ravello in Italy where Michel finds a spring located high above the plain. After suitable exposure to the sun—"I offered my whole body to its flame" (p. 401)—and three trips[43] to the spring, he plunges in. "Quickly chilled, I left the water, stretched out on the grass in the sun. There, odorous mint grew; I picked some, crushed the leaves, rubbed them all over my damp but burning body. I looked at it for a long time, no longer feeling any shame, with joy rather. I found myself, not yet robust but capable of it, harmonious, sensual, almost beautiful" (p. 402). Here, Michel seems close to becoming a well-integrated person. The forces of nature (Dionysus) and of rationality (Apollo) are in harmonious balance. He cuts his beard, protects Marceline, and while begetting his child begins a new life free of the limitations of his former existence. "Our happiness during the end of this trip was so unchanging, so calm that I am unable to tell anything about it" (p. 408). Perhaps it is significant that the plant with which Michel dries himself is mint, Jupiter's plant, for Jupiter is normally considered to correspond to the virtues of judgment and will.

The happiness and equilibrium established when he consummates his marriage appear as the apex of his moral and physical development. He experiences a moment of happiness so intense that it can never again be equaled: "Nothing prevents happiness like the memory of happiness. Alas! I remember that night" (p. 405). Nonetheless he maintains a sort of plateau, characterized by happiness,[44] tranquility,[45] and confidence (p. 410). In addition, both Marceline and Michel are fruitful—he begins to work and she is pregnant (p. 410). Unfortunately, a hint soon appears that the equilibrium established in Italy and maintained in Normandy is about to go out of balance. Michel looks at the Normandy land, where "from this ordered abundance, from this joyous submission, from this smiling cultivation, harmony was established. It was not fortuitous but given, a rhythm, a beauty that was both human and natural" (p. 410). And he begins to imagine not just order, but perfect order: "I constructed a set of ethics which was becoming a science of the perfect utilization of one's self through intelligent constraint" (p. 411).

His desire for perfection spills out onto the farm, and he decides to repair a leaking pond. As the workers drain it, Michel considers leaving to seek Marceline. But suddenly the eels are sighted. He forgets his wife, enters the water, joins hands with

Bocage's son Charles, addresses the latter in the familiar form, and allows himself to be covered with mud. Michel, clearly attracted to Charles, begins to neglect Marceline in order to be with him. The eels suggest an erotic attraction, and the mud adumbrates the eventual end of the unconscious choice Michel makes at the pond. He does not go after his wife, and "already, I no longer regretted her absence. It seemed to me that she would have impeded our joy somewhat" (p. 413).

The image of the *leaking water* appears later: "I leaned over her [i.e., Marceline] the way one would over deep, pure water where, as far as you could see, there was nothing but love. Ah! if this was still happiness, I know I tried from then on to hold it back, the way one tries, in vain, to hold leaking water in one's hands; but even then beside the happiness I felt something other than happiness, which certainly gave my love color, but the way autumn colors" (p. 420). This passage recalls the images discussed above. We have the pure water which appeared in the spring near Ravello related to Marceline. The leaking water reminds us of the episode in the pond at La Morinière, and the reference to time already noted in relation to running water is clear. The passage also prepares Ménalque's image: "Ah Michel! all joy is similar to . . . water from the fountain of Ameles which, according to Plato, cannot be held in any vase....Let every moment carry off everything that it brought" (pp. 436-37).

Given Gide's later public stance on homosexuality, perhaps I should insist that the episode at the pond provides no indications that Michel is on the right track. To the contrary, the mud puts him back to the beginning of what we shall see to be a metaphorical evolution. Further, where Marceline has been clearly associated with his equilibrium and with the pure water of the spring of Ravello, here, after the water has escaped, he begins to reject her. The following day, a new movement begins. In the company of Charles, "Both of us went toward the woods" (p. 413). Soon, "we reached the edge of the woods" (p. 417). When he actually enters the woods to poach (prepared by the already mentioned etymological relationship of Silas to the forest), he reveals a new preference for water near the ground: "I went home across the fields in the grass heavy with dew, drunk with night, with uncivilized life and anarchy, soaked, muddy, covered with leaves" (p. 449).

To return to the first stay at La Morinière, the watchword is order, excessive order that runs in the face of reality. Simultaneously, he pushes in the other direction by exalting the wild and untutored ethic of the Goths: "By a sort of natural reaction, while my life was becoming ordered, regulated and while I was enjoying regulating and ordering everything around me, I became more and more infatuated with the rough ethics of the Goths" (p. 418). The order stays only on the surface, affecting his external life and everything surrounding him. It is nothing but apparent order. Naturally, because of his unwillingness to recognize the availability of farm labor, when he departs for Paris he leaves La Morinière in worse shape than he found it—"with more than a hundred hectares on his hands." In Paris, empty formulations are the rule; art occurs at the opposite extreme from life. Most novelists and poets "did not live, were content to seem to live, and it would not have taken very much for them to consider life an annoying hindrance to writing" (p. 423). Writing and teaching are but empty words: "How well I understood from then on that the almost entirely moral teaching of the great philosophers of antiquity was by example as much as and even more than by words!" (p. 429). Encouraged by the example of Ménalque, his course finished, he begins to undermine the forms of his life by poaching, by deciding to sell the farm, and finally by attacking Marceline herself. The willed abandonment to sensation eventually leaves him helpless, like flotsam after the water has receded.

At Neuchâtel, he loved the swamp-like lake (p. 454). Later he finds the little lake high in the Alps a "hideous, blue lake" (p. 456), and when Marceline begins to mend, they leave. The trip south, which has "all the dizziness of a fall" (p. 458), ends only in the midst of the desert at Touggourt. During this trip, Michel repeatedly leaves bodies of water, despite the fact that they seem beneficial to Marceline. Not only did he leave the Engadine valley, but he leaves Palermo ("The Palermo bay is mild, and Marceline liked it there"— p. 462) and the sea ("When we were at sea, Marceline improved..."— p. 464). Rain and humidity, on the other hand, prove harmful to Marceline (pp. 459, 465), but in Naples we find Michel enjoying this humidity: "I breathed in the night's humidity" (p. 461). Finally, at Touggourt, they drink some tea, "which the salty water of the area gave a detestable taste" (p. 468). The wind stirs up the sand, the sand which appears repeatedly in the last pages.[46] Michel cannot resist the night and leaves his dying wife alone.

When one considers the earth, sand, and water imagery, the various references support what is actually happening to Michel in much the same way as do light and darkness. Indeed, there seems to be a value distinction between the types of water. While Michel's body and mind gain strength in Biskra, he follows a river in which "the heavy water is the color of earth."[47] The metaphorical progression continues to a reasonably healthy state and to what might be called "upper waters," the spring of pure water near Ravello. "Lower waters" appear in conjunction with Michel's unconscious rejection of Marceline and his homosexual tendencies at La Morinière. Michel likes the lake at Neuchâtel, "this lake with the seagreen banks. . . which has nothing alpine about it. Its water, like that of a swamp, mixes long with the earth and filters between the reeds" (p. 454). He despises the subsequent altitudinous lake. At sea level, in Palermo (p. 462) and Syracuse (p. 463), he joins "the society of the worst people" (ibid.). When he finally reaches the desert, there is only the vilest of drinking water and sand. At this point Michel has lost control to the forces of "the sinister god" (p. 467), a state of helpless disintegration which becomes almost complete by the time his friends arrive at Sidi. There, he tells his friends, he likes to play with "white pebbles" (p. 471). If names have importance, as I have suggested in reference to Denis, Daniel, Silas, and Will, it may be significant, in relation to the pebbles, that Pierre (French for "stone") the farmhand at La Morinière, is a brute "uniquely led by instinct" (p. 442).

Coming back to the water imagery, humidity, as distinct from bodies of water, appears in conjunction with transition. At the spring when Michel approaches integration, his body is "humid but burning" (p. 402); moistness, dew or humidity appears at La Morinière during his comradery with Charles (p. 417), when he goes to visit Ménalque (p. 435), when he joins the poachers (p. 449), and as Marceline dies.[48] One might summarize by saying that Michel's progression from sickness and near death, to health and happiness is highlighted by a system of images that moves concomitantly from earth-laden water to pure water at high altitudes. The spiritual disintegration is accompanied by a movement to low water, and finally to sand, pebbles, and night. This complex of imagery closely follows the traditional symbolic divisions between darkness, a state of destruction or of unrealized potential, and light, the gold of wisdom and self-integration. Earth appears at the lowest symbolic level of evolution; when it occurs as sand or pebbles, it signifies disintegration. Water, a transitional element, has more freedom and may be transformed into air by fire, which is related to light and gold. Those seeking salvation and the light traditionally turn to the flaming aridity of the desert. Michel also seeks the desert in the final portion of *L'Immoraliste*, but he refuses the sun, taking instead the easy path in the shadow of the night. If, as Goodhand has reasonably suggested, Marceline "*is* the earthly representative in this novel of

the forces of light,"[49] Michel should have sought his salvation
through her. Significantly, as has already been pointed out, it was
only when he was attending to his husbandly duty that the sun entered
his window.

The system of imagery contradicts what Michel attempts to
make his listeners believe. Despite his assertion to Marceline—"Oh
Marceline! Marceline! Marceline! Let us leave here. Elsewhere I will
love you the way I loved you at Sorrento. You thought I was
changed, didn't you? But elsewhere, you will clearly sense that
nothing has changed our love..." (p. 453)—the frantic voyage south
does not mean a search for the values he espoused during his first
visit to North Africa. Nor is it the quest for a new, future-oriented
ethic ("What more can man do?"), for in seeking the "old man" he
voyages to the places where past joys occurred. And finally, his night
is not like Ménalque's knightly vigil of arms, it represents almost
total incapacity. He can do nothing but ask for help. At La
Morinière, in willfully relaxing the control over his sensations, in
neglecting to continue the balanced self-discipline he developed in
North Africa, in abandoning his future-oriented ethic, Michel makes
the fatal error which results in his final helplessness. Enslaved to the
night, to his unconscious, to sensualism, incapable of conscious
choice, he follows the whim of the moment. Consequently, his
disintegration does nothing but increase in velocity. Michel and, in
the process, Marceline are doomed.

As we follow the covert structure of significant images, an
interesting thing occurs. The overt structure is subverted. Neither
the three main parts, nor the thirteen chapters are related to what
are actually the formative developments of Michel's life. Although I
agree with Porter that the spaces and numerals which mark the
chapter divisions result from the "implied author" which Gide
introduced in the preface to the second edition in 1902,[50] I would
maintain that the markers merely render blatant what is already
obvious in the structure of Michel's discourse. I shall, however,
suggest that the *author*, rather than the "implied author" or the
protagonist-narrator, is responsible for the symbolic pattern which
contravenes Michel's exculpatory patterns. The latter approaches
integration in chapter 6 when he plunges into the spring of pure
water. Only in chapter 8, when he makes love to his wife, does
happiness and equilibrium arrive. The "plateau" of happiness is
recounted in chapter 9 (the last chapter of part I) and in the first few
pages of part II. Where, earlier, while under the seductive sway of
Michel's account, it seemed that the death of the child and the

meetings with Ménalque (which occur, as mentioned, at the "center" of the book's formal structure—chapter 2, part II) are responsible for Michel's rejection of all restraints, in fact, they only emphasize his already well-established tendency. The formal structure, then, corresponds to what Michel wants his listeners to believe. But it is far removed from having anything to do with what actually happened. In that sense, it corresponds to the kind of "art" Michel finds in Paris, that is, it reflects a preconceived idealization which ignores reality.

The disparity between the formal divisions of L'Immoraliste and the reality of the events as they happened provides an astonishingly powerful support for one pole of Michel's moral dilemma. It is an extreme, exactly as was Michel's decision to make his life and La Morinière conform to his idea of perfection: "the perfect utilization of one's self through intelligent constraint." In the light of what Michel subsequently does, it is clear that by "intelligent" he does not mean "constraint based on understanding." He means "constraint that reveals the workings of the intelligence." It is intellection run wild, without any regard for the realities of farming in Normandy or of his own capacities. He thus presents vivid proof that culture can kill life, as he prophetically suggests in his course (p. 424). By the time Michel reaches Paris, he conforms to his image of its inhabitants. However much he disdains them for being and living empty forms, for guiding their lives according to appearance, for writing "art" that has nothing to do with life, the plain truth is that when he rejects all constraints, whether self-imposed or not, he attempts to conform to his intellectual ideal of an unrestrained Gothic leader. If logic or directness were the standards of judgment, one would have difficulty faulting Michel's actions. As he systematically attacks every restraining bond, all fall, even will power and the orderly use of his mind that successfully overcame the effects of his sickness. His intellectual goal leads to control by unconscious sensation.

When this occurs, Michel coincides with the quality he sees in North Africa: "Land on vacation from works of art. I despise those who are unable to recognize beauty if it has not already been transcribed and completely interpreted. The Arab people is admirable in that they live their art, they sing it and dissipate it from one day to the next. They do not make it rigid and do not embalm it in any work. It is the cause and effect of the absence of great artists..." (pp. 464-65). Michel, like his conception of the North Africans, accepts his lot and floats with the current. "I sense that art is leaving me" (p. 467). One minute follows another, the expected effect always follows the cause. There is no attempt to overcome chronological or causal relationships. Nothing is fixed, everything flows. "Here, it is impossible to seek, so quickly does voluptuousness follow desire. Surrounded by splendor and death, I feel as though happiness is too much present and one's surrender to it too uniform" (p. 471). Michel has left Paris to become North Africa, a development that is structurally supported by the apparent artlessness of Michel's account. On the surface, the story is of the simplest variety, ordered only by the normal sequence of cause and effect and by chronology. It appears perfectly natural and ineluctible when, from innocent beginnings, the events concentrate and, with a vertiginious rush, turn into tragedy. This aspect of *L'Immoraliste* perhaps best satisfies the demands of a story. A reader is encouraged, after all, to read in a linear fashion, line by line, page by page, from beginning to end, accepting each word as an ordered event and as it comes. Michel's discourse superficially resembles "life" and not "art." While Michel touches two opposing extremes: a strait jacket and anarchy, Paris and North Africa, *L'Immoraliste* incorporates artificial, nonlinear order and unilinear discourse: in short, image *and* process structure. In respect to Michel, the first visits to both Italy and Normandy also serve as a middle term. There he attained happiness and fruitful activity, a situation that seems to be echoed structurally by the integration of those verisimilar, unobtrusive elements which serve as the primary conveyance of meaning and as the most important means for providing *L'Immoraliste* with the equilibrium Gide expected of art.

Art, as Gide clearly understood, must be natural. "Do you know what makes today's poetry and, especially, philosophy dead letters? It is because they have been separated from life" (p. 435). Carried to an extreme, however, nature can be destructive. "The true return to nature is the complete return to the elements: death."[51] In the work of art, nature must be balanced by order (a sort of Maxwell E. Perkins for a Thomas Wolfe). Gide puts it this way in "Les Limites de l'art": "In nature, nothing can be isolated or arrested; everything continues. Man can attempt, propose beauty; immediately nature takes it over and disposes of it. This is the opposition that I was talking about. Here, man is in submission to nature, but to the contrary in a work of art he submits nature to him" (ibid., p. 407). In *L'Immoraliste*, not only does *God propose*, not only does *man dispose*, but also "God proposes and man disposes [which] is [a] work of art" (ibid., p. 408). This happens to Michel and to the book.

After having suggested that irony undermines the credibility of Michel's account, that this interplay stimulates an alternating involvement and rejection, participation and judgment from the reader, and that one is finally forced to turn to the imagery underlying the account, it is difficult to avoid the thought that such complex games are at worst precious and at best unlike life. Perhaps this represents the final irony. Still, it seems to me that the book is preserved from preciosity because it continues to elicit active participation from readers even after they are very familiar with the book. Even on the last of numerous readings, I felt the same sort of horrified revulsion, the same desire to close the book before the end that I have felt before.[52] The only relief came from the very artificiality of the tale. And, on completing the reading, on looking back over the highly integrated style, motifs, images, and structure, I experienced a pleasure similar to gazing down into a pool of pure water, where the wind-caused ripples and the shifting angle of light made widely varying visions of what is essentially the same object. In the end, although I should not like to slight *L'Immoraliste* insofar as it provides insights into one form of individualism,[53] it seems to me that its primary success resides in having encouraged an active participation in the act of reading, in permitting the reader to see multiple levels of meaning integrated into one significant work where Gide has, indeed, succeeded in what he attempted: to "paint and illuminate his painting well" (p. 368).

That said, it is more important to speculate on the implications of the pressures Gide placed on the novel by subverting the normal ways of giving form to the romanesque universe. In the first place, the conflicting structures show extraordinary insight into how authors organize novels. A first reading leaves one full of admiration for the control the author manifests over the plot, the leisurely flow of the first two-thirds gradually giving way to the rush to Marceline's death and Michel's passivity. That Gide would then place this process structure in conflict with an image structure shows both awareness and daring, for the initial effect of noticing the schema suggested by the three parts is to arrest the movement. Of course, this conflict eventually adds piquancy to the reader's experience of the text. It further indicates the degree to which traditional process and image patterns of organization had become so familiar that they had few mysteries left, so common that Gide could expect the reader to pick up on his many subversions and recognize the novel's artifice. When artists reveal such awareness, the devices are destined soon to fall victim to the satirist. Indeed, Gide's *Les Caves du Vatican* (1914) offered the public a biting satire of the whole craft—artifice and artificer. Of course, awareness of pitfalls and limits is not enough. It remains to create new, more effective ways of bringing readers to live the aesthetic experience. From the standpoint of structure, at least, Huysmans was a striking innovator. He not only pushed the novel to its apparent limits, he began to form it into something quite, though not entirely, different.

## Chapter 6

# Negative Representation in Huysmans's *En rade*

IT IS WELL KNOWN THAT LITERARY FORMS are in a constant state of flux. Viktor Shklovsky said, for example, "Each art form travels down the inevitable road from birth to death; from seeing and sensory perception, when every detail in the object is savored and relished, to mere recognition, when the object or form becomes a dull epigone which our senses register mechanically, a piece of merchandise not visible even to the buyer."[1] The mechanism is most obvious in popular literature. One thinks, for instance, of Dashiell Hammett's tough, capable private detectives and the later degradation in the brutish heroes created by Mickey Spillane, which in turn led into the comic-satires by such writers as Donald E. Westlake. Shklovsky would however have us believe that all literary transformations follow the same path. In fact, though minor literary fashions indeed seem to pass through literature in this way, radical changes in significant aesthetic categories or structures are not so easily schematized. They occur seldom, and they involve such profound reordering that readers are frequently incapable of perceiving any structure at all in the results. When the time arrives that some sort of organization once again becomes perceptible, it is then still difficult to find adequate vocabulary to describe what has happened.

As I have done the reading required for this study, I have become increasingly convinced that the turmoil in the arts of the late nineteenth and early twentieth centuries signaled growing dissatisfaction with the old ways of making aesthetic objects and an important quest for new subjects, techniques, and forms, perhaps even for a new vision. Thomas S. Kuhn's *The Structure of Scientific Revolutions*[2] has been extremely helpful in coming to terms with the agitation and confusion of this period, despite the fact that he is interested only in the way scientists renounce one scientific "paradigm" for another. By paradigm, he means both "the entire constellation of beliefs, values, techniques, and so on shared by the members of a given community" and concrete models or examples which can replace explicit rules as a basis for the solution of scientific problems (ibid., p. 174). At a certain point, scientists notice more and more anomalies. There is then a "gradual and simultaneous emergence of both observational and conceptual recognition" (ibid., p. 62). The shift from one paradigm of categories and procedures to another is far from easy, however, and it frequently meets considerable resistance before successfully gaining the adherence of the majority (ibid.). "The proliferation of competing articulations, the willingness to try anything, the expression of explicit discontent, the recourse to philosophy and to debate over fundamentals, all these are symptoms of a transition from normal to extraordinary research [leading to a paradigm change]" (p. 91). Finally, of course, the shift takes place and, barring a few diehards, scientists acknowledge the existence of a new paradigm.

I do not advance Kuhn's model as an exact analogue, rather as a fillip for understanding. While the signs Kuhn lists as evidence of transition admirably characterize the years from 1885 through 1917 (which resulted in those major revolutionaries, Proust and Joyce, whom the period formed), one would be wrong to suggest that the artistic community shows the unanimity of opinion generally found among scientists. Even in the most authoritarian times like the French classical age artists are notorious for their independence. The ability to comprehend what was happening in the fifty or so years at the end of the nineteenth and beginning of the twentieth centuries is further complicated by the cataclysmic events of the First World War. The death toll was appalling; village after village was left with no adult males whatsoever; the injured and maimed remained a living reminder of the horrors of modern warfare; and writers committed their art to finding and propagating solutions to mankind's ills. The best novelists (and dramatists) between the two wars, indeed until the early 1950s, were strongly didactic. The result was that the artistic ferment prior to 1914 had little result until almost ten years after the Second World War. Even Proust, whose novel is unquestionably revolutionary, had few French readers until then.

Perhaps it is not surprising that it has taken so long to assimilate the changes from endomorphic to the kind of novel Proust exploited. The earlier shifts in major organizing device were, though important, not nearly as profound. Eighteenth-century readers had relatively little difficulty adapting to works by Marivaux, Crébillon fils, Voltaire, which were organized for the most part around plot rather than depending primarily on character and character development, as had been the case of La Fontaine's, Racine's, Molière's works. Even in respect to Balzac and the realists, where theme takes the predominant structural role, character and plot continued to be sufficiently apparent, and readers did not normally feel disoriented. By late in the century, however, writers were less willing to cater to the expectations of their public.

Huysmans, in particular, could not be bothered, especially from *A rebours* (1884) on.

Of the fine nineteenth-century French writers who have not received their due recognition, Joris-Karl Huysmans must surely come at the head of the list. On the rare occasions that his work is considered, the results are generally disappointing. Michael Issacharoff puts it this way: "Huysmans criticism has often been rather unliterary. Religious and occasionally political considerations have prevailed with several commentators. Moreover, in the stead of precise analyses which limit themselves to the work, one often finds 'recollections' or a super-abundance of irrelevant biographical details."[3] Indeed, it seems that "if critics have judged Huysmans, and in truth judgments of him are not lacking, it is the man who has too often been judged to the exclusion of the work" (ibid., p. 11). There are, however, a few bright spots. Baldick's biography is excellent, for example, as is Cressot's stylistic study.[4] And I must neglect neither Brombert's fine investigation of the claustration theme in Huysmans's work nor Livi's engaging consideration of the decadent movement leading up to *A rebours*.[5] But for those of us interested in criticism that treats individual works as wholes, there is little to assuage our thirst. Although I do not agree with Ruth Plant Weinreb that in *A rebours* "the sequence of chapters could be shifted without consequence," her dissertation provides a welcome exception.[6] Issacharoff's "Huysmans et la structure métaphorique du récit," a perceptive consideration of *A vau-l'eau*, is another.[7] Most important for the present chapter, however, is Ruth B. Antosh's *Reality and Illusion in the Novels of J.-K. Huysmans* (Amsterdam: Rodopi, 1986). Her perceptive reading of Huysmans's oeuvre allows her to demonstrate conclusively that Huysmans's predominant and increasingly successful effort concerned portraying the inner life of complex characters. And I shall return to J. H. Matthews's insightful work on *En rade*.

*En rade* particularly interests me, for it makes use of a startling device which was to have profound effects in more recent novels. Perhaps that explains why it has been so misunderstood. Certainly, I can think of no book so undeservedly neglected. It was poorly received when it appeared in 1887,[8] and subsequently, for the most part, it has been granted only the nod of almost always negative judgments made in passing on to other things. At first it seems to have been the three dreams that disconcerted reviewers.[9] Later critics were drawn especially to the difficulty of classifying the novel. George Ross Ridge is typical. After an eleven-line summary of the plot, which he says represents "the substance of the novel," he states that it is

> structurally the portrait of a soul-state of the Naturalist-Decadent protagonist Jacques Marles, and hence the evocation and, to a large extent, the picture of the evolution of the novelist himself. . . . Here, in this analysis of the fictional hero, and thereby in his own self-analysis, Huysmans achieves his most lasting effect. Otherwise, the novel leaves much to be desired. Indeed, it is even somewhat ineffective. The style, for instance, is rather undistinguished. It is neither Decadent nor Naturalistic, and it cannot be classified as representative of either of Huysmans' great periods. . . . [And] from the philosophical standpoint, the novel is far from a major achievement. . . . In it Huysmans is not a Catholic writer, as he later is; or a Decadent writer, as most assuredly he can be. . . . or even a Naturalistic writer, as he was.[10]

Ridge's conclusions are interesting because of his criteria for evaluation. After praising the novel because of the autobiographical elements, he condemns both style and philosophy because they cannot be classified according to norms which are *per se* external to the novel. It would make as much sense for a zoologist to castigate *En rade* for being neither fish nor fowl. Such judgments are common in periods of paradigm change.

Most critics have been content to call attention to the auto-biographical nature of the protagonist,[11] to term *En rade* pessimistic[12] and, thereafter, to dismiss it to the oblivion from whence it came. Not infrequently, they echo Huysmans's letter to Zola in an apparent attempt to justify their lack of attention. G. Vanwelkenhuyzen says, for example: "In a letter to Zola, J.-K. [Huysmans] recognized, moreover, that his book, [*En rade*] was badly constructed."[13] But the letter itself should be read more carefully and put into a context: "As for your opinion about the different legs of these pants, one real and the other up in the air, it is, alas! mine. Your reflections are absolutely right. I got in trouble because of a preconceived idea of a division decided ahead of time—day, reality—night, dream. Notice that, given this idea, I would have been infinitely better off to apply it in all its rigor."[14] Could Huysmans's deep affection and gratitude for the master of Médan have anything to do with the deference revealed in the letter? Although there was no longer any question about his independence, Huysmans wanted to maintain as friendly a relationship as possible. Matthews goes further and subjects the letter to keen analysis: "While agreeing with the naturalist leader, Huysmans does not state the problem in quite the same terms. Zola would like to see the dream element kept apart from the stern picture of reality. . . .Huysmans, without facing this criticism, condemned himself on other grounds—for not applying his method more systematically; in fact, for not stating more plainly in *En Rade* his true intentions."[15] Of course, even if Huysmans really did believe he had failed by not making his novel more obvious (a statement which contrasts rather strangely with what he wrote earlier to Jules Destrée: "I haven't finished *En rade* which is coming out now—it's already raising a big uproar—naturalists reproach me for my nude Esther, in a dream—Others for my peasants that they think are too real—Nobody is happy—I don't give a damn!"[16]), nothing absolves the reader from making an effort to understand or, even, guarantees that Huysmans was right. Valéry's judgment seems pertinent: "When a work has appeared, its interpretation by the author has no more value than any other by anyone at all."[17] Suffice it to say that no one has taken up Matthew's suggestion that the dreams and the realistic description function, not as two unrelated entities, rather as one.[18] Perhaps the time has come to look carefully at *En rade* in the attempt to formulate an aesthetic reason for accepting or rejecting the novel.

There is no question that the work poses serious difficulties if one seeks what recent writers call a "traditional" novel—that is, the realistic representation or projection of a minutely described character who, across causally and chronologically arranged episodes situated in appropriate settings, develops in one way or another to the tune of the narrator's patient, if professorial, explanations. Granted, the characters are vividly described. Huysmans catches the tone of peasant speech in an admirable fashion, and with a few deft strokes, he allows us moreover to see them, to "project" them. Jacques Marles also provides an excellent vehicle for the author to unleash the full range of his rich vocabulary. Doubtless, "he was good for nothing, incapable of becoming interested in the occupations sought by men, inept at making money and even at keeping it, indifferent to the attractions of honors and to what may be gained from position."[19] "He had," however, "done an enormous amount of reading and gathered considerable erudition from remote but scattered sources" (ibid.). Prehistory, theology, the Cabala had in turn drawn and held him. He had searched libraries, exhausted cardboard filing cases, and his mind had become congested from skimming the surface of this farrago of useless knowledge" (p. 121). Not only does Jacques have the background to render a sophisticated interpretation of his thought and dreams possible, his luxurious lexicon of revulsion is perfectly in character. He might well describe the courtyard of Lourps in the following terms: "Before him extended a vast courtyard boiling with dandelion bubbles that furred above the green leaves crawling on the marl bristled with hard cilia" (p. 45). In short, although within the narrative sequence the effects follow the causes, although there is for the most part a strict adherence to chronology, nothing much seems to happen. Viewed as a projection of a pseudoreal world, Jacques Marles gives every indication of remaining to the end the same incompetent dilettante he was at the outset.[20]

Where the events of Julien Sorel's and Emma Bovary's lives appear the inevitable results of carefully prepared causes, the occurrences of *En rade* are by comparison poorly motivated. One is reminded of such eighteenth-century novels as *Manon Lescaut* where a blind destiny having little if any connection with Manon and Des Grieux afflicts the two lovers with one randomly chosen catastrophe after another. In the whole of *En rade* only two incidents can properly be termed "motivating": one, which occurs prior to the formal opening of the story, accounts for Jacques and Louise Marles's arrival at the château of Lourps—through poor management, Jacques has lost his fortune. The other permits the couple's departure— Jacques receives some money. The same cannot be said for other events. What realistic motivation could explain the order of such episodes as Jacques's battle with the owl, his inability to draw water from the well, the arrival of the cat, the bull servicing the cow? And if the narrator is supposed to pontificate, one can scarcely fail to notice that, despite numerous analytical passages, little is explained and less justified. Consequently, should we accept the recently formulated canons for the "traditional" novel, *En rade* fails miserably.

These problems dissipate, however, when the novel is read with an understanding of the symbolic or connotative implications of the objects and actions described. There are, of course, many symbolic traditions. Still, because *En rade* refers specifically to the Cabala (pp. 121, 213), to alchemists (pp. 211-14, 228) and to such specific writers as Porphyrius (p. 59), Paracelsus (p. 228), and Del Rio (p. 217), the novel suggests a reading in the light of Occidental black magic, cabalism, and alchemy. Huysmans's sources are not exhausted by the authors provided by the text. Indeed, it would be difficult, if not impossible, to discover exactly where Huysmans gained his knowledge. The nineteenth century was as interested as our own age in such topics, and the possible sources are legion. I have consequently used excellent, well-organized scholarly works of recent vintage, though in all cases this material has been controlled by wide reading in those less systematic texts Huysmans might have known.[21]

Generally, Huysmans is not considered to have made consistent use of traditional symbols until the composition of *Là-bas* or later.[22] The author himself must bear part of the responsibility for this misconception. In the "Preface written twenty years after [*A rebours*]," he specifically disclaims having used such loaded language in the novel in question: "*A rebours*. . . .is a perfectly unconscious work, imagined without preconceived ideas, without intentions reserved for the future, without anything at all."[23] He goes on to deny having had any knowledge of "the idiom of symbols" in respect to precious stones (ibid., p. xv) and flowers: "*A rebours*," he says, "does not consider them from the point of view of contours and tints, not at all from the point of view of the meanings they disclose" (ibid., p. xviii). Despite this explicit disclaimer, it should not be forgotten that in the twenty years separating the composition of the novel and the preface, Huysmans may well have become a little vague about the chronology of his education. In respect to flowers, the text proves, as a matter of fact, that he was not absolutely uninitiated. While Des Esseintes considers "the sacred flower of Egypt and India, the great lotus," which appears in one of Gustave Moreau's paintings, the narrator recounts Des Esseintes interpretation: "Des Esseintes sought the meaning of this emblem. Did it have the phallic significance that the primordial Indian cults lent it? Did it announce to old Herod an oblation of virginity, an exchange of blood, an impure wound solicited, offered with the explicit condition of a murder? Or did it represent the allegory of fecundity, the Hindu myth of life, an existence held between a woman's fingers, torn away, crushed by palpitating man's hands that were invaded by insanity, that a crisis of the flesh led astray?" (ibid., p. 87). One would admittedly not have to be a scholar to have accumulated this information, especially in this period of sustained interest in such matters. But few would share Huysmans's knowledge that "the pumpkin [is a] symbol of fecundity" (ibid., p. 69).

The most convincing proof of Huysmans's far from elementary awareness of various ancient symbolic traditions would come from demonstrating the consistent patterns of meaning that arise from his novels when read with the necessary insight. This can and should be accomplished for *A rebours*.[24] For the moment, however, *En rade* poses more interesting problems.

As the book opens, Jacques Marles hurries through the dusk toward the château de Lourps. Jacques is only thirty, but already his life has been ruined. A comfortable fortune and a good strong wife of peasant stock were supposed to shield him from the world and allow him to continue his dilettantish games without interruption or worry. But the well-laid plans had a short-lived success. First of all, his wife, Louise, fell ill. "And little by little, a fissure was produced in the house's hold, a fissure through which money leaked. Louise, so attentive in her look-out, beginning with their marriage, had gone to sleep, letting the maid steer the boat. They immediately entered a dirty waterway" (p. 116). Then the bankruptcy arrived and the conjugal ship is in dire straights. Jacques "had remained struck with consternation, without defense against the financial worries that iced his mental bursts of speed and tossed him brutally back into the inextricable systems of real life" (p. 121). The young man, however, has no choice. He must take command of the bark. What they need, he decides, is a *rade*, that is, a large natural basin opening onto the sea where ships can find a good mooring. Louise's Uncle Antoine, fortunately, is the caretaker of a château in Brie. Since he and his woman, Norine, have frequently invited the "Parisians" to visit, this will be their haven. *En rade* then tells the story of Jacques and Louise Marles "in the haven." The title might well make the reader expect an account of calm happiness, were it not for another French expression. Indeed, Jacques and Louise are not "en rade," they have been abandoned, *laissés en rade*.

As Jacques approaches the château in the opening pages of the novel, sky and buildings burst into flames. Slowly, "the solemn din of the fiery sunset was succeeded by the bleak, silent firmament of ashes. Here and there, however, unconsumed embers glowed in the cloud's smoke and lit up the château" (p. 11). The protagonist continues on the "Way of Fire" (ibid.) to the door. This is the first indication that the novel deals with more than a simple account of Jacques Marles's financial problems, more than a description of city dwellers discovering country life. The "Way of Fire," like the two-edged sword, symbolizes initiation which may destroy or lead to a rebirth.[25] But what kind of an initiation? Much later the protagonist recognizes, "This stay at Lourps . . . will have mutually initiated us into the abomination of our souls and our bodies!" (p. 245).

Jacques has far to go before he will understand this. When he arrives at Lourps, he is absolutely ignorant of his soul, body, and, as well, his spirit. Everything in his life has been planned to protect him from the knowledge. He lives as though only one part of him were important, and that one, his mind, is very poorly controlled because it has been cut off from, rather than integrated into, the whole man. His momentary enthusiasms, though of sufficient force to drive him through many volumes in quest of knowledge, tend to die as suddenly and inexplicably as they arose, leaving him bored and disgusted. He should have known it could not continue. The cabalists, whom he brags of having read (p. 213), could tell him that there are three sides to man: body, soul, and spirit. The first step of the cabalist is to understand these elements. Eliphas Lévi explains: "When the sage has arrived at lucidity, either with the intermediary of a pythoness or a somnambulant or by his own efforts, he communicates and directs magnetic vibrations at will throughout the mass of astral light, whose currents he divines with the help of a magic wand."[26] Though much against his will, Jacques Marles is about to begin a voyage of discovery. He will be thrust into his body, into physical matter; he will plumb the depths of the unconscious, of unreasoning fear and of instinct; and he will be forced to integrate them with his intellect. Only then will he be ready to face the real world of struggle in Paris.

The château of Lourps, his sick wife, the rapacious Antoine and Norine, the cat, every element of his new environment will serve to teach him the cruel lesson of his own being. As he leaves the "Way of Fire," he confronts, not a haven, but an enormous ruin lacking the most elemental niceties. It takes five minutes of hard work to raise a bucket of water from the well. And, although Louise "finally discovered one room in the whole château which was almost habitable" (p. 14), it is hideous, humid, cold, and filled with the unpleasant odors of old wood and wet plaster. "Decidedly, a bath of sadness fell from the too high ceiling onto the tile of the floor" (p. 17).

When Antoine and Norine finally leave the Marleses alone, Jacques sits at the table and begins to sort through his papers. "In spite of the long distance he had traveled, he did not feel that exhaustion that makes one's limbs feel lukewarm, but he felt feeble, stupified by infinite spiritual fatigue, by limitless discouragement" (p. 27). He begins to nod off. "An indefinable sensation of malaise obsessed him. He seemed to have behind him in the obscurity an expanse of water whose lapping breath chilled him" (p. 28). After the already mentioned sunset of fiery red and ashes—signifying the loss of all force—after arriving at the château and the initiation in darkness, it seems appropriate that his dream begins with water. Water has long been considered the source of life, a means of purification and of regeneration. When agitated, as in this case, it points towards disorder or evil.

Huysmans went to great trouble to integrate this dream into the narration and to insist on its importance. For later dreams, he did not take the same trouble, either because he felt it was no longer necessary or because he wished to draw attention to the discontinuity.[27] This first time, however, we watch Jacques doze at the table, wake up, go to bed, and drift off again: "He counted the lozenges of the paneling, noting with care the pieces of wallpaper added whose designs did not match. Suddenly a bizarre phenomenon took place. The green latticework of [the wallpaper's] trellis began to undulate, while the brackish background of paneling ruffled like a stream" (pp. 28-29). The next day, because the protagonist attempts to analyze his dream, the text encourages the reader to do likewise. Jacques realizes rather rapidly that it was a re-creation of the story of Esther, Mordecai's cousin, who married King Ahasuerus and thus saved the Hebrews (pp. 57-58). But recognizing the source leaves him dissatisfied as, consequently, it should leave the reader.[28] "This explanation seems right, he said to himself, but why had the image of Esther assailed him?" (p. 58). "He remained thoughtful, for the unfathomable enigma of the Dream haunted him" (p. 59). Were these visions the result of his spirit wandering loose in occult regions, Jacques wonders. Was Artemidorus Daldianus right when he suggested that dreams are fictions of the soul? Or, the protagonist continues, did Porphyrius see things correctly when he attributed dreams to a guardian spirit warning us of the trials life was preparing? Did they forecast the future? Or were they nothing but a metamorphosis of previous impressions? Was there, on the other hand, some sort of a mysterious association between the present and the long forgotten past which suddenly illuminated "larvae of images" (p. 60)? Asking such questions, alternating between natural and supernatural explanations, he continues to speculate. But the sun begins to warm his back, and he leaves his ruminations to explore the grounds. This is in fact what his dream proposed.

Had Jacques continued his analysis he would doubtless have ended with a combination of the possibilities suggested by his musing. The very Porphyrius whom he cites said explicitly that the philosopher need not go to diviners. By searching within his own integrated self he will find the necessary precepts. And on those special occasions of need, "there are good daemons, who, in the man living after this manner, and who is a domestic of divinity, will indicate and prevent, through dreams and symbols, and omens, what may come to pass, and what is necessarily to be avoided."[29] Such guiding spirits "presignify to us the dangers which are impendent from malefic daemons, unfolding these through dreams, through a divinely inspired soul, and through many other things; so that he who is capable of explaining what is signified, may know and avoid all the perils with which he is threatened. For they indicate to all men, but every one cannot understand what they indicate, nor is every one able to read what is written by them; but he alone is able to do this, who has learnt their letters."[30] Indeed, a careful reading of the dreams indicates that Jacques's unconscious mind—rather than a daemon for which there is no evidence—has recognized what is happening to him and what he must do. This dream and the others describe and prescribe. Paracelsus, the sixteenth-century alchemist, whom as already mentioned Jacques also cites, was very plain on the subject in *Astronomia Magna*: "Dreams must be heeded and accepted. For a great many of them come true."[31] With Jacques's considerable background in such matters, he should have been able to understand, and he should have known enough to heed their warnings. He does not, of course. But then he lacks the integrated, controlled personality of Porphyrius's philosopher.

After the water, Jacques's nocturnal muse turns his room into an arch, beneath which he sees a road. The arch represents the beginning of knowledge; the road, the path he must follow. At the end of the road rises a hugh palace, which is worth a few words. Obviously, the palace may be explained on one level by the unrealistically rosy dreams he had of the château. The luxurious splendor of the dream then provides striking contrast which emphasizes the ruin he actually inhabits. But a palace is also considered the image of the world and of the man. Because the palace and the château are so intimately related, it is worth continuing to their incorporated symbolic meanings, though they occur not in relation to the dream, but to the reality of the château of Lourps. Basements refer to the unconscious; upper stories or attics to spiritual elevation and conscious mastery. Here, however, after the palace approaches and turns the fluid arch into a frame with a round top and straight sides (because the frame is precisely described, it reinforces rather than negates the arch's sense of a unification of the upper and lower), Jacques suddenly finds himself in the heart of the building, in a huge room from which extend lateral galleries. During Jacques's later analysis of the dream, he says that the columns surrounding him were phallic (p. 57). If so, they parallel the floor of porphyry, a dark red stone, and the king's red robe. Red symbolizes love, blood, passion, in short, the experience of the material physical world. The dream does not yet turn wholly in this direction, however. First there is another incarnation of integration. Within the room, "an incombustible vinestock [composed of precious stones] flamed everywhere" (p. 30). Gems suggest spiritual truths. Having originated in the earth, they constitute a synthesis of the upper and the lower. But the vinestock, which Jacques later terms a "vine" and relates to the Hebrew Messianic lineage (p. 58), is far more interesting. It represents life. Because it burns without being consumed and because of the Biblical associations, it seems proper to remember the words of Christ: "I am the vine, ye are the branches: He that abideth in me, and I in him, the same bringeth forth much fruit. . . . If a man abide not in me, he is cast forth as a branch, and is withered; and men gather them, and cast them into the fire, and they are burned" (John 15: 5-6). The Huysmansian incombustible vineyard unites everything, for its vines creep everywhere from top to bottom.

The text begins to converge on the physical. "Here and there in the disorder of the foliage and creepers, the woodstocks spread out at random, catching each other again with their tendril so that the branches formed a cradle. At the end of the branches hung symbolic pomegranates whose carmine colored hiatuses of bronze caressed the points of the corollas shooting up from the ground" (p. 31). The cradle's suggestion of birth will be repeated shortly when the "furnace of the vineyard" begins to growl at the approach of the king. In the philosophical furnace, unity is elaborated and rebirth prepared. The pomegranates are, of course, central to the passage as is their symbolic significance—multiplicity reconciled in unity and fecundity. The fact that the carmen-colored, bronze[32] hiatuses of the pomegranates caress the phallic corollas thrusting from the ground emphasizes the importance of the physical side of existence. Significantly for Jacques, who has carefully isolated himself from the world, this is precisely the side he has most neglected.

The king, who now appears, echoes Jacques's disorder. Normally, one would anticipate that the king would represent terrestrial equilibrium, an ideal of harmony. "The king is sacred, he is the god of the earth," explains Lévi.[33] The king is at the center of the kingdom and represents man's "center," that is, his heart or soul. Jacques, having arrived at the heart of the palace, finds its king who, contrary to expectations, is sick. Although his face reveals the ravages of physical decay, it soon becomes clear that he suffers from a spiritual malady. "He looked at his feet, . . . tired perhaps of the uselessness of unlimited power and of the inaccessible aspirations it gives birth to . . . You felt the dearth of all joy, the abolition of all suffering" (p. 32). He raises his eyes and sees an aged man with an egg-shaped head and a nose like a gourd. Old men are traditionally the guides, the sages, the physicians. Judging from his physical characteristics, this one has abnormally powerful capabilities. Both eggs and gourds symbolize the occult source of latent and immortal life. Moreover, his eyes, organs of perception and understanding, are set awry on his nose. Since the nose represents clairvoyance, his powers can only be increased. He presents the ill king with a girl, whom he disrobes for the monarch's inspection. Finally, the king extends the tulip shaped diamond of his scepter for her to kiss. After mentioning that tulips symbolize love, while scepters, like rods, legs and arms represent masculine virility, there is no need to carry this explanation further. As the dream ends, we leave the couple: "the woman ... tipped back, very white, on the red knees, her bust elevated beneath the red arm which stirred her" (p. 36). The king has decided to follow the Old One's prescription. He turns toward the potential of reality and physical experience.

Jacques's similar return from the land of nod to the real world of Lourps is, to say the least, a rude awakening. He hears a terrible cry, and he leaves cane in hand to seek out the intruder. The succession of dilapidated rooms smelling of the grave makes him uneasy. He decides to explore them the next day. In the meanwhile, however, "the lamentable solitude of these rooms gripped him and, with it, an unexpected, atrocious fear, the fear not of a known, certain danger, because he sensed that this fright would disappear before a man hidden over there in a corner, but a fear of the unknown, a terror of nerves exasperated by disquieting noises in a black desert" (p. 40). Suddenly a frightening commotion fills the air. Jacques advances, strikes out, fights with all his might, and kills an owl. In his first successful combat, Jacques has begun his initiation at the lowest level of reality. By vanquishing the owl, he symbolically overcomes solitude, melancholy, cold, night, and death. Naturally, it is not quite that easy, for the next day, while exploring the grounds, he continues to be obsessed by the château's "hollow, morbid melancholy," by the "disoriented state of [his] soul" and his "abraded nerves in revolt against his reason" (p. 55). He struggles to turn his mind to other things. If one can believe Ély Star, he could have taken encouragement from the obsessions themselves: "When the beacon of our soul is illuminated by the divine torch of integral knowledge, diabolical spirits . . . come immediately to obsess us. Obsession is the revenge of the temptation which we did not wish to give in to. It is the illusory dread of the evil we did not wish to commit."[34] Jacques's fears continue, compounded by Antoine's warning not to go near the woods at night. The poachers might take it amiss. Nonetheless, he struggles against "this vague and tyrannical fear . . . this preoccupation with security . . . this inexplicable dream which even now obsessed him" (p. 67). He pursues his explorations, this time in the château itself, wandering through one filthy, decaying room after another. Louise has indeed chosen the only possible room.

The birth motif joins that of reality in the next chapter as Jacques watches one of Antoine's cows calve. More and more he is thrust into the company of Uncle Antoine and Norine, with whom he has nothing in common, and makes the acquaintance of the mailman, a disgusting, wheedling drunk who brings a letter from Paris that confirms Jacques's worst fears about his fortune. Furthermore, the expenses of establishing themselves in the country are burdensome. The château is so isolated that tradespeople refuse to bring them their daily needs. Only the baker will deliver, and he refuses to climb the steep hill to the door. The bread will be left below, subject to the elements. To get their other supplies, they will have to hire a local girl. "Jacques began to believe that the savings from living in the country were a decoy and that solitude, which is so beguiling when you evoke it while living in the middle of Paris, becomes insupportable when you go through it far from everything, without servants and without transportation" (p. 91). Not only are there menacing animals and men in the area, the château lacks comfort, water, and its humidity seems glacial.

The last straw, however, is Jacques's discovery that in the whole château, there is only one small room designed to serve as a toilet. It is in such bad repair that one can use it only at great risk. When he complains to Antoine and Norine, they propose with noisy amusement that he use the great outdoors like the rest of them. For the second time, Jacques has an indication of the peasants' deep-seated hatred for Parisians. In general, he nonetheless feels better. Unfortunately this new found peace is constructed on quicksand that will soon swallow him. "The country's sedative action still coddled him. . . . He was still in the sluggish period, this blessed lassitude from fresh air which blunts the acuteness of worries and bathes the soul in the dozing sensations of syncope, in inert, dim impressions" (p. 92). The minute evening comes, however, this sense of physical well-being dissipates, and he is once again prey to the ravages of his spiritual malady. To add to his problems, Louise looks worse. She suffers from a mysterious, incurable psychoneurosis which causes her great suffering and makes Jacques feel even more helpless. "And this almost cozy discomfort, which results from powerlessness to dominate oneself, changed in Jacques to unmistakable anxiety" (p. 93).

Jacques's progression towards self-integration has clearly suffered a setback. The first dream suggested that unconsciously at least he realized the need to take firm control of his life. Only in that fashion could he survive in the world. And his victory over the owl made it seem as though he would take the advice of his dreaming mind. But he resumes the old patterns of behavior, passively accepting whatever comes his way, lethargically drifting with the current, and, thus, inexorably becoming the helpless victim of his unconscious. Because of his inability to dominate himself, he will plumb the horrifying depths of his soul.

One night, after the couple has taken a moonlight walk on the grounds, Jacques dreams that he and Louise are on the moon. Later, he ties the dream to the evening stroll: " 'This time,' he said to himself, 'the source of my dream is clear, the filiation easier to follow than that of Esther, since the evening before my departure for the old star, I looked at the stars and the Moon, and I remember that at that moment I clearly recalled details from the selenographic maps I own' " (p. 139). He would have done well to continue his speculations and thereby spare himself some painful lessons, for the dream divests him of mind and body, thus setting his psyche at liberty. Far from representing an advantage, such freedom is a state which must be overcome. As Eliade explains, "Plutarch wrote that man had two deaths: the first took place on earth, in the domain of Demeter, when the body became cut off from the psyche and the *nous* [mind] and returned to dust . . . ; the second takes place in the moon, in the domain of Persephone, when the psyche separates from the *nous* and returns to the moon's substance."[35] According to tradition, lunar life represents an elementary form of existence. "It is a regression, rather than a total extinction. While waiting to return into the cosmic round (transmigration), or to be finally delivered, the souls of the dead *suffer* and that suffering is generally expressed as a thirst" (ibid., p. 198). Jacques and Louise do not appear to suffer. The text mentions several times, however, the lack of water. Here, because Jacques did not heed the warnings of the first dream and take firm control of his body, he reaps his reward. Lost in unconscious instability, Jacques must exert himself. He must dominate his soul or unconscious. Otherwise, he will remain the plaything of dark forces.

The chapter of this lunar dream opens without preparation or transition, if we except the description of the evening stroll. The reader is simply confronted with the vision of a barren landscape and expected to understand that it is a dream. Jacques looks out over "an immense desert of dry plaster, a Sahara of coagulated whitewash in the center of which rose a gigantic, circular mountain with rough sides . . . [and] a crest of hard snow hollowed out in the shape of a saucer" (p. 99). Deserts are the settings for transcendence. When anchorites formerly sought the desert, they hoped the all-consuming sun would burn away earthly attachments and allow them to join with God. But in Jacques's dream, no sun yet shines. True, the first mountain also suggests spiritual illumination, for it leads up to the cup-shaped peak which symbolizes the mystical center. Had this mountain been alone, we could have assumed that Jacques was on his way. Unfortunately, another mountain rises nearby. In such cases, the pilgrim faces a choice between life and death, between light and darkness, between consciousness and an unrestrained psyche. Jacques must choose.

Strangely enough, given his previous passivity, he does just that. After carefully surveying the terrain,[36] the protagonist "explains in a few words that it would be imprudent to venture out into the middle of this star, for the volcanic zone, an agglomeration of extinct craters, is there" (p. 101). Another explanation has nothing to do with natural features. In Porphyrius's words: "The southern parts are adapted to that which is immortal."[37] In this direction, life is dissolved and sent to the sun. On the other hand, "the northern parts are adapted to the mortal tribe, and to the souls that fall into the realms of generation" (ibid.). When Jacques turns around and leads Louise toward the North, he has decided in favor of regeneration. He has taken control of his unconscious. Still, as the couple moves purposefully on their way, they cannot help but pause occasionally to marvel at the fantastic moonscape. "The Moon appalled one's reason, terrified one's human weakness" (p. 109). Momentarily, he is calmed by the sight of his wife, "a familiar creature, whose existence was level-headed and dependable" (p. 110). This reassurance is uncomfortably like his previous dependence on his wife. He still has not learned that he can rely on no one but himself.

Then, he felt empty beneath his clothing, like tubulous mountains without metalloid entrails, without a heart of rocks, without granite veins, without metal lungs. He felt light, almost fluid, ready to fly away if the unfamiliar winds of this star came alive. The exacerbated cold of the poles and dismaying canicules of the Equators succeeded one another around him without his even noticing them, for he experienced the sensation of being finally freed of the temporary shell of a body but the horror of this bleak desert, of this sepulchral silence, this mute knell was suddenly revealed. The tormented agony of the Moon laid down beneath the funeral stone of a sky threw him into a panic. He raised his eyes to flee. (p. 110)

In this passage, Jacques has come to a full realization of just what the moon represents. The symbolic archetype of the feminine, it stands for the unconscious, instability, and death. Though he wants to flee, there is nowhere to go. Once again, however, his dreaming mind provides a solution. The sun, which rises and illuminates the violent mountain range before them, symbolizes the intellect, what should, according to the cabalists, be the dominant force of man. As Adolphe Franck put it in his study, *La Kabbale* (1843), the "mind... represents the highest point of [man's] existence" (p. 232). Apparently the light has some effect, for when his wife comments, Jacques finds her silly. In dream, he asserts himself.

In reality, life at the château de Lourps grows increasingly difficult for Jacques who does not cope. Louise has another attack, as mysterious and horrifying as the others. Her physical sickness parallels in an exaggerated fashion what is happening spiritually to her husband. "That had dragged on for years, affecting only her physical health, then, little by little, it infiltrated her spirit, undermining her at the very base of her being and finally arranging a lamentable equilibrium between the heaviness of metritis and mental torpor, between fainting fits caused by a ravaged stomach and the languors of a fallen will" (p. 116). When all this started, Jacques simply complained. Soon, however, "He also consented to sit back and let things go, frightened by this failure of energy, by this dolorous mutism from a woman that he had known as a lively, hard worker" (p. 118).

He becomes more and more irritable, increasingly indecisive, less capable of directing his mind. "Was it his fault that he was the kind of a person who couldn't stand to have things adrift and that, with his curiosities and infatuations, he needed rest at all cost?" (p. 120). The text leaves no doubt about the answer: there is no excuse and no protection for those who cannot or will not dominate themselves. His reward, as he himself recognizes, will be "mental and physical collapse, complete wretchedness" (p. 122). Of course, he believes such are the results of his financial rather than volitional bankruptcy. Both he and his wife lose themselves in daydreams of the life they could have had with other mates or with none at all. Unable to put the blame where it belongs, each petulantly blames the other for their problems, until finally the very exaggeration of their thought makes them come to their senses and feel shame. The narrator then explains that they are fundamentally nice people who, nonetheless, "clearly incarnated the lamentable example of decent souls' unconscious ignominy" (p. 129). "These unreasoning, morbid, secret impulses, these simulacrums of temptation, these diabolical suggestions (to talk the way believers do) especially occur in the lives of unfortunates whose lives are unmasted" (p. 130).

Nothing, however, seems capable of reversing Jacques's mindless passivity. Even when he does occasionally show "practical common sense" (p. 136), as when he refuses to give the postman twenty sous to release the owlet (he realizes that the postman would have kept the money and sold the baby bird nonetheless to an amateur taxidermist in the region), it remains a negative act. He apparently lacks the ability to pay the money, take the young owl, and release it himself. His other "practical" resolution—"tergiversate with my wife and deal tactfully with the old folks, since otherwise life would not be bearable" (p. 168)—however practical, is of the same sort, the decision of an ineffectual man. He knows that, "everything carefully considered, it would have been better not to run away to the country, but rather to face up to the assailants, come to grips with the problems in Paris, settle himself in a different fashion, not use his limited money uselessly at the château of Lourps" (pp. 138-39); he knows that "the provinces take the outer shell right off a man!" (p. 139); still, he is unable to leave.

To add to his problems, he fails to draw water from the well. It must be dry. And that would be a catastrophe, for life at the château would be impossible. As Louise's attack grows more serious, Antoine and Norine are half frightened, but simultaneously allow their disdain for the Parisians to show clearly. They do not hesitate to cheat them shamelessly. Jacques, on his side, despises the peasants. Nothing, except parhaps the fear of jail, stands in the way of their vile rapacity. To Jacques's distress, Louise sympathizes with them. "Here," she says, "money is everything" (p. 162).

The fact that the well is not dry—Jacques simply did not know the trick of tipping the bucket to make it fill—helps little. Louise is now selfish and crabby. Furthermore, she clearly is contemptuous of Jacques for his ineffectiveness. Though he recognizes the problem and though the physical and mental numbness which has characterized much of his stay at Lourps ends, rather than doing something, anything, he complains of boredom and yearns to lose himself once again in dilletantish amusements. He thus repeats the destructive pattern. When the summer heat arrives, "Like most nervous people, Jacques suffered unspeakable tortures from this weather which made your head feel as though it were melting (p. 170). Like Louise, "He no longer ate and stomach weaknesses began to manifest themselves" (p. 171). Then the harvest-ticks appear and inflict what seems to him the ultimate torture. Finally, he is drawn to decide to return to Paris . . . as soon as money arrives.

Such inoperative decisions have no affirmative importance, for there is no action which would signal a change. Consequently, "irritated by his fiery skin, nervous from the suffering, he was caught up again by fear, a mysterious, impulsive fear, a sort of waking dream . . . a fear whose relationship with the anguish of dream seemed certain . . . . Greased and set in motion by boredom, the mechanism of his mind had started again, and the foster-mother of nightmare and fear (his imagination) immediately carried him away, suggesting exaggerations, multiplying the aspects of dangers, working his entire nervous system in all kinds of ways. The delicate network oscillated with every jolt and discharged its energy" (pp. 181-82). Because of the solitude, "their spiritual sickness" (p. 183) is clearly visible to both Jacques and Louise. Jacques discovers that he can no longer maintain interest even in Baudelaire. "The atmosphere of Lourps positively changed his points of view, blunted the fine edge of his mind, made sensations of refinement impossible" (p. 188). The rains come, and the humid château is unbearable. "Jacques fell into a dreadful depression, hit his lowest point" (pp. 189-90). The protagonist looks in the mirror and sees that he has become, at thirty, an old man. "He felt finished, he and his wife, emptied to the marrow of their bones, unable to make the slightest effort of will, incapable of any incentive" (p. 191). At this point a cat arrives to keep them company and to give them something other than themselves to occupy their thoughts. The cat, a lunar creature, serves to illustrate the results of the couple's spiritual sickness, should they not take energetic action. Louise in fact is specifically compared to a cat (p. 120), and the similarities between her symptoms and those of their feline pet, who dies horribly, are inescapable.

In the midst of this misery, Jacques begins to change. "He resolved to explore the cellars" (p. 193), and he actually bestirs himself. Although Antoine is frightened of the place and refuses to join the endeavor, the protagonist's decision has considerable symbolic importance. It suggests that Jacques is about to turn the light of his reason towards the frightening depths of his unconscious. The actual exploration continues the established theme of demythification, which began when the postman showed Jacques the owlet, a pathetic little creature that puts the terrifying combat with the owl into proper perspective. A similar reaction greeted the harvest. However much Jacques tries, he is unable to view it through the mythic eyes of poets. It is not very impressive at all when compared to modern industries—just hot, dirty work which would have seemed heavenly to miners. The château's basement is equally unimpressive. For the first time, Jacques persists in his exploration, and he broadens it to include a better acquaintance with Antoine, Norine, and the postman. With understanding, his horrified revulsion and fear dissipate. He even arrives at the point of joking about death. Having read that ptomaine was discovered as a sweet-smelling oil in decaying bodies, he imagines, or dreams, he is not sure which, a burlesque scene where ancestors are celebrated by partaking of delicacies flavored by the "precious liquid extracted from the ancestor's decomposed viscera" (p. 209).

The third and last major dream begins, like the second, without preparation. Jacques is climbing a dark spiral staircase (the symbol of integrated ascension towards knowledge) when he meets a man dressed in a bizarre greatcoat of green and pink and coiffed with a blue sanitary sloppail.[38] The colors are important. "Red, blue and green correspond to the three celestial spheres: the first to the sphere of love, the second to wisdom and the third to action or creation. The three degrees of initiation and regeneration are equally represented by these three colors."[39] Jacques follows his guide into a room in which scalded calves' heads hang from hooks shaped like the number eight. This numeral symbolizes regeneration and dynamic equilibrium, thus paralleling the significance of the guide, who turns out to be an alchemist, and of the colors he bears. The tongues of the lunar calves point to the right, that is, towards unconsciousness, and the military headgear, which Jacques also sees, suggests masculine action. The alchemist begins to mutter something about sowing the earth's menstrua into his bubbling pot, but Jacques is not impressed. "I have read the ancient books of the Cabala, and I am not unaware that this expression, the earth's menstrua, designates very simply coarse salt..." (p. 213).

Nothing in the room is pleased with the protagonist's demystification, for it demonstrates his lack of seriousness and understanding. Where the other dreams were never overtly menacing, this one from this point on confronts Jacques with explicit threats and danger. The alchemist's bucket falls from his head, revealing vermillion hair; he roars, the calves tongues begin to wag, woolen snakes of primordial forces emit intestinal rumbles, and shakos produce the sound of drums. The cosmic side of the dream escapes Jacques. He understands only the warning and the necessity to contribute his watch to the pot. Since Jacques has left the timepiece (which represents the creation and existence in time of autonomous beings) hanging above his bed, he has no recourse but flight.

Without any specific goal in mind, he escapes to the stairs which soon become a well, a microcosm of the universe that unites the three centers: heaven, earth, and hell or mind, body, and soul. In the dim light of an October sunrise, another indication that his time is short, he makes out an enormous bell. This instrument repeats the symbolism of the well, for it serves as a means of communication between heaven and earth. The bell tower also contains broken ladders suspended without supports in the emptiness, which, added to the fact that the well is "stopped up at the top" (p. 214), suggest that Jacques is not meant to rise heavenward. He tries descending towards some stars below and finds himself in a cultivated gallery planted with pumpkins. Normally this fruit signifies an integrated self-contained relationship between the upper and lower worlds, but *En rade* emphasizes its sense of fecundity.

Jacques perceives that the pumpkins are really yellow buttocks, and, filled with obscene curiosity, he stretches out his hand. The fruit open to display their seeds, the symbols of occult forces. For some reason he connects them to stars and "enormous pity overcame him for these scraps of the firament which had doubtless been veiled and interned for centuries perhaps in this room" (p. 216). The association presents no difficulty if we remember that numerous stars (in contrast to the single North Star), which appear in all three dreams (pp. 31, 102, 215), represent dispersion or disintegration.

By opening, the integrated pumpkins have dispersed the force which is theirs because of their closure. But Jacques hears the sound of arms and, remembering a warning from Del Rio's *Disquisitionum Magicarum,* he realizes he has wandered into the sabbath of sodomistic sorcerers. Such magicians are the opposite of alchemists. They serve the devil and the unconscious. Sensibly, Jacques "draws back. No, not at any price did he wish to attend the disgusting effusions of these animated cultures and of these larvae!" (p. 217).

Cut off from the heavenly state of pure mind, the protagonist decides against the lower world of the occult. Where the first dream pointed Jacques toward reality and the second warned him against the unconscious, the third forces him towards an integration of the three centers.

Dazed, he finds himself at the bottom of the bell tower, looking up at an old woman dressed in red and blue. The fact that she has varicose veins is perhaps explained as a transformed image of Louise whose attacks are manifested in painfully twitching legs. Using a pocket-violin, she plays "How You Hurt Me, Handsome Grenadier" to a legless cripple across from her. A grenadier is of course a kind of soldier; it is equally important, however, to remember that, in French, *grenadier* also means pomegranate-tree. Pomegranates, as previously mentioned, symbolize fertility. The cripple, though he lacks legs (symbols of virility), has eyes of the green that the old woman's red and blue lack and, thus, complete the integration. Jacques assumes the couple are his aids, since he has become the church bell-ringer.

It suddenly occurs to him that the tower probably lacks water. Perhaps he can convince the old woman to fetch some. As he starts forward to request her help, he receives another reminder that only he can solve his problems; his regeneration comes not from without but from within. Straddling a beam, he notices that it slips between his legs until it finally disappears under his stomach to drop him into the space below. Then, on Honoré-Chevalier Street, this less than "honored chevalier" (or knight) remembers the cane he has misplaced. "He knew in a peremptory way that his life, his entire life, depended on this cane" (p. 220). Indeed, it does. Unless he aggressively takes control of his life, he will soon be irreparably lost. Little time remains.

Out of the water in front of him rises a young, small-breasted, childless woman. Her solemn, tragic beauty changes to reflect indescribable suffering as the jaws of an enormous jack bite into her hip. The shaken protagonist leaps forward to help her, when he hears two sharp cracks and sees her blue eyes drop from empty sockets into the green river Seine. The eyes regenerate only to fall again. Does this women represent what happens to Jacques's ideal of intellection cut off from body and soul? The fact that she rises to the top of one of the spires of Saint-Sulpice might suggest as much, for the Saint-Sulpician devotional representations were known for the bad taste of their idealization. However the case may be, the women changes into a sordid old strumpet laughing lewdly beneath flaming hair.

Bewildered, Jacques tries to comprehend and succeeds in persuading himself that the spire is a well. As already pointed out, it makes little difference whether he sees it as a well or a tower, for both represent the integration of body, soul, and mind.[40] Then he arrives at the final goal of the cabalists. He recognizes that the "abominable slut was Truth" (p. 224).

> In fact, what was astonishing about that? Isn't Truth the great Tart of the mind, the street-walker of the soul? In fact, only God knew how much, since genesis, she had noisily sullied her name with anyone at all! Artists and popes, canteen-keepers and kings, all had possessed her, and each had gained the assurance that he alone possessed her and, at the least doubt, furnished unanswerable arguments, irrefutable, decisive proofs.
>
> Supernatural for some, terrestrial for others, it sowed conviction indifferently in the Mesopotamia of elevated souls and in the spiritual Sologne of idiots. She caressed each depending on his temperament, depending on his illusions and idiosyncrasies, depending on his age, offering herself—as he wished, in every position and on every side—to satisfy his lust for certainty. (pp. 224-25)

But not even Truth impresses Jacques. He decides she looks as phony as a counterfeit coin. And once more, rather like what happened when he displayed a similar lack of comprehension with the alchemist, his sleeping mind loses patience. The whiskey-voice of a coachman tells him he is a fool. "So you don't recognize her! Why it's old Mrs. Eustache's daughter!" (p. 225). The daughter of "the beautiful ear of grain," the "happy harvest," the only thing that life has to offer. One ignores the truth of life at great risk; ignorance leaves one defenseless. And the drunken coachman screams demented oaths, spits tomato sauce into the chief magistrate's cap, and carries out the implicit judgment by attacking Jacques. Fortunately for our helpless protagonist, he wakes up mortally tired and drenched with sweat.

Although he continues his attempts to understand the reasons for his dreams, he does not succeed. He does better. Taking control of himself for a change, he abstains from brandy, waits until his food is digested before going to bed, uses lighter bedclothes, and takes long walks in the area. The horrifying dreams stop. With a bit of luck, he obtains the key to the Lourps church and continues his explorations. He finds to his amazement by reading the names on the tombstones that Lourps derives from the combination of two names: "Lours" (the bear) and "Loups" (wolves). For alchemists, the bear corresponds to the *nigredo* of prime matter and is thus considered a symbol of the dangerous side of the unconscious. The wolf, for Eliphas Lévi, represents impiousness and ferocity, or, more specifically, since it is associated with Mars (the God of war and destruction), Lévi ties it to the brutal forces that oppress intelligence.[41] Wolf and bear, then, symbolize the two centers to which Jacques has been initiated at Lourps: on the one hand the destructiveness of unreasoning matter and, on the other, the dangers of the unconscious mind.

There seems to be a profound change in Jacques. With his body and mind firmly in control, he takes everything in stride. When he accompanies Antoine to have one of his cows serviced, the protagonist finds the whole business rather banal. "Jacques began to believe the bull's 'epic grandeur' was no different than that old platitude, 'golden grain,' that old rag patched up by today's versifiers and novelists! No, truly, there was no reason to get all excited, pull on one's soft boots and sound the horn! It was neither imposing, nor haughty" (pp. 242-43). He calms his wife, handles the peasants with diplomacy, and plans for the new life of struggle awaiting him in Paris. Not even the terrifying foreshadowing of his wife's end, as they watch the cat die, suffices to undo his self-mastery. He makes the effort and wins his composure.

The next day the money will arrive and allow Jacques and Louise to leave for Paris. Though Jacques is almost sorry to quit this place of trials, he knows that he has to face his life. However much he would like to, he understands that he cannot really make any firm plans. "What good would that do? He was penetrating the unknown. The only plans he could reasonably dare make ahead of time were the following: As soon as he arrived he would have to set out, visit one person, wait for another, renew his contacts with people whom he despised, so as to procure advantageous work or a good position for himself" (p. 259). It would be difficult and degrading, "the expiation of my disdain for utilitarian things is ready!" (p. 260). But he will do what has to be done. When the money is finally in hand, he pays the inflated debt to Antoine, puts up with the final evidence of venal friendship, and departs with Louise. Jacques leaves, not defeated, rather as a soldier goes off to war, somewhat apprehensive, perhaps, but prepared for battle.

Particularly when one pays attention to the symbolic significance of the dreams, it becomes clear that quite a lot actually happens in *En rade*. Although there is no striking action which signals the change in Jacque's character, such as can be found, for example, in Hemingway's "The Short Happy Life of Francis Macomber," *En rade* is a *Bildungsroman*. The novel even has a plot, at least, if by plot we mean, not a sequence of interelated events taking place in a fictional world, rather a character's progressive discovery of the elements that constitute his entity, the integration of those elements, and the consequent change in his attitude towards reality. Indeed, the "action" is intense. It simply takes place primarily in the mind.

Of course, some might well criticize Huysmans for using such esoteric knowledge as the central vehicle, but then the novelist knew by the time of *En rade*, even if he had previously deluded himself, that he was not a "bestselling" writer. The astonishing success of *Là-Bas* later left him dumfounded. There is, however, no question that Huysmans's use of symbolism poses certain problems for the reader. Where a writer like Proust used his symbols in repeated and varied contexts, thus allowing the reader to apprehend their meaning within his text, Huysmans employed such images in the same way as he used the well-defined code of language. Apparently he felt that symbolism required no special effort on his part to be understood. Rarely does the text define the symbols. Occasionally, one finds an explanatory context, for example, in the instance of the otare, but most commonly the symbolic object or being occurs only once with no hint of explanation. Even when there is repetition, the Huysmansian black humor might encourage grimacing and passing on with little further thought. Furthermore, *En rade*'s repetitions add little to aid interpretations. In fact, the only convincing evidence that the novel employs symbols grows from studying the whole interrelated system of *En rade*'s meaning.[42] Then, it seems to me, one must conclude that the text is consistently articulated by means of the symbolism from the cabalists, the alchemists, and such writers as Porphyrius, Paracelsus, and Del Rio, whom, as previously indicated, the novel specifically mentions.

This does not mean, of course, that one can accurately translate a symbol by another explanatory word. Nonetheless, symbols have traditionally been rather too much set apart and invested with a certain mystery that tends to render them untouchable. Goethe, for example, says, "Symbolism transforms the phenomenon into an idea, the idea into an image, so that the idea remains forever infinitely effective and inaccessible in the image, and unspeakable even if expressed in all languages."[43] I do not quarrel with this statement. I would suggest simply that artists normally employ *all* language in this fashion. Aesthetic language operates not as a one-to-one ratio, "word" equals "thing" or "idea." It functions as a complex of interrelated meaning.

The dreams themselves are integrated into several levels of *En rade*. They create a separate "surreal" world of beauty and mystery for the displaced protagonist. They provide a marvelous vehicle for Huysmans's wild black humor, perhaps the best example in the whole of his work, about which, regrettably, I have said almost nothing. The Huysmansian comedy might make him "unFrench," but it fits him into a strong Occidental tradition including Petronius, Rabelais, Günter Grass, and, in the States, Thomas Pynchon or Kurt Vonnegut. It consequently deserves serious consideration. Perhaps most important, the dreams set off Jacques Marles's desperate struggle to do what all men must do, to understand himself, to bring himself under control and thus to find self-integration. For this aspect of the novel, the reader must come equipped with special information. Those who have or seek out and inform the reading experience with the necessary knowledge will be rewarded with a masterpiece. Those who have not or do not will waste their time.

Still, the most serious difficulty is somewhat different. Readers then and now are accustomed to plots which are objectified or projected off into the distance, thus allowing the reader to view the events as though watching a movie. Huysmans, however, "subjectified" his action. In truth, of course, he only pushed the pathetic fallacy to an extreme. While in *Atala* (1801) the raging storm serves merely to intensify the maiden's tumultuous feelings which are elsewhere expressed at length, in *En rade* such scenes provide the only indication of Jacques's psychological state. Readers are consequently forced to make several shifts. Once they have understood the objectified story of Jacques and Louise at the château of Lourps, the three dreams remain. Even when readers have made sense of them, the analysis has not been completed. It remains to integrate dream and reality and to read them as the outward projection of an inward phenomenon.

Huysmans presents a mold, leaving the reader to make the casting. There is no direct indication that the surface represented by the text may not be the positive form one generally finds in sculpture galleries or on reading novels. When the pieces make no sense, one is perhaps encouraged to suspect that one might be confronted by an intaglio, a negative surface which must be filled and cast off in order to reveal the true figure at the center of the narration. I am reminded of those strange hollows archaeologists found in and around Pompeii. Only when some clever person thought to fill the empty spaces with plaster of Paris and chip off the shell of hardened lava, did they discover the forms of dogs and men writhing in the agony of death by burns.

What makes *En rade* doubly difficult is its use of a narrator who is not Jacques Marles but who knows everything the protagonist thinks and sees. From today's vantage point of considerable sophistication in narrative point of view, one might accuse Huysmans's narrator of holding back essential information and, thus, tricking the reader. Of course, such withholding is far from uncommon, if for no other reason, because the minute an aesthetic device is explained it is of no—or little—effect. Without a sense of discovery (what Arthur Koestler in *The Act of Creation* called the "Eureka act"), where readers actually take part in the creation of a work of art, novels, poems, plays, like paintings, symphonies, and dance remain insipid indeed.

It is, I believe, precisely this sense of discovery, that Huysmans's negative structure permits and encourages, that makes *En rade* so important. It was a significant part of the new paradigm in formation. Of course, this paradigm was rather long in coming, but, after the hiatus of committed or *engagée* literature, which occupied most writers of the twenties, thirties, and forties, the recent novel has once again turned in upon itself, and artists are now busily continuing the experiments of the turn of the century. In the process, the New Novel has institutionalized negative narration, which no longer disconcerts readers as it did in Huysmans's day. At the time of *En rade*, however, such construction was in direct contradiction with the prevailing practice. It was, I suggest, an indication of dissatisfaction with the accepted paradigm of the novel, and it was not alone. As I shall say in the next chapter, Proust was to make a far more radical innovation, which went to the very core of the novel. *A la recherche du*

*temps perdu* reveals an awareness of the various structural possibilities
of the genre, an awareness at least as clear as that of Gide. In
addition, he advances a completely new way of organizing his fiction.
This change was to have significant repercussions in the recent
novel. I suspect it may have even more impact in the future.

# Chapter 7
## Proust and the Paramorphic Novel

IN MANY WAYS, *A la recherche du temps perdu* (1913-27) represents
the apogee of the traditional novel, as it had developed over several
centuries. It did not arrest all use of the well-worn devices that had so
powerfully served the great novelists of the nineteenth century.
Doors seldom close either so firmly or so rapidly in matters of artistic
change. The more usual course of events, and the one which
occurred in this case, is to have devices that have lost much of their
effectiveness continue for many years in popular fiction. The
cataclysmic occurences of our century may have been responsible
for the "former" novel's even more marked afterlife. A frightening
sense that mankind may be doomed does not encourage artistic
experimentation, at least not until people become used to, thus
comfortable with, the idea. With Marcel Proust's masterpiece,
however, the *Mene, Mene, Tekel, Upharsin* was there for all to see. Of
course, not everyone perceived that an event of considerable
importance for the future of the novel had taken place. Not
everyone was a Daniel.

While Proust's search for new ways of organizing literature was
apparent in his early, long unpublished attempts at fiction and his
mastery of the minute mysteries of style in his *Pastiches*, the clearest
evidence of his command of the expected tools and tricks of the
novelist's trade occurs in *A la recherche. Un Amour de Swann,* the
second compartment of Proust's fictional edifice, would satisfy the
most hidebound traditionalist. One has no difficulty following the
action. Swann meets, pursues, vanquishes Odette, before becoming
jealous, losing her, and moving on to other loves. The characterization
is impeccable. Told in the third person, we watch and understand
how a well-bred rake like Swann could fall in love with a woman
"who was not [his] type."[1] And the secondary characters are equally
vivid, from walk-on figures like the pianist's aunt, "[i]n black because
she believed that it is the most distinguished color possible and that
one is always well dressed when in black" (I, 204), to Mme Verdurin
whose clichéd thought, behavior, and language indelibly stamp the
little clan. Every personage comes alive, enabling the reader to settle
back and view the marvelous comedy in comfort. If *Un Amour de
Swann* were all alone, it would be a closed, endomorphic novel of
process—expert, perhaps, but like thousands of others.

When joined to the rest of *A la recherche*, the matter is not so clear-cut, for the novel as a whole has such obvious disarticulation that it has brought acerbic reactions from numerous critics, among whom one might cite Melvin Maddocks: "Proust," he says, "simply couldn't finish things. When he finally did assemble his masterpiece, it was the same way he assembled himself as a man. He put all the uneven bits and pieces together and let them stand."[2] The chronological and causal interstices occurring at the end of *Combray, Un Amour de Swann, Nom de pays: Le Nom*, and elsewhere are undeniable. What, for example, brought Swann to marry Odette? The embarrassment of an illegitimate child cannot have made him forget the difficulties engendered by such an unsuitable marriage. Though later we realize the importance of his hunger for an heir, the ellipsis is as bothersome as the hole in time and causation which led the protagonist to and from the nursing home many years later (III, 854).

Most readers have nonetheless treated *A la recherche* as though it were a particularly fine endomorphic novel. Taking passages which insist that the work tells the account of "a vocation,"[3] critics study "the story of how a little boy becomes a writer."[4] More adequate interpretations view the novel as what I have termed "serial." They suggest that though the conclusion indicates a prolongation, the future is so well defined and delimited that it does nothing to negate the closure. The protagonist's search for something to give his life meaning—whether Albertine or social success—stops at the discovery of a subject for literature, and the movement is reversed. He begins to plumb the life he has lived. "When the second movement (the one which is oriented toward a search for the work) receives its object, it nullifies the first movement (the search for a Good from life), or rather it inverts the sense: from progressive, this movement becomes regressive—no longer the search for something *to live*, but the search for something *lived*; it is intermingled with the creation of the book."[5] Still, the conclusion contains this new movement in essence, the reader is left with no significant questions about the future, and the novel remains closed (for very different reasons, I shall, however, later suggest an important means of opening).

Emphasizing the protagonist and his realization, after a series of "blessed moments" (*moments bienheureux*), that he himself is the subject of what he will write has the advantage of centering on the "I," rather than on the unquestionably fascinating view the novel presents of the end-of-the-century world. Indeed, one may be led to recognize that the positive or objective portrayal of *Un Amour de Swann* serves to set off the negative representation of the whole. As I suggested some years ago, neither the characters nor the places to which the hero first looks for truth have ultimate significance to *A la recherche*. The only completely developed character is the "I"; the only completed action is his gradual absorption of sufficient experience to permit the final integration of that experience into a whole.[6] At the moment he understands that he is what he has seen and thought of Combray, Balbec, the aristocratic Faubourg Saint-Germain, his mother, Gilberte, Charlus, and, in fact, the Swann of *Un Amour de Swann*, then he becomes the narrator. All those fragmentary views into various characters and worlds come to be the sum total of the protagonist. The cast is shucked off; we turn from the intaglio, and we confront the "I."

While this view of *A la recherche* as negative presentation of a central protagonist may be helpful, it still leaves unexplained the numerous breaks in the narrative structure. It seems unlikely that a novelist seriously interested in recounting the process of his hero's development would be so cavalier about providing the links. It seems even more improbable that if the narrative process were of the essence there would be so much emphasis on the "blessed moments" which signal the way to ultimate truth. If the key to Proust's novel resides not in the story of a boy's education, rather in a marvelous image which can be expanded or explored, *A la recherche* like other image novels has subordinated narration to description.

The "blessed moments' have attracted the attention of virtually every critic who has considered *A la recherche du temps perdu* at any length. In fact, as Leo Bersani has pointed out, "The passages that describe these experiences have been subjected to so many complicated exegeses that it is only too easy . . . to forget our original impression of them."[7] Although I am rather partial to Eméric Fisher's capsule explanation (a revelatory moment is a "meeting-sensation-memory-by-analogy"[8]), the clearest analysis doubtless came from Proust's hand. On reflection the phenomenon seems simple, perhaps because it has been studied so often and in such detail. The protagonist experiences something; he forms an image composed of many different elements, some of which he absorbs unconsciously. The image is then stored and forgotten. When, at some later time, he experiences a sensation identical to the previous one, the current sensation recalls the stored image, which seems new because it was previously "lost." Real effort must be expended to resuscitate and identify the recollection which metaphorically joins the more recent image to create another and, thus, bring a marvelous feeling of oneness.

The problem with the episodes of involuntary memory is that Proust intellectualized the experiences to such a degree that his analyses, though they may well explain, tend to kill any drama. It is difficult not to sympathize with J.-F. Revel when he says in exasperation: "Yes, all that is true, all that happens to us, but, I must say, it has hardly any interest for anyone but ourselves. . . . We have our own from our own experience. It is not the general fact that is precious; it is the personal content, which only touches the one who lives it."[9] But if one were to have "put aside a few theoretical hors d'oeuvres" (ibid., p. 40), as this critic would prefer, the truth of the matter is that an enormous part of Proust's novel would end up in the waste basket. Though some of Proust's readers would consider this a decided improvement,[10] I suspect the power of *A la recherche* would be considerably diminished.

Proust explains, it seems at but one remove, virtually everything in great depth. By the time he finishes with a thought, there can seldom be any doubt about his opinion. This tendency appears especially strange in the light of his repeated disdain for the intelligence (e.g., III, 880). The reason the "I" elevates music over literature resides precisely in the fact that music does not sin in this fashion: "This music seemed somehow truer than all familiar books. There were moments when I thought it depended on the fact that because what we sense in life is not in the form of ideas, its literary— that is to say intellectual— translation takes it into account, explains it, analyzes it, but does not recompose it the way music does when sounds seem to take on the inflection of being, to reproduce that internal and extreme point of sensations which is the part that gives us this specific intoxication that we find from time to time and which, when we say: 'What beautiful weather! What a beautiful sun!' we do not at all communicate to our neighbor, in whom the same sun and the same weather awaken completely different vibrations" (III, 374). If Proust really believed that "the truths which the intelligence grasps directly and openly in the world of full light are somewhat less profound, less necessary than those which life has, in spite of our conscious efforts, communicated in an impression, material because it entered through our senses, but whose meaning we can discern" (III, 878), why did he refuse to leave his analyses aside, why did he thrust his undoubted intelligence on us, why did he give us those long sequences where his thoroughly masticated ideas are offered up for consumption?

Such passages help explain why many critics would maintain that *A la recherche du temps perdu* is about life. Still, it seems safe to say

that Proust preferred Rivière's opinion: "It is life itself!"[11] This was
precisely the quality he sought. For Proust "art recomposes life
exactly" (III, 898) and, like Berma's performance of Phèdre, is
composed of "rich, complex elements . . . that the fascinated
spectator took, not for one of the artist's successes, but for one of
life's givens" (II, 48). When a reader confronts a novel he must find
more than a treatise about life, he must find life. Art provides
experience, provokes conceptualizing, and, most important, incites
creation. The difference between a book about life and a work of art
which is life has enormous significance for Proust. In the first case,
the book has failed and, in the second, succeeded in its primary
function: to teach. Either as a success or a failure, it may have taught
some valuable truths, but the types of pedagogy are at odds, as is the
relative success of the instruction. If Proust's novel is but about life,
it has succeeded only in transmitting descriptive, bookish, pedantic,
or dead knowledge; if it is life, the reader has had the opportunity to
experience and discover directly himself and his world. Nonetheless,
as Proust knew and stated, the artist can use the intelligence to set
off the real meat of his work: "I felt, however, that these truths which
the intelligence discerns directly from reality are not to be entirely
disdained, because they may enshrine with material that is less pure
but still penetrated with meaning these impressions that the essence
common to past and present sensations bring us from outside of
time" (III, 898). This, I would suggest, is the primary role of Proust's
analyses and explanations: they set off, they prepare, and they
encourage the reader to discover for himself the great lessons of
A la recherche.

The emphasis I place on teaching is not accidental. That A la
recherche du temps perdu is a didactic novel will not surprise us if we
remember that the only overt justifications for art in Proust's novel
concern education (e.g., I, 84-85). Only art allows us to enter
another's mind: "Only by means of art may we go out of ourselves
and know what another sees of this universe which is not the same as
ours" (III, 895). Doubtless, had Proust's thought stopped there, it
would scarcely provide sufficient recommendation for art. He goes
on, however. After the moments of revelation at the Princess de
Guermantes', the protagonist changes to become an artist and, thus,
realizes a life-long dream. The development occurs because he has
struggled and succeeded in understanding the significance of his
moments bienheureux. He, as a narrator, perceives what most men,
inundated by the confused and confusing fragments of life, do not.
Through art, he will be able to allow others to read within themselves

and find the great human truth (which is objective, but only in that it can be subjectively true in all men): each individual constitutes the unifying factor of his own life. Thus, the seeming denial of the importance of art: "The objective value of art is small in and for itself," in fact, points to what is potentially its true utility and grandeur: "what it is a question of releasing, of bringing to light are our sentiments, our passions, that is to say the passions, the sentiments of everyone" (III, 907). Art, to repeat his marvelous analogy, is a lens which allows the reader to read within himself (III, 911, 1033). The mechanism remains subjective, and the objective truth known to the artist depends upon its inner actualization by others. The reality taught is not the objective, physical world, which is indifferent (III, 910), rather "our thought, our life, reality" (III, 895).

Unfortunately, as Proust well knew, there are people like Swann and Charlus who are for one reason or another incapable of using their sensitivities and minds for deep reflection. Perhaps because of laziness, they suffer from "inertia of [the] will."[12] Such a person needs a doctor who will provide the necessary impulsion "until the day arrives when his varying organic will has been little by little reeducated" (*CSB*, pp. 178-79). In *A la recherche*, the analytical passages, each of which incorporates what might be termed "a truth which may be copied in a notebook" (*CSB*, p. 183), begin the cure. But it must not be forgotten that they are only the beginning, only the first step. In all instances, such a truth "is less, to speak precisely, truth itself than its indication or proof, thus giving way to another truth that it announces or verifies and which is at all events an individual creation by [the reader's] mind" (ibid.).

In his examination itself, Proust may provide a little exercise for the reader's development. He does not say that the three trees of Hudimesnil remind the protagonist of "Martinville's three steeples," for example, but he mentions the steeples as the Hudimesnil episode begins (I, 717). When the protagonist wonders what they remind him of, why they affect him, and then leaves the questions without a response, Proust has effectively asked the reader a question not much more difficult than the famous "Who is buried in Grant's tomb?" but which nonetheless must be answered. It is the second small step on the road to the ultimate and essential discovery.

The third appears in the characters, those marvelous creations that succeed in having their own personalities, individualities, manners of speaking and acting, in short, their own distinct selves. Few authors have created so many fully individualized characters. And, indeed, in *A la recherche* it is important that they be clearly

differentiated one from the others, that the protagonist's mother
not be confused with the grandmother, that Gilberte be neither
Albertine nor Rachel, that Swann be separated from Bloch and
Charlus from Saint-Loup. It is important because it enables the "I"
to find and surprise the reader with analogous qualities which join
them in a metaphor. He tells us that Swann prefigures the protagonist
(e.g., I, 193) and that the mother becomes the grandmother (II, 769);
he points out the resemblances between Gilberte and Albertine
(e.g., III, 501-02); he dwells repeatedly on the qualities shared by the
Guermantes (e.g., II, 438-39); he remarks on Saint-Loup's echoes of
Charlus (e.g., III, 685); he mentions how Charlus's and Saint-Loup's
beloved Morel resembles Robert's former mistress, Rachel (III,
682), and how Gilberte, with a little effort, resembles her as well (III,
702). The same thing occurs with places which, in numerous
passages,[13] the protagonist sees as virtually interchangeable. Then,
having prepared us with a quantity of similar models, Proust leaves it
to us to discover other similarities—for example, those joining
Charles Swann, and Charlus, both of whom are obsessed in love,
elegant, brilliant, learned, talented, and tragically, both of whom
waste their potential—and to form other metaphors. He leaves it for
us to join Bloch and the late Charles Swann who is anxious about his
wife's social position—both are Jews and both crass arrivistes.
Furthermore, however true it is that many images and allusions
exert considerable influence on the form Albertine finally takes in
the readers' mind, Proust leaves her, his most magnificent creation,
for the reader to create.[14] Slowly the characters coalesce, exactly as
they did in the mind of the "I." "Thus, the spaces of my memory
little by little covered by names which, in being ordered, in being
composed in connection with each other, in being tied together by
more or less numerous relationships, imitated those finished works
of art in which there is not a single touch that is isolated, where each
part in turn receives from the others its justification just as it
imposes its own on them" (II, 537).

The passage just quoted mentions names, which serves to
introduce another of what Proust called "Incitations" (CSB, p. 176).
The importance of names to A la recherche is attested by the subtitles,
"Place Names: The Name," "Place Names: The Place" (which
appeared in the published version), and "People's Names: The
Duchess of Guermantes" (which, though projected, was not printed),
by the numerous pages devoted to the protagonist's dreams inspired
by names, and by those filled with the Curé de Combray's and
Brichot's etymologies. Revel has reproached Proust for not realizing

that the protagonist's dreams cannot be shared by the reader: "Everything that a name may evoke in us through its sonorousness alone is as little required of other people as the frame of mind colors produce in us."[15] This statement suggests an interesting observation: Proust no more explained the train of thought his protagonist followed in attaching certain colors to people and places than he did for the images elicited by names. We are given only a few vague references to history, guide books, and railway schedules, the dreams themselves, and the information that actual experience and etymology dissipate the charm. Apparently the dreams result from the protagonist's private associations, for which numerous scholars and critics including myself have proposed explanations. It remains, however, to point out that Proust apparently chose names which would provoke revery, which would indeed charm his readers. Some become particularly significant only in the context of *A la recherche.* I think, for example, of the green in the names Verdurin and Saint-Euverte, which, as I have suggested elsewhere,[16] highlights their obsessive idealization of society, or *morelle,* the feminine form of *moreau* or "black" in (Charlie) Morel(le). Proust, making use of a device he doubtless learned from Balzac,[17] saw to it that Mme de Cambremer's significant distortions of names include "Moreau" in respect to Morel (II, 1095). Later we are told that he was "excessively black" as well (III, 705). And, although it is widely known that Odette was one of the swan-maidens in *Swan Lake,* perhaps it is also worth remembering that as long as swan-maidens have the power of transforming themselves into swans or, put another way, as long as they retain their freedom, they remain youthful.[18] Even when well along in years, Odette, whose "appearance . . . seemed a more miraculous challenge to the laws of chronology than the indestructibility of radium to those of nature" (III, 948), manages to dominate the duke de Guermantes, thus preserving both her youth and freedom. If the reader has been consciously or unconsciously provoked into attempting to follow the hero's apparently random associations inspired by names, if the names have worked their magic, there should be no surprise in discovering that Gilberte, the daughter of a swan and a swan-maiden enters the family of Gilbert le Mauvais, Gilbert and Marie-Gilberte de Guermantes. It would not be the first Gilberte or the first swan in the family. After all, a legendary duchess de Brabant married the Swan-Knight, the Guermantes descend from Geneviève de Brabant (I, 104), and the family is said to have "originated with a nymph's mythological impregnation by a divine bird" (II, 439).

As a means of preparing readers to experience *A la recherche*, it would be difficult to overestimate the importance of characters, settings, and names, but I suspect the most telling device consists of the narrative sequence itself. Nonetheless, because it seems, as Revel would have it, "a gathering of pieces with haphazard seams, from several freely followed currents of inspiration."[19] it poses serious difficulties. Proust was of course aware of the problem. He pointed out in 1920: "In *Du côté de chez Swann* [*Swann's Way*], certain people (even some who are very well read), misunderstanding the rigorous though hidden composition, . . .thought that my novel was a sort of collection of memories tied together according to the fortuitous laws of the association of ideas" (*CSB*, pp. 598-99). Insisting on the rigorous composition, he points to his use of "a phenomenon of memory" as a means of juncture. Here he is discussing the madeleine sequence, though in fact the whole novel was constructed according to his understanding of the analogical workings of the human mind. One need only think of the perhaps unorthodox way *Un Amour de Swann* is prepared by the heavy emphasis on love and obsession throughout *Combray*: Geneviève de Brabant's problems with Golo, the drama between mother and son on the fateful evening of the boy's revolt, *François le Champi*, Léonie, Uncle Adolphe and "the woman in pink," Françoise and the kitchenmaid, Gilberte and the hawthorns, the protagonist's masturbation, the associations of Roussainville, and Montjouvain. More and more critics are turning to the difficulties posed by the sequence of Proust's narration, and the results more and more frequently support Proust's contention.[20] The sequence is ordered along analogical lines. Though the episodes indeed are "tied together according to the . . . laws of the association of ideas," the laws are anything but "fortuitous." They do, however, contravene the traditional rules for predominantly chronological and causal motivation in novels. Thus, they force readers who sense that the order is rigorous and right, though perhaps not of the kind one might expect, to seek other rules. It was particularly difficult for earlier readers who did not have the advantage of distance or the benefit of more recent literature to grasp the structural relations of *A la recherche*.[21] Even today it is not easy, but, then, as Proust makes clear in his preface to *Sésame et les lys,* no worthwhile reading is. To read successfully requires effort. Proust pointed out that in Victor Hugo's early poems, he "is still thinking, instead of being content, like nature, with giving the material for thought" (II, 549). The author of *A la recherche* did not make the same mistake.

Although Proust did everything in his power to hasten understanding of his book, he recognized that "each time someone looks
at things in a somewhat new way, almost without exception people
do not see anything of what he is showing them. You need at least
forty years for them to succeed in making it out" (II, 522). Forty
years and more have passed, and thanks to recent novelists, perceptive
critics, but especially, I think, thanks to the program of learning
Proust inserted into his novel, we are now beginning to read *A la
recherche* properly. We know that our "memory does not ordinarily
present our recollections in their chronological order, but rather
as a reflection where the order of the parts is reversed" (I, 578); we
accept the truth of what Balzac said long ago: "There is nothing
absolute about words. We act more on a word than it acts on us; its
force is because of the images that we have acquired and that we
group with it"[22]; we are willing to admit that "reading acts only as
an incitation which in no way substitutes for our personal activity"
(*CSB*, p. 180); we have learned that the rationalistic order taught in
logic classes need not be the only logic, that "this absence of a logical
and necessary connection . . . is, more than the facts recounted, the
sign of truth" (III, 96); and with full knowledge that "truth has no
need to be said in order to be manifested" (II, 66), we are devoting
the effort necessary to uncover those richly woven "mysterious
threads" of our experience of *A la recherche* which form "a rich
network of recollections [that] leaves only the choice of the path to
take between them" (III, 1030).

A la recherche du temps perdu* is unquestionably didactic, which
makes it a novel of its day, since most novelists between the two
great wars were bent on teaching solutions to the world's problems.
Nonetheless, Proust, as perhaps no one else, knew that the novel
constitutes what René Godenne has called an "anti-didactic genre
*par excellence*."[23] "People reason," says Proust, "that is to say that
they meander" (III, 882). Where Jean Ricardou has suggested that
"great narrations are recognized by the sign that the fiction they
propose is nothing but the dramatization of their own functioning,"[24]
Proust, it seems to me, not only dramatized, he permitted the
actualization of his fiction.

The difficulty which *A la recherche* poses for readers may be
explained by Proust's awareness that although exhortation, explanation, description, and vicarious experience may help direct a
reader's quest for truth, only real-life discovery can teach. There
exists "a remarkable and moreover providential law of mental optics
(a law which perhaps signifies that we can receive truth from no

no one and that we must create it ourselves)" (*CSB*, p. 177). "What we have not had to decipher, to illuminate by our personal effort... is not ours" (III, 880). The extensive, detailed exposition around the various episodes of the protagonist's involuntary memory serves as little more than a guide for the reader. In no sense does it satisfy the goals of *A la recherche*.

All the characters, all the settings, all the episodes, all the devices, all the systems of meaning, the whole of the novel work to produce a blessed moment in the reader. This glorious synthesis cannot be explained into existence. Because it "would be impossible by direct and conscious means" (III, 895), it occurs only when provoked by unconscious, subjective stimuli. And it can germinate only where it has been sown and cultivated: in the reader's mind. For *A la recherche du temps perdu* to come alive, and thus succeed, it must produce involuntary memory. Consequently, where the thought of submitting his work to the mercy of a reader revolted Valéry and reduced him to silence, Proust permitted and encouraged his audience to read within themselves. "The recognition within oneself, by the reader, of what the book says is the proof of its truth" (III, 911). The writer must provide many lenses and allow "the reader the greatest possible freedom in telling him: 'Decide for yourself whether you see better with this lens, with that one, with that other one" (III, 911). Proust could be tolerant of the major causes for the disparate perceptions different people may have of an event. I see or hear differently, depending upon my position in relation to objects, my perspective and the intervening temporal and spatial distance. This relativity is abolished by literature. The distance of a book from the reader's eyes has no importance, as long as he is able to make out the print. The artist controls perspective, and, thus, he necessarily controls that of the reader. The author either says a tree is at a certain distance, or he describes it in such a way that we visualize it from afar. He may announce that a trip takes several hours, or he may describe it so as to convey an impression of lapsed time.

The other type of erroneous perception—often an aberration— is beyond the control of an artist. Two people watching the same event will experience it differently, depending upon the imperfections of their senses, their background and education, their prejudices, etc. Proust assumed, probably correctly, that this category of aberration did not matter, for it would be consistent. That is, the person who never "sees" red, but who hears G-flat when confronted with the color, would always do so. The homosexual who transforms fictional mistresses into young boys (III, 910) would consistently do so. He has not impaired the quality of his experience, for his aberration is invariable. The narrator could then accept such psychological and physiological flaws, for they would always produce the same pattern of response.

Without the reader, Proust knew quite well that his work could not live. For this reason he was most concerned with finding a public, very aware of the reviews of his book as portions appeared, and anxious to encourage people to study it. He asked only that his book be read with care. In this light, it is interesting to note that only once does the narrator leave his role as an impartial observer of Charlus. The sharp, overt criticism that results concerns neither Charlus's snobbishness, nor his homosexuality, nor his cruelty, rather his sloth. And it culminates with a condemnation of his careless reading habits (II, 567). One may read in any optic one wishes, but one must read attentively.

As is evident from what precedes, *A la recherche* gives the reader a great deal of importance. A text, as an objectively independent entity, may have been organized, but it cannot have structure until a human mind establishes the relationships implicit in the organization and forms images. A text, the formalization and translation of a writer's thoughts into words, remains a mere sequence of hiero-glyphics until they are retranslated or decoded into ideas and images by a reader. Where a completed building has foundations, load-bearing walls, braces, etc., which support it independent of an onlooker, a literary work only gives the material. It lacks the final step. Leaving aside questions of aesthetic value for the moment, a literary text may be said to resemble a prefabricated building, which is sophisticated enough to permit certain, limited variations in the final form, and which is all laid out, awaiting the assembly crew. A book or a poem is little more than a pile of smudged paper until the reader, through his knowledge of the conventions of the written language, puts the parts together, bonds the dispersed materials, and gives the work structure.

As far as *A la recherche* and its reader are concerned, style is vision *and* revelation (III, 895); communicated by style (ibid.) and images (III, 882), art is the spiritual equivalent (III, 879), and it has no value except insofar as it becomes transparent, a lens serving the reader. Proust saw that everyday language, a convention which we accept and which allows communication of sorts, was and is by nature incapable of transmitting the particular, individual secrets of one human being to another. Because words always represent the common denominator, what is unique to an experience cannot be communicated by ordinary language. "Is it not so that these elements, all of this real residue that we are obliged to keep for ourselves, that conversation cannot transmit even from friend to friend, from master to disciple, from lover to mistress, this ineffable which makes a qualitative difference between what each person has sensed and that he is obliged to leave on the threshold of sentences where he can only communicate with someone else in limiting himself to external points common to everyone and without interest, art, the art of a Vinteuil as of an Elstir, causes it to appear, exteriorizing in the colors of the spectrum the intimate worlds which we call individuals and which we would never know without art?"[25] For a writer, there are two obvious resolutions to this dilema. Proust did not disdain the first, Mallarmé's answer: to put language under extreme pressure and thus force it, by using rhythms, rhetorical devices, lexical precision and imprecision, imagery and symbolism, to mean, not the quality common to us all, but the particular reality of the protagonist. The power of Proust's style to spellbind is undeniable.

The way Proust worked suggests his second important tool. One of the first things that strikes the scholar studying his manuscripts is the number of times one finds formulas like: "Put elsewhere," "Don't forget elsewhere," "Put someplace here or there," "At some point in this chapter, or before, or for something else," "[P]ut (Capitalissime [)] at the place where it can fit in our life," "Intercalate some place farther on," or "Put this some place or other for Elstir. *Important*."[26] In addition, he not infrequently would write a whole development—for example the one which takes M. Vinteuil from our first introduction (I, 112) to the posthumous resurrection of his works[27]—and then disperse it across thousands of pages. Indeed, he frequently does not know where, when, or, elsewhere, in respect to whom[28] he wishes to place an image, a thought, or even, on occasion, a whole episode. One begins to suspect that these considerations are not among the most important. Some understanding of his priorities may be gained in considering another passage, originally a unit, now separated.[29] After describing the odors and sounds of Léonie's house, he seems to have begun to worry that the conjunction of the descriptions interfered with the impression he wished to make, for he wrote himself the following note: "To be put someplace else. Doubtless these odors are not striking."[30] His decision to put the olfactory images in one place and the auditory images in another apparently rose from the desire to set off each.

It would of course be foolish to argue that chronology and casuality had no influence on the final position of a passage. Obviously, the protagonist cannot talk about forgetting his grandmother until she has died.[31] Nevertheless, I have come to believe that his most important consideration was for each significant passage to be highlighted, while lesser ones took their proper place in relative obscurity. Proust wanted the reader to perceive some images fully, to "fix" them, and to record them. This is where the protagonist began: "Even at Combray I attentively fixed in my mind some image which had forced me to look at it: a cloud, a triangle, a steeple, a flower, a pebble" (III, 878). The reader must imitate him. Proust scorned those who would not do likewise: "I leave it for people of taste to decorate their homes with the reproductions of masterpieces they admire. By confiding them to sculpted wood frames, they relieve their memories of the need to conserve precious images" (*CSB*, p. 167).

If *A la recherche* succeeds, the reader will resemble Louis Lambert, whose knowledge came from books, but for whom "the image [of things] impressed on his soul could not have been more vivid if he had really seen them."[32] Then these images are stored and, for the most part, forgotten until they are recalled to the conscious mind. The resurrection of the image may be caused by a mere word or name, or by a character, a scene, or even the whole of an episode. It may include any sensory perception, whether actually perceived or just suggested, and, when stored in the mind, it constitutes an organization of interrelated or interacting parts. Though the image tends to be retained in the same form as received ("the gesture, the simplest act remains enclosed as though in a thousand closed vases each one of which is filled with things having absolutely different colors, odors, temperatures"—III, 870), it may combine with other images by joining analogous elements.

As each image stimulated by Proust's novel and impressed in the attentive reader's mind is followed by another, and another, and another, eventually "all these memories added to each other no longer formed anything but a mass" (I, 186). Sooner or later, however, the reader will be struck by something he has sensed before; the sensation caused by an element of the passage before his eyes will establish a relationship with the similar stimulus of a previous text and, thus, with a previous experience; and he will discover the proof that this "mass" is in truth like a work of art, "harmoniously regulated by a general idea on which [the images] were suspended" (I, 737). Because the image has to have been forgotten for the revelation to have its full effect, *A la recherche* stands in opposition to the theories of Edgar Allan Poe, who insisted on the necessity of an uninterrupted reading.[33] "If, thanks to forgetfulness, the memory has been unable to establish a tie or link between it and the present moment, if it has remained in its place, at its date, if it has kept its distances, its isolation in the hollow of a valley or at the peak of a mountain, it suddenly causes us to breathe new air, precisely because it is air that we previously breathed, this purer air that poets have tried in vain to establish in Paradise and which could not give this profound sense of renewal had it not been breathed before, because true paradises are those we have lost" (III, 870). The length of Proust's novel assures that no one can read it at one sitting. The days, weeks, months required for a confrontation with this reality subject it to time and, perhaps more important, to forgetting.[34] Only when a reader has forgotten some image which impressed him will the sudden sensation of a significant repetition allow him to grasp, not just the "point . . . common to one person and another," but as well the "general essence common to several things which nourished and filled him with joy" (III, 718). In short, like the protagonist, on receiving an impression "that brings us from outside of time the essence common to past and present sensations" (III, 898), we are expected to form a new image which will retain the integrity of its constituents metaphorically. The reader will have seized one of the proffered *lenses* and discovered a world within himself (III, 911).

I do not know what if anything will cause this experience. It may be the sudden closure of all the disparate visions of a particular character. It may be the unexpected realization that the bedrooms, the dreams, or the closed social groups, from the family in Combray to the Guermantes's circle, form meaningful extensions. It may be Swann's desire to possess all of Odette (I, 314) when it reappears in the protagonist (I, 794). It may be the birds, the fish, the windows, the churches, the bells—all of which form systems of more or less extensive ramifications. It may be the instantaneous comprehension that Gilberte, Oriane, and Albertine are more than mere characters... they are settings. Or, it may be a color.

As I have argued in *The Color-Keys to A la recherche du temps perdu*, color provides an excellent "lens." It is absolutely consistent; each color-complex forms a system of relationships; each provides the opportunity for a "blessed moment." When viewed as a constellation, all of the incidences of a range of colors form a global unity within which "the smallest facts, the smallest events are nothing but the signs of an idea which must be disengaged and which often covers others as in a palimpsest" (II, 109). Any one of the parts could fulfill the function of keying the others and thus stimulating the reader's discovery of the whole. Though Proust did not, except by inference, explain what he was doing with the colors, he did say in one of his notebooks that artistic reality is a relationship or law which unites different sensations through the synthesis of a penetrating impression.[35] To have gone much further might have impaired the reader's opportunity to uncover his own unification.[36]

Each incident of a color, name, character, place, or whatever, functions as a "parameter." It is a variable whose value or meaning not only depends upon the relationship in which it is found but changes significance depending upon the particular relationship involved. A simple example will illustrate. The pink hawthorns the young protagonist sees in *Combray* fit into the long, poetic tradition of floral imagery and, especially when joined to the imagery of *Les Jeunes Filles en fleurs* [*The Flowering Girls*], render the theme of *carpe diem* inescapable. When, on the other hand, it is included in the extension the color pink establishes across the novel, it suggests the process of sensation and desire. But it is equally important to recognize that these flowers work within a realistic framework encouraging readers to recreate the scene in detail. In the latter function or relationship, the pink has mimetic value; in another it acts symbolically, and in another allusively. The pink then constitutes a parameter, for, though fixed, its value changes depending upon the relationship the reader seizes. I think there is no question that Proust intentionally laid out the possibility that readers would perceive one or more of these relationships, but, I shall suggest, I am not at all certain that the reader must be open to them all.

Once the reader has sensed an incipient metaphor (or relationship) of involuntary memory, another discovery awaits him if he follows the author's directions: It is essential to "oblige yourself to make an image go through all the successive states that end with its fixation" (III, 882). Because every impression or image bears "the reflection of things that logically are not tied to it" (III, 870), because each element of the image leads to the contiguous complexes, because virtually every element reappears in other contexts, there occurs "a complicated, flowery magician's book" (III, 879). The revitalized, unified image of involuntary memory will be prolonged "in every direction and dimension, with every sensation that I had experienced, uniting the square to the church, the quay to the square, the canal to the quay, and to everything eyes see the world of desires which is only seen by the mind" (III, 876). Clearly, the famous phrase, "The whole of Combray . . . came, city and gardens, from my cup of tea," is much more than an awkward stunt to get into the heart of the author's story. It demonstrates, rather, one of Proust's basic insights into involuntary memory. By insistently plumbing the impression resulting from a blessed moment, one will eventually arrive at the whole, as constituted within the self. As an intermediary step, a person who has pursued and attained this goal will recognize both "the unity of composition" and the fact that "the creator only used one and the same patron for all organized beings." (Here I am quoting from Balzac's discussion of the importance of Geoffroy Saint-Hilaire in the "Foreword" to the *Comédie humaine,* which may have been the source of Proust's idea for the name of the Combray church.) Saint-Hilaire becomes the symbol for the unity of *A la recherche*: "an edifice occupying, so to speak, four dimensional space—the fourth being that of Time" (I, 61). Like this monument in four dimensions, Proust's novel stands in the reader's mind, and, as Jean Cocteau put it, "In the space of a second, you can dream the equivalent of Marcel Proust's work."37

But perhaps a better symbol for this unification would be the setting where it takes place—within the "I" of the novel. I have already pointed to the importance of Proust's negative narration, where the protagonist-narrator is the sum of everything he sees. He is all the characters, all the places, all the events, all the thoughts, and all the errors. "He is nothing but the place for sensations," to use Martin-Chauffier's words.38 For this very reason, Proust's "I" serves as an effective vehicle. As Michihiko Suzuki saw in his remarkable article, "Le 'je' proustien," the first person acts as a means of generalization. The reader "fixes" the images of the "I," thus transforming them into his own images, and Proust's fictional first person becomes the reader's "I."39 It was not by accident that Proust chose the image of a book when the narrator says, "This [internal] book [of unknown signs (of signs in relief, it seems, that my attention, exploring my unconscious, was seeking, collided with, skirted, like a diver sounding)], the most arduous of all to decipher, is also the only one that reality has dictated to us, the only one whose 'impression' was made in us by reality itself. . . . The book with figurative characters, not traced by us, is our only book" (III, 880).

"During [the] reading" of *A la recherche*, Proust's ideal reader does not execute "incessant movements from within to without" as does the young protagonist in Combray (I, 84); he goes "from without to within" and thus "toward the discovery of truth." While following the process that leads from the first person of *A la recherche* to that of the reader, we gain insight into the author's understanding of art and of reality. In a period when artists were tortured by the conflict between the real and the illusory, Proust considered as our experience, our life, our reality, not the physical substance which surrounds us, rather our idea of it. The book which "recomposes life exactly" (III, 898)—not imitation, let me insist, but recomposition— offers an experience through time and space which has real existence. As with other real objects, only the reader's idea of it exists— "Everything is in the mind" (III, 912)—though the novel includes many sets of lenses which control to an enormous degree his point of view. "Things—a book with its red cover like the others—, as soon as we perceive them become something immaterial in us, of the same nature as all our sensations and preoccupations . . . and combine indissolubly with them" (III, 885). Art, then, is no more illusion than life. Indeed, art is life or, to be more precise, "true life, life finally discovered and explained, consequently the only life really lived is literature" (III, 895).

Comments which suggest that "the supreme truth of life is in art" (III, 902) might even make one believe that for Proust art was better than life. And, in fact, there is some evidence to support this contention. He mentions in the margin of one of his notebooks, for example, that we need art because life is an imperfect realization.[40] I take this to mean that for those of us who have been unable for whatever reason to find unification in the shifting multiplicity of our daily lives (the world we see is a chaos, the narrator says—I, 834), artists like Proust create carefully ordered, essential reality at man's level and within his grasp. When *A la recherche* succeeds in causing readers to experience involuntary memory and discover the novel's unity, Proust has not only succeeded in transmitting his own unity, for the book is his reflection, but he has communicated one of the two great lessons of his masterpiece: Unity (the other lesson is Time). If both the reader and Proust are unified, and if the author can make others sense this quality, then there exist universals which rise above the obstacles separating men.[41] In short, though the mechanism of involuntary memory and of artistic creation remain particular and subjective, the fact that many accomplish the process proves the subjective event to be an objective, universal truth.

It is even possible, the narrator thinks, that such a reality overcomes death. When the unenlightened protagonist despairs that the images of his past are "in reality dead to me" and possibly dead forever (I, 44), art provides him with reasons for more optimism. He notes that musical phrases, like that of Vinteuil's sonata or of the *Tristan* theme, are subject to the future of those who hear them. Should we die, they must accompany us. "And death with them has something less bitter, less inglorious, perhaps less probable about it" (I, 350). Finally, while musing on Bergotte's death, the narrator conceives of art, and the devotion required for its creation, as one of the major reasons for believing that there are universal, governing laws directing men, "so that the idea that Bergotte was not dead forever is not improbable" (III, 188). Whatever the case may be, the Countess de Monteriender is nowhere near as ridiculous as one might think when she says of the performance of Vinteuil's sonata: "It's prodigious. I've never seen anything so great... . . . . nothing so great... since table turning!" (I, 353).

Despite literature's undoubted importance in eliciting universals, Proust never forgets that art is subordinate to man. The author may guide the reader by means of explanations and other "incitations" to those potential systems imbedded in the work; still, only the reader can provide the revelation capable of creating complexes of meaning and significant truths. However important art was for Proust, he recognized that "reading is at the threshold of spiritual life; it can introduce us to it; it does not constitute it" (*CSB*, p. 178). He had little choice but to echo Gide's "Nathanaël. . . .when you have read me, throw this book away... and leave," to warn his readers against "idolatry," and to urge them to create their own lives and works. "Certain minds which love mystery want to believe that objects conserve something from the eyes that look at them, that the monuments and paintings only appear before us beneath the sensible veil that the love and contemplation of many adorers have woven during the centuries. This chimera would become true if they were to transpose it onto the only reality for each person, into the domain of his own sensibility" (III, 884).

Rather then being dismayed by literature's dependency on readers, Proust views its capacity to incite, to stimulate, to create creators as one of its greatest glories:

And there, in fact, is one of the great and marvelous characteristics of beautiful books (which will cause us to understand the role, both essential and limited, that reading can play in our spiritual life) that for the author could be called "Conclusions" and for the reader "Incitations." We sense very clearly that our wisdom begins where the author's ends, and we would like him to respond to us, when all he can do is give us desires. And he cannot

> awaken these desires in us except by making us contemplate
> the supreme beauty which the utmost effort of his artistry
> has permitted him to attain. . . . What is the end of their
> wisdom appears to us nothing but the beginning of ours.
> (*CSB*, pp. 176-77).

The true test of the success of a work of art in Proust's eyes was in
whether it provoked the viewer to artistic creation. It is not enough
to meditate quietly on the glorious vision of artistic unity, the reader
must go beyond, as the protagonist did on finally understanding
Vinteuil's "mysterious call" to artistic creation (III, 877-78). Every
man must create his own unity and his own work of art.

This interpretation of *A la recherche du temps perdu* has important
repercussions in respect to its coherence and economy. For the
critics who have denied these qualities to Proust's novel,[42] the
author's goal was to recount the development of a young man who
finally becomes capable of art and to explain the process of his
discoveries. Should that in truth have been the case, the book clearly
contains large amounts of extraneous material. If, however, I am
correct in suggesting that, while both the protagonist's quest and the
narrator's explications are important, they represent only the first
small step ("incitations") towards a true understanding of the
masterpiece, the exposition and the rather disconnected account of
the vocation constitute but a part of the *novel's* vocation, which is to
stimulate the reader's discovery of his unified self and to incite him
to undertake his own act of creation. They can therefore not be used
as criteria for judging either coherence or economy. Should that
indeed be the case, analogy is not only functional but essential to the
triggering of metaphor. Analogy and the rigorousness of its connections
then become the only valid touchstones. Overviews by such previously
cited critics as Rousset, Bolle, and Tadié have provoked a number of
studies in detail, which, as mentioned before, indicate that analogy
rules supreme in governing the narrative sequence. Whether viewed
as a reader's sequential progression through time or as the instantaneous
vision of the whole in all its complexity, the harmoniousness of the
parts is absolute.

Since economy must also be determined in the light of
function, it seems essential to recognize the need for sufficient
length to permit forgetting and, moreover, to fix the systems of
imagery indelibly. From this point of view, one imagines with
difficulty that the novel could be shorter. Given those who deny the
unity of *A la recherche*, one might even wonder whether the novel
should not have been longer. That would have rendered the

parameters or variables more obvious and, thus, facilitated an understanding of the whole. Unfortunately, the novel would have lost something as well. As Jan Mukarovsky suggested, "Unity should not be understood as something static, as complete harmony, but as dynamic, as a problem with which the work confronts the viewer. . . . If the task faced by the viewer is too simple, that is, if in a given situation similarities outweigh differences, the effect of the work is weakened. . .since the work does not force the viewer to remain or to return. Therefore a work having a weakly based dynamics rapidly becomes automatic."[43]

In the end, of course, the solitary reader must be the judge of all such problems, for Proust planned his novel as an individual, subjective experience, and that is how he would have wished it. Each reader must be his own Magellan; he must set out on his voyage *A la recherche du temps perdu* in the effort to discover his own structure and meaning, his own new world. On disembarking, because Proust's structure means the reader, all distinctions between form and content, all separation between subject and object are suppressed. Granted, the voyage may fail and leave unity unproven, the call to art unheeded, and the earth flat. Though both Magellan and Proust died in their endeavors, there is perhaps encouragement in the knowledge that Magellan's men completed the task. While Proust did his part, the rest depends on those of us who follow his charted course.

One should not be overly impressed with the enormous freedom which Proust allowed the reader. Although the author is certainly responsible for the analogical chains crossing the novel—whether colors, bells, churches, characters, or places—I find no evidence that he preferred one over another. Proust's interest was not in one or more sets of variable relationships, for any one could produce the effect he sought. Proust's interest was in the effect. However it happened, and he provided numerous opportunities, he hoped only that *A la recherche* would provoke involuntary memory, that the reader would then bring back to mind the elements of an extension, and, finally, that because of a blessed moment, it would be possible to incite artistic spectators to create their own lives and works. There is no doubt that Proust's masterpiece constitutes what I would call an open novel. Though the author has provided a text, the reader has considerable freedom in the way he treats the preestablished creation. But I am not suggesting that the reader has been granted the right to create from the novel in unauthorized ways. Those who take it upon themselves to deform Proust's creation, do so on their own accord.

In fact, despite the many variables, Proust's novel remains rigorously structured. It resembles a form similar to what in mineralogy is called a *paramorph*, that is, a structure formed by changing the physical characteristics without changing the chemical composition. In this sense, *A la recherche* is paramorphic. By whatever extension the reader may consciously—or more probably, unconsciously—choose, he must grasp the central issue of involuntary memory or the novel has failed. Whether the reader seizes on the plot, or one or more characters or objects makes no difference. The result will differ, but in unimportant ways.

Although every work of art requires the "consumer's" participation, in general this involvement follows a more well-defined path. To allow numerous alternative patterns with seeming lack of prejudice for the reader to attain aesthetic satisfaction was unusual in the first few decades of the twentieth century. Proust's novel is the first that I know of which can be properly called paramorphic. There may be others, but I am less interested in the question or originality than in the clarity with which Proust laid out his understanding of the relationship possible between his work and the reader.

As in respect to Huysmans's *En rade* and its negative structure, the further exploitation of Proust's innovative paramorphic novel had to wait until recent novelists began seriously to turn again to radical experimentation. I do not believe Proust's success has been surpassed in our time, but there have been very interesting, provocative variations on the pattern. That is one topic for discussion in the next, the concluding chapter.

# Chapter 8
## Conclusion

IT MIGHT SEEM THAT THE VERY PLETHORA of the New Novelist's innovations makes it impossible to choose the most significant. One would be hard put to question the importance of Nathalie Sarraute's characterization as she attempts to capture the very mechanism of consciousness in, say, *Tropismes* (1938). Or Marguérite Duras's sensitive revelations of the evanescent moment in novels like *Le Square* (1955). Or the haunting melancholy Pinget succeeds in communicating as he builds the dossier of Clope's loneliness and crime, with scarcely a mention of the title character (*Clope au dossier*— 1961). Or the pronominal development in Butor's *La Modification* (1957). Or Robbe-Grillet's largely unsuccessful attempt both to separate signifier and signified and to allow his themes to "self-generate" in *Projet pour une révolution à New York* (1970). Or any number of other developments which touch plot, character, theme, image, syntax, lexicon. In no sense do I wish to question the importance of these aesthetic events. New Novelists have been quite right to stress them. Indeed, one could correctly say that we have yet to appreciate these and other innovations fully.

I do wonder, however, whether any such changes succeed in thrusting to the heart of the genre. With but slight adjustments of definition, easily discernable plots, characters, themes, settings, and so on, exist in all of these novels. Butor's *La Modification* and legions of other novels could have served just as well as *La Chartreuse de Parme*, for instance, to exemplify endomorphic novels of the process variety. *Clope au dossier* could have replaced *Gobseck* as an exemplary image novel. And this despite significant, but I think peripheral, changes. Especially when one considers the kind of figural construction that Zola used in *Germinal*, one has to admit that most recent novels maintain the same basic structural patterns as those consecrated by tradition.

My point is not to belittle the contributions of the New Novel. Not only does that seem an empty, useless exercise, it would do a grave disservice to the many admirable novelists who, after the detour into didactic literature during the nineteen twenties, thirties, and forties, have picked up the gauntlet cast down at the turn of the century. Calling standard conceptions of plot or character or whatever into question is not a negligible or an idle task, especially when it is, as in this case, consciously pursued. As with Gide, one of the salient features of current artists is their awareness of theory. Robbe-Grillet, Sarraute, Butor, Ricardou, and others have had major impact on literary criticism. We may indeed one day decide that Ricardou, at least, made his primary contribution in that area.

I am very interested in understanding what seem to me the most significant contributions of recent novels. The prospect of enriching my experience of past masterpieces adds an inducement, as well. And in this regard I believe we may justifiably concentrate for a moment on structure. Certainly, negative representation such as that found in Huysmans has had important repercussions in recent years. One might even say it constitutes a sign of the New Novel.

Alain Robbe-Grillet's *La Jalousie* (1957) is just one of many possible examples. As in *En rade*, we are nowhere told to deduce the true focal point from what is given, and, as in *En rade*, the author withholds information, for the narrator never poses the questions he surely would have asked, for example, "I wonder whether A... had an affair with Franck?" Without positing a husband, however, the novel makes no sense: it remains a sequence of disconnected, repetitious images. The fact that the reader is introduced to "the look which, coming from the back of the bedroom, passes over the balustrade"[1] might even suggest the existence of an omniscient narrator rather like that found in *En rade*, though it should be stated that most of the images in the text could be the direct transcription of the husband's thoughts. Certainly, unlike *En rade*, the text never includes a physical description of the source of either the "look" or the perceived and remembered images which mix in what Robbe-Grillet has called "an ordered system of extremely high character."[2]

At first, the text resembles the native song which has no discernable structure. "Doubtless it is always the same poem which continues. If sometimes the themes become blurred, it is to return a little later stronger, almost identical" (p. 101). Images of apparently past events recur in the text, occasionally changing, frequently interspersed with views of the present reality. On the one hand, glimpses of A...'s undulating and "opulent black hair. . . .[t]he cascade of heavy curls" (p. 133) return obsessively, and, on the other, we watch replays of the time Franck usurped the husband's role of protector and killed a centipede which frightened A....In one reconstruction, A...'s hand clenches her knife handle (p. 63), in another the tablecloth (p. 97). Perhaps they were different hands. Finally, the centipede dies in an (imagined?) hotel room, while A...'s hand clutches the sheet, before Franck joins her in bed (pp. 165-66). As for the place on the wall where the insect was first smashed, the resultant mark is "scarcely visible" (p. 69), though later it is so "perfectly visible" (p. 90) that it is "perfectly distinguished (p. 129).

At some point most readers will doubtless begin formulating the questions the text does not ask. Perhaps it will be in regard to the pale blue letter, folded twice, which A... holds (pp. 14, 105), when we later view a pale blue letter—folded four times, however—protruding from Franck's shirt pocket. Eventually, a vision of A... and the "pale blue sheet" mingles with an attempt to efface the remains of the centipede from the wall (pp. 131-32). Did A... write a letter to Franck? Or, after the overnight trip to town, when A... leans back through the car window, does she kiss Franck good-by? As though to prove that objective knowledge is possible, precise descriptions of a shadow and the house's setting (e.g., p. 9) or of the geometrical pattern of a field of banana trees (e.g., pp. 32-37) occur intermittently. Why does A... call Franck a poor mechanic? Is it, as Bruce Morrissette suggests, "sexual disappointment on the part of A...?"[3] Or is it A...'s reference to Franck's (successful or unsuccessful?) ruse to spend the night with her? Or is it merely a teasing reference to Franck's inability to repair a simple mechanical failure? The text offers no solutions. But in asking the questions, the reader effectively incarnates the invisible narrator.

Inevitably, it seems that the true focus of La Jalousie resides, not in A...'s virtue or adultery, but in the husband and the pattern of his obsession. Through the projected images, the reader sees the mold, the negative of the real subject. That the main character exists only negatively does not mean that there has been "a *more or less radical disappearance of personage and a no less considerable, correlative reinforcement of the autonomy of objects,*" as Lucien Goldmann has suggested in his analysis of modern literature.[4] To the contrary, as the reader follows the pattern of the obsession, the very absence of the husband has the effect of stressing his existence, while the objects that serve as what Morrissette calls "objective correlations" and Robbe-Grillet "supports for his passion"[5] become, not autonomous, but signs pointing directly to the absent, positive figure of the husband.

In fact, of course, negative structure has few surprises for modern readers. For a while, it confused critics, but those days are long gone, and educated readers grasp material organized in this fashion with little or no difficulty. The same cannot be said for paramorphic structure. With the exception of Proust, few truly major authors have exploited the device; it remains primarily the property of the avant-garde and most commonly in the fine arts. I think of Calder's mobiles, effectively communicating a soaring sense of freedom within rigidly controlled patterns. While many museum pieces likewise allow spectators to change the position of panels or parts, novels have been less fruitful in this regard. Still, several novelists have shown their awareness of the potential of such structures. I think in particular of Marc Saporta's *Composition No. 1* (1962), which is *almost* paramorphic. Its use of parameters differs radically from that of *A la recherche*, while it also succeeds in producing a unified whole. The novel may be referred to as a deck-book, for it consists of 149 unbound pages, each of which contains a unit of narration or description, which may be shuffled. This provides considerable liberty to the reader.

Saporta has been very explicit about the work's theoretical premises: "Françoise Giroud. . . .has said that according to the time when things happen, events take on a different meaning. Contrarily, there was Sartre's old theory, according to which we are the sum of our circumstances, or our phenomena, of all that we have 'existed.' . . . I kept saying to myself that if we add the same events in a different order, the sum is not the same. I had to find for my mobile-novel a way of making that explicit. And that's what I did."[6] After inviting the reader to shuffle the book's pages, the flyleaf of *Composition No. 1* goes on to suggest that, depending on the order of the pages, the protagonist's mistress, Dagmar, may date either from before or during his marriage, his rape of Helga may have occurred during his adolescent or adult life, the theft may have taken place during the war and under the direction of the Resistance or it may have occurred during peacetime, and the automobile accident where he was injured may be connected to the theft or the rape. The blurb ends with the statement that "the number of possible compositions is infinite."

On considering the novel, one discovers that the reader has not been granted such unlimited license. There are a number of episodes which are dated by the obvious age of the narrator—for example, when he is caught in a childish lie, when he plays marbles, when he passes out anti-Nazi tracts at the university. Other sequences are dated historically, in particular his participation in the Resistance and in the army occupying Germany. During this period he was · responsible for stealing a dossier containing Nazi interrogation reports of fellow resistance fighters.

Other sequences are intimately interrelated. We know that he rapes Helga during the period of his affair with Dagmar; in one place he compares Helga's facial expression to Dagmar's, and in another Dagmar's to Helga's.[7] Furthermore, we learn that he not only drives a car during his acquaintance with Dagmar (fol. 54), he works then in an office (fol. 125). Both are unlikely activities for a French adolescent before World War II. His financial troubles, employment, gambling, and the unfortunate marriage are contemporaneous (fols. 19, 134). Despite the flyleaf's suggestion, the first interview with Helga will simply not allow this episode to have taken place during his adolescence, for she is clearly talking to an adult (fol. 73). Likewise, his amorous expertise would find few equals among "16 or 17 year old boys" of the 1930s or early 40s, his age when Mama hired a girl to take care of her younger children (fol. 56). In short, his wife, Marianne, gambling, work in an office, Dagmar, and Helga probably date from after the war. One theft may have taken place during this period (there may have been several in addition to the wartime activities). All we know is that he was strongly tempted (fol. 119).

Not every episode or leaf is incontrovertably a part of one or another of the sequences I have mentioned. The police staked out at an intersection (fol. 14), the instructions for potting flowers (fol. 20), the description of pruning a rose (fol. 25), the motorcycle police stopping the driver who has just run a red light (fol. 127), and the description of a parish church (fol. 100) could be put in any of a dozen places. Other episodes are anchored to a sequence though not absolutely fixed in time. We know for example that the protagonist-narrator was involved with Marianne when he picked up the hitchhiker, for Marianne "explodes. . . [claiming] that she was in danger of death" (fol. 24), but we have no further clues. It could have occurred early or late in their relationship. The moment before breaking into a house could be a part of any one of several thefts, whether real or imagined (fol. 17). We have no way of knowing when, in a moment of fatal charity, he pays for the little secretary's abortion (fol. 31). Still, most episodes are relatively fixed in time and cause: he grew up prior to World War II when, perhaps because of the young woman engaged by his mother, he gained a preference for green-eyed (Marianne, Dagmar, Helga), blond (Dagmar, Helga) women with German accents (Dagmar and Helga). After passing out tracts against the occupying Nazi forces, he joined the Resistance and robbed an interrogation center, later passed into the French Army and was a part of the occupying force in Germany. Then came work, marriage to Marianne, two children, his wife's increasing mental problems and their related financial difficulties, gambling, a possible robbery or robberies, an affair with Dagmar, the rape of Helga, the au pair girl caring for his children. While the robbery might have occurred earlier then indicated here, if one uses some of the skills honed by modern novelists and reads to solve a puzzle, there are numerous clues scattered across the novel that make anything but minor variations on the above pattern impossible.

In short, if Saporta's intention while writing the novel was indeed as he expressed it afterwards—that is, to provide readers with the opportunity to create completely different stories from the base of 149 episodes—he failed. With some careful editing, however, *Composition No. 1* could easily have come to resemble Saporta's subsequent descriptions, a perspective of considerable interest, for it would then be a paramorphic novel.

On reflection, the chronology and what actually happens seem of little interest and less importance. The justification for the fragments has to do with an automobile accident which leaves the narrator delirious in a hospital. As he lies in his hospital bed, the bits and pieces of his life float through his mind. "Dagmar comes in, dressed completely in white and moves aside for a bride [Marianne] who, with a contorted, pale face beneath her veils, controls her nerves as she stands before the altar" (fol. 95). "Dagmar wanders across the sky. . . .She leans Helga's face above the bed" (fol. 70). We realize that the lack of chronological and causal sequence is explained by the narrator's delirium. "The hospital room is nothing but an accumulation of disordered memories" (ibid.). But whatever the order of the narrator's confused memories, his condition remains constant. His gambling, for example, has little to do with his financial difficulties, as becomes clear when he gives away his winnings (fol. 43). It appears instead but one side of his compulsively self-destructive personality, and it joins the senseless lies that finally destroy his relationship with Dagmar. It is hardly surprising to find that he is in addition a robber. The portrait finally emerges of a mythomanic, compulsive gambler, rapist, and thief, bent on his own destruction. *Composition No. 1* draws the reader not so much to the events of this life, rather to what the narrator is, to the shape and quality of his character.

If I may then imagine *Composition No. 1* without the markers giving it a reasonably rigid chronology, I have an example of a paramorphic novel which differs radically from *A la recherche.* While Proust's novel establishes numerous systems or functions, each one of which would allow the reader to grasp the whole in a moment of involuntary memory, Saporta's creation (reincarnated flawless for the present purposes) provides a deck of fragments susceptible of many orders, each one of which presents the same pathological personality. In both cases the structure changes but the "chemical composition" remains the same; the form varies but the essence rests immutable.

Other varieties of paramorphic novels are possible. Julio Cortázar's *Rayuela* (*Hopscotch*—1963) begins with a "Table of Instructions" which proposes two orders of reading. One may begin with the first chapter and finish with the fifty-sixth. This sounds more traditional than it is, for the novel also contains another ninety-nine "expendable" chapters of quotations and text, some only a few lines long. These additional portions may be included in alternative readings indicated at the end of each chapter and in the "Instructions." After beginning with chapter 73, one goes to 1 and 2, then 116, and, while this version of the novel maintains the original order to chapters 1 through 56, it both skips chapter 55 and intersperses other chapters here and there in the sequence. Furthermore it does not end with chapter 56; the previously terminal chapter is now followed by chapters 135, 63, 88, 72, 77, 131, 58, 131-, in that order. A reading limited to chapters 1 through 56 concludes ambiguously: we do not know whether Oliveira actually followed through on his threat to "lean just a little bit farther out [of the insane asylum window] and let himself go, paff the end."[8] Still, the fact that in the longer version he does indeed drop and live through the experience is of no importance. The emptiness of these trivial lives has been well established and does not change in the coda. The principal characters are the living dead.

Insufficient attention has been paid to the sign following the last chapter indicated in the "Instructions," that is, following chapter 131. It is not a period[9]; it is a dash, which consequently invites the reader to make other combinations. As Cortázar says in the "Table of Instructions," "In its own way, this book consists of many books." The dash is indeed weighted. Before one makes the most obvious assumptions and concludes that one is invited to either reorder the chapters or add an additional story, thus pushing the chronological account of Oliveira farther into the future, it is worth considering that the effect of Cortázar's "Expendable Chapters" is neither to provide a new chronology for the first section nor to lengthen the period covered. Instead, the additional chapters expand the fictional world, including previously unmentioned events and characters or adding new facts and facets to the personages and activities presented in the shorter version. I wonder whether the reader is being encouraged to create new details, new situations, new characters which will give further depth and nuance to Cortázar's image of futility? The result of such an invitation would not change the author's vision, if done in the spirit of what precedes, but it could, like the best of paramorphic novels, increase its richness and profundity.

A very different kind of paramorphic novel appears in Jean Ricardou's exploitation of textual repetitions in *La Prise de Constantinople* (1965). Tobin Jones suggests perceptively that the reader may view such passages "as the material elements of an expanding form or as poetic motifs marking points of thematic intersection."[10] It is the lengthening form which interests me, for it allows the reader much freedom and marks the novel as paramorphic in form. On running into and recognizing a passage which he has seen before, the reader is encouraged to reconsider the new values given by the new context and perhaps even to return to the original, "seminal" text, which, itself, has now changed. Given what the reader has read and learned since first encountering the passage, it now has a new context. The unnumbered pages encourage the reader to refuse the ordinary sequence of reading, from the first page to the last. As the narrative voice of *La Prise* puts it, "[P]eople would simply be induced to reread certain paragraphs, to go through the volume in one direction then in the other until they notice unexpected figurations susceptible of prolonging and refining—without a break, it seems—the cycle of these reversals."[11] Of course, there is no way of knowing whether the reader will notice, or reconsider briefly, or actually reread—and if he does reread, how much of the intervening text he will go back through. The reader then has considerable freedom in determining the shape of his reading and, thus, the shape of the book.

These examples fall into two categories which parallel those of the endomorphic novel. Proust's Saporta's, and Cortázar's works encourage readers to form an image, while Ricardou's creation emphasizes the potential of variable sequences. Just as we have process and image fiction within the bounds of endomorphic structures, so, likewise, does paramorphic fiction break into patterns of process and image, of action and inaction. That is not surprising since, as said before, these modes of conceptualization are basic to the human mind.

A reminder of *A la recherche du temps perdu* serves to conclude this volume. Viewed through the lens of preceding novels, it provides an example of negative, process, and image structures in endomorphic fiction. As argued before, it is essential for readers to realize that the protagonist is constituted by the images of characters, places, events, activities that he has stored away on the pages presented to the readers. We must then construct him by projecting the light of our understanding through these negative images and thus reverse them, creating a positive representation. Likewise, the reader follows the protagonist as he evolves, as he changes, as he ages, until, in a flash, he discovers the subject which will allow him to create a work of art. In short, we read a process novel, whose development remains essential to adequate understanding. Nonetheless, the discovery at the Princess de Guermantes' *matinée* completely reorients the conclusions to be drawn about the process of the protagonist-narrator's life. *A la recherche* becomes an image novel. In fact, the entire development over the several thousand pages which precede these revelatory moments may be conveniently summarized as "lost" time. The protagonist's discovery of his own unity depends upon his instantaneous perception, due to involuntary memory, that he, as he existed in the past, is not dead but alive and present. Past and present are unified within his own person. In short, the causal and chronological sequence of his life is negated in favor of an all-encompassing conception that keys the whole. What was process is subverted and becomes image structure. Simultaneously, where the reader's attention has been focused on the people and events of the protagonist's life, the frame shifts and the image blurs. Despite the vivid sights, sounds, smells, and sensations enregistered in the projections, we understand that none of them—whether characters, places, events, anticipations, or memories—have importance except as they detail the projecting "I." *A la recherche* provides a negative, a cast which must be shucked off to reveal the narrator-protagonist.

Were this all, Proust's novel would admirably fit into the aesthetic turmoil of the turn of the century. It would display for everyone to see the author's firm control of traditional devices and conventions. Like Gide, he has taken process and opposed it to image structure; like Huysmans, he neglects positive for negative representation. Proust would then join other artists of the period whose experiments show decided discontent with the prevailing paradigm, but who give little indication of alternative possibilities. I do not mean to suggest that the authors on whom I have concentrated were alone in attempting to break out of what apparently seemed an aesthetic cul-de-sac, for that was not the case. It would take several volumes to describe in any detail what was taking place at the time. Furthermore, some of the experiments were interesting and deserve further work. I think in particular of the importance given to the "collective hero" in such authors as Zola, Octave Mirbeau, Maurice Barrès, Jules Romains. Still, I would maintain that my concentration on Gide, Huysmans, and Proust is justified, for it emphasizes not just a break with the past but new departures as well, new departures that appear increasingly significant since midcentury.

Proust, as I have shown, was aware that passivity kills art. Somehow or other, the reader has to go beyond mere appreciation to become an active partner in the discovery and creation of aesthetic works. Proust's awareness of this need appears so explicitly across his oeuvre that it cannot be denied. What is less obvious is his means of revitalizing the relationship between reader and text. I believe he subordinated those elements that suggest an endomorphic novel in order to exploit a revolutionary, paramorphic structure. While it is true that a reader must cooperate before any text can succeed as a work of art—otherwise the sign-systems will not be translated into meaning—readers' freedom to pick and choose between unifying devices is for the most part severely limited. Proust established numerous variables which the reader is encouraged to use in constructing one or more of many possible systems. On considering Proust's novel, one thinks of paramorphs, whose structures change without affecting the underlying chemical composition. *A la recherche* may legitimately take a number of different forms, each one of which maintains the work's meaning. The particular formula Proust employed for his paramorphic novel is, however, not the only one. Other modern authors indicate its potential richness.

It is considerably more difficult to find examples of open works. Few authors have been willing to run the risks involved in challenging their readers to react, not as in Balzac's case to bring about a reactionary revolution, but to create his own work of art. True, a traditional reading of Proust's masterpiece would view it as closed, for the hero completes his task in finding the source for his future writings and, the concluding pages suggest, he will finish his novel. In short, *A la recherche* explicitly brings one action to a conclusion and implies the completion of the other. But on paying attention to the number of times the novel calls the reader to go beyond Proust to his own personal work, there can be no question that *A la recherche* dramatically opens beyond the pages of a book to real life. While Gide claimed that the novel must turn around an opposition between life and art, in fact, his works enclose the conflict within the realm of fictional similitudes. Proust made a work which, when successful, encourages overture that continues on long after the reading has ended.

Endomorphic structure still occurs frequently in recent fiction, and it provides rich opportunity for authors as varied as Thomas Pynchon, Robbe-Grillet, and Borges. I have no doubt that it will persist in allowing authors to tantalize readers as they experiment with such components as plot, character, description, theme, images. Though *Madame Bovary* and *Les Gommes,* for example, are both endomorphic process novels, they seem very different because of the divergent handling and, indeed, concept of character. But the potential of paramorphic fiction, while indicated by Proust, Saporta, Cortázar, Ricardou and a few others, remains largely for future exploitation. As readers become more demanding and insist increasingly on being allowed more of a part in the creative process, I suspect writers will rely with greater frequency on the paramorphic structure. It allows them sufficient control to assure a sense of the order necessary to art, while providing the reader with the opportunity to make his own aesthetic work from the materials the artist has previously selected. But whatever the writer uses to give his fiction form and thus to turn it into an edifice of sorts, the development of the relatively new paramorphic structure and the rich variations possible in this and more traditional forms indicate the continuing vitality of the novel.

# Notes

## Preface:

[1]*Fable's End: Completeness and Closure in Rhetorical Fiction* (Chicago: Univ. of Chicago Press, 1974), p. 19.

## Chapter 1

[1]Philippe Hamon, "Qu'est-ce qu'une description," *Poétique*, No. 12 (1972), pp. 484-85.

[2]I refer specifically to Hirsch's *Validity in Interpretation* (New Haven: Yale Univ. Press, 1967) and his *The Aims of Interpretation* (Chicago: Univ. of Chicago Press, 1976).

[3]*The Well Wrought Urn: Studies in the Structure of Poetry* (New York: Reynal & Hitchcock, 1947), pp. 178-79. A useful introduction to some of the more recent developments may be found in Robert Scholes, *Structuralism in Literature* (New Haven: Yale Univ. Press, 1974).

[4]Stevick, "Scheherezade Runs Out of Plots, Goes on Talking: The King, Puzzled, Listens: An Essay on New Fiction," in Malcolm Bradbury, ed., *The Novel Today: Contemporary Writers on Modern Fiction* (Manchester: Manchester Univ. Press, 1977), p. 199. It is particularly the works of Barthelme, Brautigan, and Coover that bring Stevick to this pass.

[5]*Problèmes de linguistique générale* (Paris: Gallimard, 1966), p. 9. Cf. Claude Ollier's statement: "My 'procedure' consists in choosing and combining the words most likely to resound and to constitute the autonomous being composed of internal dependences—which is fiction"—"Interview with Bettina Knapp," tr. Alba Amoia, in B. Knapp, ed. *French Novelists Speak Out* (New York: Whitston, 1976), p. 154—and that of Claude Simon: "The work must be a whole, composed, rigorously constructed; the different parts must correspond to each other"—"Interview avec Claude Simon," by Bettina Knapp, *Kentucky Romance Quarterly*, 2 (1970), 187.

[6]"The Liberation of Sound," ed. Chou Wen-chung, *Perspectives of New Music*, 5, No. 1 (Fall-Winter 1966), 16.

[7]Nathalie Sarraute, in André Bourin's "Le Roman jugé par Nathalie Sarraute, M. de Saint Pierre, Claude Simon, Jean Hougron, J.-R. Huguenin," *Nouvelles Littéraires*, No. 1764 (22 juin 1961), p. 7.

[8]Louis Hjelmslev, *Prolegomena to a Theory of Language*, tr. Francis J. Whitfield (Madison: Univ. of Wisconsin Press, 1963), p. 11.

[9]Frank Kermode, "Sensing Endings," *Nineteenth-Century Fiction*, 33 (1978), 147.

[10]Paul Valéry, *Littérature,* in *Oeuvres,* Bibliothèque de la Pléiade, II (Paris: Gallimard, 1960), 554. E. K. Brown says in this regard, "Repetition is the strongest assurance an author can give of order"—*Rhythm in the Novel* (Toronto: Univ. of Toronto Press, 1950), p. 115.

[11]Kenneth Burke, *The Philosophy of Literary Form: Studies in Symbolic Action* (New York: Vintage, 1957), p. 75. Sheldon Sacks's *Fiction and the Shape of Belief* (Berkeley: Univ. of California Press, 1964) and Mary Doyle Springer's *Forms of the Modern Novella* (Chicago: Univ. of Chicago Press, 1975) have developed a different concept of function tragic, comic, satiric—which, however, is subject to the same reservation I advance in regard to Burke's theory.

[12]Jean Starobinski, "Psychanalyse et critique littéraire," *Preuves,* 16$^e$ année (mars 1966), p. 29.

## Chapter 2

[1]E.g., Claude Ollier, in the interview with Bettina Knapp, p. 154; Nathalie Sarraute, *L'Ère du soupçon: Essais sur le roman* (Paris: Gallimard, 1956), pp. 60-64; Alain Robbe-Grillet, *Pour un nouveau roman,* Collection Idées (Paris: Gallimard, 1963), pp. 39-40; and in Jean Ricardou and Françoise van Rossum-Goyon, eds., *Nouveau Roman: Hier, aujourd'hui,* Communications et interventions du colloque tenu du 20 au 30 juillet 1971 au Centre Culturel International de Cerisy-la-Salle, 2 vols. (Paris: 10/18, 1972), statements by Claude Simon (II, 88, 96-97), Robert Pinget (II, 317), Ricardou (II, 404, 407-08).

[2]Robbe-Grillet, *Pour un nouveau roman,* p. 33.

[3]*Linguistics and Literary History: Essays in Stylistics* (New York: Russell & Russell, 1962), p. 10.

[4]*Pour un nouveau roman,* p. 39. Robbe-Grillet is referring to "didactic literature," by which he means any work which reveals "the slightest regard for didacticism or even for meaning" (p. 42). He explicitly mentions the relationship "between the Balzacian [or nineteenth-century] novel and the triumph of the bourgeoisie" (p. 40)

[5]Robert Pinget, in, *Nouveau Roman: Hier, aujourd'hui,* II, 322. Though Pinget is here speaking as a writer, both he and the others would claim that the reader's activity does not differ in quality from that of the artist. For other passages having much the same thrust, see, e.g., Ricardou, *Pour une théorie du nouveau roman* (Paris: Seuil, 1971), p. 24; Robbe-Grillet, *Pour un nouveau roman,* pp. 17-18, 29, 31-33, 36-47; Saurraute, *L'Ère,* pp. 55-57, 60-64, 83-84, 108-109, 124. Leonard B. Meyer's *Music, the Arts and Ideas: Patterns in Twentieth-Century Culture* (Chicago: Univ. of Chicago Press, 1967) provides a cogent response to those who claim that modern readers cannot establish vital relationships with the works of writers who employ the "norms, forms, and procedures" of the past—pp. 186-87.

[6]*Nouveau Roman: Hier, aujourd'hui,* I, 21.

[7] *The French New Novel* (London: Oxford Univ. Press, 1969), p. 36.

[8] Jan Mukarovsky, *Aesthetic Function, Norm and Value as Social Facts,* trans. Mark E. Suino, Michigan Slavic Contributions, No. 3 (Ann Arbor, Mich.: Dept. of Slavic Languages, the University of Michigan, 1970), p. 72.

[9] Robert Scholes and Robert Kellogg, *The Nature of Narrative* (New York: Oxford, 1966), p. 207.

[10] The first quotation comes from Balzac's "Etudes sur M. Beyle (Frédéric Stendhal)," reprinted in Victor Del Litto's and Ernest Abravanel's edition of *La Chartreuse de Parme* by Stendhal, vol. 2 (Geneva: Cercle du Bibliophile, 1969), p. 451; the second from Balzac's letter to Mme Hanska, dated 14 avril 1840.

[11] Pierre-Louis Rey, *La Chartreuse de Parme: Stendhal* (Paris: Hatier, 1973), p. 24. Of the many criticisms he makes of the novel, I refer only to the "poorly composed" advanced on p. 26. Elme-Marie Caro termed the novel "an accumulation of scenes, without any plan, without a shade of unity"—*Études morales sur le temps présent* (1855; rpt. Paris: Hachette, 1887), p. 245. Émile Zola pronounces "[I]t is useless to prove the lack of logical composition in Stendhal's novels; this lack of composition is blatant, especially in *La Chartreuse de Parme*"—"Stendhal" (1880), in *La Critique stendhalienne de Balzac à Zola,* ed. Emile Talbot (York, S.C.: French Literature Publications, 1979), p. 264. Pierre Brun exclaims: "What an accumulation of scenes with neither plan nor unity and what trifling hors-d'oeuvres!"—*Henry Beyle, Stendhal* (Grenoble: Gratier, 1900), p. 52. A. Lytton Sells concludes, "Had [Stendhal] spent a day or two in studying *Andromaque . . .* he might have learned how to construct a novel—which, in any case, is easier than a tragedy"—"*La Chartreuse de Parme:* The Problem of Composition," *Modern Language Quarterly,* 12 (1951), 207-08. For quotations from other detractors, see: ibid., p. 205, and Hans Boll Johansen, "Notes sur la structure de la *Chartreuse de Parme,*" *Revue Romane* numéro spécial 1 (1967), p. 194, n. 1.

A few have talked as though the apparent flaws were virtues. Henri Martineau, e.g., mentions "the spontaneity and charming abandon"—*L'Oeuvre de Stendhal: Histoire de ses livres et de sa pensée* (Paris: Albin Michel, 1951), p. 558. Maurice Bardèche suggests that Stendhal "lets himself get carried away with the joy of writing. There is no hierarchy of interest. . . . The *Chartreuse,* in the end, is a poetic, picaresque novel"—*Stendhal romancier* (Paris: La Table Ronde, 1947), p. 396. Marcel Gutwirth states that, though the conclusion is "slapdash," it is because it has no importance "once the cycle of [Fabrice's] *gesta,* of his high deeds in the service of a noble destiny, crowned by love discovered, has run its meteoric course"—Marcel Gutwirth, *Stendhal* (New York: TWAYNE, 1971), pp. 96-97.

[12] "La Réponse de Stendhal: Premier Brouillon," in the previously cited second volume of Del Litto's edition of *La Chartreuse,* p. 518. Regarding the "Problem of [Stendhal's] Literary Language," see the important chapter iii of Emile Talbot's *Stendhal and Romantic Esthetics* (Lexington, Ky.: French Forum, 1985).

[13] In respect to characters, Ginette Ferrier says, e.g., "Mosca is not the hero of the *Chartreuse de Parme,* but an essential cog in the novelistic plot, an obscure cog whose functioning commands all the others"—"Sur un personnage de *La Chartreuse de*

*Parme*: Le Comte Mosca," *Stendhal Club*, 13 (1971), 39. Many critics have felt that the novel found its unity in Fabrice: see, n. 23, below. In re irony, see, Grahame C. Jones, *L'Ironie dans les romans de Stendhal* (Lausanne: Grand Chêne, 1966), pp. 129-70. In re setting, see, Louis Kronenberger, "Stendhal's Charterhouse," *Encounter*, 27 (July 1966), 38. In re imagery, Klaus Englehardt suggests: "Only a view of the whole of the visual complex can give the measure of the spectacle side of the novel. It seems, in fact, that the esthetic unity of the novel, often called into question by critics, is essentially related to this complex"—"Le Langage des yeux dans *la Chartreuse de Parme*," *Stendhal Club*, 14 (1972), 159. In re thematic structure, Gérard Genette states, "Stendhal's novelistic unity is . . .incontestable, but it is not because of cohesion, still less because of continuity, it results entirely from a kind of constancy that is in fact thematic: unity of repetition and of variation"—*Figures II: Essais* (Paris: Seuil, 1969), p. 178.

[14]"L'Unité artistique de *La Chartreuse de Parme*," *Communications présentées au Congrès Stendhalien de Civitavecchia* [1964] ed. V. Del Litto (Florence: Sansoni Antiquariato, 1966), pp. 229-30.

[15]"La Réponse de Stendhal: Second Brouillon," p. 526. I am of course not the only one to agree with Stendhal. See, for similar stances, e.g., Maurice Bardèche, *Stendhal romancier*, pp. 417, 421; Jean Bellemin-Noël, "Le Motif des orangers dans *la Chartreuse de Parme*," *Littérature*, 5 (1972), 32; Georges Blin, *Stendhal et les problèmes du roman* (Paris: Corti, 1954), p. 152; Johansen, "Notes," p. 196; Mairit Nordenstreng-Woolf, "Waterloo: Étude sur le troisième chapitre de *la Chartreuse de Parme*," *Stendhal Club*, 16 (1974), 241; Michèle Hirsch, "Fabrice, ou la poétique du nuage," *Littérature*, 23 (1976), 22.

[16]Stendhal, *La Chartreuse de Parme*, ed. Henri Martineau (Paris: Garnier, 1961), p. 12. All further references will be to this edition and cited parenthetically in the text.

[17]*Stendhal: Fiction and the Themes of Freedom* (New York: Random House, 1968), p. 173. In respect to prisons, see also Brombert's "Stendhal et les 'Douceurs de la prison,' " in *La Prison romantique: Essai sur l'imaginaire* (Paris: José Corti, 1975), pp. 67-92; Gilbert Durand, *Le Décor mythique de* la Chartreuse de Parme: *Contribution à l'esthétique du romanesque* (Paris: Corti, 1961), pp. 159-74; Leo Bersani, *Balzac to Beckett: Center and Circumference in French Fiction* (New York: Oxford Univ. Press, 1970), pp. 119-21; Emile J. Talbot, "Stendhal, the Artist, and Society," *Studies in Romanticism*, 13 (1974), 213-23.

[18]H. W. Wardman, "*La Chartreuse de Parme*: Ironical Ambiguity," *Kenyon Review*, 17 (1955), 463.

[19]Stephen Gilman, *The Tower as Emblem: Chapters VII, IX, XIX and XX of the* Chartreuse de Parme (Frankfurt: Vittorio Klostermann, 1967), p. 58.

[20]Chaitin, *The Unhappy Few: A Psychological Study of the Novels of Stendhal* (Bloomington: Indiana Univ. Press, 1972), p. 153; and, e.g., Robert M. Adams, *Stendhal: Notes on a Novelist* (1959; rpt. n.p.: Minerva Press, 1968), p. 97.

[21]Pp. 345, 363, 366, 374. Chaitin's discussion in *The Unhappy Few* is pp. 153-55.

[22]"Notes," pp. 199-200.

[23]*L'Oeuvre*, pp. 552. For similar views, see, e.g., Sells, "Problem of Composition," pp. 212-13; his "*La Chartreuse de Parme*: The Problem of Style," *Modern Language Quarterly*, 11 (1950), 489; Matthew Josephson, *Stendhal or the Pursuit of Happiness* (Garden City, N.Y.: Doubleday, 1946), pp. 432-33; Robert O. Stephens, "Hemingway and Stendhal: The Matrix of *A Farewell to Arms*," *PMLA*, 88 (1973), 277.

[24]Though I have consulted the facsimilie edition of the Chaper text (Paris: Cercle du Livre Précieux, 1965), I quote from V. Del Litto's subsequently published transcription of Stendhal's notes for the second volume, as published in *La Chartreuse de Parme: Exemplaire interfolié Chaper* (Paris: Cercle du Livre Précieux, 1966). The following additional references indicate passages in volume two which are pertinent to this matter: "Face verso du titre," "Face p. 375," "Page 375," Page 392, 11. 10 et 25," "Face page 434, 1. 14," "Face p. 445." In respect to "Face p. 364," which may also be of interest, see Del Litto's commentary, ibid., pp. 35-36.

[25]"La Réponse de Stendhal: Premier Brouillon," p. 522. The importance of Sandrino's death is mentioned elsewhere as well. I quote it because it too stresses the importance of the end point towards which the whole creation is directed: "The page that I write gives me an idea for the following: the *Char[treuse]* was written that way. I thought of Sandrino's death: that alone made me undertake the novel. . . . Now, making hardly any overall plan, I dampen my ardor with the foolishness of *expositions* and *descriptions* which are often useless and which must be suppressed when I arrive at the last scenes"—note in the ms. of *Lamiel*, published by Victor Del Litto, ed., t. 44 of the *Oeuvres complètes* (Geneva: Cercle du Bibliophile, 1971), pp. 340-41.

I should perhaps stress that these statements bring no light whatsoever to bear on the last five paragraphs of *La Chartreuse*, where Fabrice withdraws to a Charterhouse and dies. Nonetheless, on considering the claim Stendhal thought of sending Balzac, to the effect that Dupont prevented him from dealing with Sandrino's death at more length, one might remember other similar phrases of *La Chartreuse*, where the author excuses himself for not giving fuller details: e.g., "It would perhaps be amusing to tell about Rassi's fury, . . .but events hurry us on" (p. 416), or "Swept along by the events, we did not have the time to sketch in the comic rage of courtiers who . . . were making odd comments about the events we recounted" (p. 465). Georges Blin comments: "Unlike Balzac who is always so explicit, where Stendhal cuts the 'infinite details' short, he does so as author and not as a self-styled editor. . . . It would not have taken very much for him to tell us right in the middle of *La Chartreuse*'s story that M. Ambroise Dupont, who did not wish a third volume or a very voluminous second, obliged him near the end to speed things up"—*Stendhal*, p. 235.

[26]Gilman, *Tower*, p. 42, n. 52. Elsewhere (ibid., p. 28), he points out that these indications of the supernatural are "ways of communicating a sense of wholeness to novels which otherwise might seem amorphous and arbitrary." Jean Prévost makes the interesting suggestion that the omens bring the reader to a relationship with the text which resembles that of the improvising author—*La Création chez Stendhal* (1951; rpt. Paris: Mercure de France, 1967), pp. 361-62. David James indicated the omens'

significant function as leitmotifs in the structure of the novel—"The Harmonic Structure of *La Chartreuse de Parme," French Review*, 24 (1950), 119-24. For a distinction between the words, "prédiction," "prophétie," and "présage," see Hirsch, "Fabrice," p. 26.

[27]It is to a large degree the case of the previously mentioned dead Hussar presage. As François Michel concludes, "The Hussar's misdeeds which serve as premonitions will be noticed. The beat-up peasant will be the actor Giletti, though to be truthful he is somewhat more than beaten up, and the stolen cow, with apologies, is his mistress, little Marietta, whom Monseigneur Del Dongo will, in fact, steal from him. It seems that destiny spared Fabrice the silverware. As for prison, we know that it will be called the Farnese Tower"—"Les Superstitions de Fabrice del Dongo ou l'Humiliation de l'esprit," *Études stendhaliennes,* 2nd ed (Paris: Mercure de France, 1972), p. 59.

[28]François Michel, *Études*, p. 58; F. W. J. Hemmings, "Quelques observations sur les procédés de l'invention chez Stendhal," *Stendhal Club,* 6 (1963), 47-62; and I. H. Smith, "Brief Note on the Predictions of the Abbé Blanès," *Journal of the Australasian Universities Language and Literature Association*, 45 (1976), 96-97.

[29]Martin Turnell proposed the phallic tree and the castration symbol—*The Novel in France* (New York: Vintage, 1951), p. 207; Gilman advanced the suggestion of the "unusable past" (*Tower*, p. 46); and Henri Martineau the identification of the branch as Sandrino (I quote Martineau from Gilman, ibid.).

[30]Francine Marill provides what seems to me an excellent summary of the author's relationship to the faith of his characters: "*He confided to his characters the mission of verifying what neither life, nor circumstances, nor his own temperament allowed him to sense*; he refused fear of God for himself, but he attributed it to Clélia; he does not experience metaphysical anguish, but he never disputes this feeling and gives it the form of the anguish of remorse and repentance"—*Stendhal et le sentiment religieux* (Paris: Nizet, 1956), p. 201. I would not however oppose Robert M. Adams's conclusion that "the *Chartreuse* comes as close as anything ever written to being an amoral or immoral novel" (*Stendhal*, p. 101). Religion has implications for the unity and closure of the novel. It does not constitute a "message" to the reader.

[31]P. Veyne published the correct attribution in 1964, according to the "Carnet critique," *Stendhal Club*, 8 (1966), 193.

[32]P. 377. Prévost wonders pertinently: "Why does this sonnet give such a clear impression of Italian poetry? It is not just because of the sweetness in the choice of images, the agreeable slow way in which the thought unfolds; the rhythm is also Italian. This prose poem breaks itself into verses of uneven numbered syllables" (*Création*, pp. 362-63). Hirsch, who feels Fabrice is presented as an inferior poet, senses irony in Stendhal's indirect treatment of the poem—"Fabrice," pp. 29-30.

[33]All translations of Petrarch's poems are from Thomas Campbell's edition of *The Sonnets, Triumphs, and Other Poems of Petrarch Translated into English Verse by Various Hands* (London: George Bell, 1904).

34 Petrarch, *Petrarch's Secret or The Soul's Conflict with Passion: Three Dialogues Between Himself and S. Augustine*, tr. William H. Draper (London: Chatto & Windus, 1911), p. 123.

35 See, Alain Chantreau, "L'Utilisation esthétique et romanesque du thème de la religion dans *La Chartreuse de Parme*," *Aurea Parma*, 51 (1967), 34-42, for a balanced view. Turnell, who believes that "Fabrice is at heart... ruthless in using religion as the path to Clélia's bed" (*Novel*, p. 209), fails to recognize the degree to which Fabrice's religion constitutes an unthinking part of his life.

36 Cited by Martineau in his Garnier edition of *La Chartreuse*, p. 625, n. 720.

37 *The Masked Citadel: The Significance of the Title of Stendhal's* La Chartreuse de Parme, Univ. of California Publications in Modern Philology no. 93 (Berkeley: Univ. of California Press, 1968), pp. 5-21.

38 I hasten to add that after Leo Weinstein's convincing argument—which has had surprisingly little impact on criticism of *La Chartreuse*—I no longer see Mosca as a *brilliant* statesman—"Stendhal's Count Mosca as a Statesman," *PMLA*, 80 (1965), 210-16.

39 Turnell, *Novel*, pp. 203, 212. Françoise Michel may be correct to doubt that Fabrice was truly the illegitimate offspring of the French officer (*Etudes*, p. 65), but that matters little to my argument. Whether because of illegitimacy or xenogeny, Fabrice is *different*.

40 "Études sur M. Beyle," pp. 508-09.

41 *The Sense of an Ending: Studies in the Theory of Fiction* (New York: Oxford Univ. Press, 1967). See, as well, the special issue on narrative endings published by *Nineteenth-Century Fiction*, 35 (1978), 1-158, where Kermode's insights have received a generous admixture of deconstructive criticism.
    Other work, which I have found more useful for the present purposes, has studied the actual mechanisms of closure. I think particularly of Barbara Herrnstein Smith's *Poetic Closure: A Study of How Poems End* (Chicago: Univ. of Chicago Press, 1968) and David H. Richter's *Fable's End: Completeness and Closure in Rhetorical Fiction*. Philip Stevick has, in addition, useful perceptions in, "The Theory of Fictional Chapters," in his edition of *The Theory of the Novel* (New York: Free Press, 1967), pp. 171-84.

42 "The Idea of Order at Key West" (1934), *The Palm at the End of the Mind: Selected Poems and a Play by Wallace Stevens,* ed. Holly Stevens (New York: Alfred A. Knopf, 1971), pp. 98-99 (Copyright 1967, 1969, 1971 by Holly Stevens).

43 Pablo Picasso, "Conversation with Picasso," by Christian Zervos, in *The Creative Process: A Symposium*, ed. Brewster Ghiselin (Berkeley: Univ. of California Press, 1954), p. 49.

44 *Fable's End*, pp. 6-7.

[45] "Godard and *Weekend*," in *Weekend/Wind from the East*, by Jean-Luc Godard, Modern Film Scripts (New York: Simon and Schuster, 1972), p. 5. For an example, see the conflicting readings author and critic give William Burrough's *The Exterminator*—Ihab Hassan, "The Subtracting Machine: The Work of William Burroughs," *Critique*, 6 (1963), 10.

[46] The definition starts from Cleanth Brook's conception of structure as "resolved stresses" (*Well Wrought Urn*, p. 186). It then assumes that closure involves structure, a point that Jurij Lotman makes with considerable cogency: "The text is not a simple sequence of signs lying between two external boundaries. Inherent to the text is an integral organization which transforms it on the syntagmatic level into a structural whole. In order, therefore, to recognize a certain aggregate of phrases in a natural language as an artistic text, we need to be convinced that they form a secondary structure on the level of artistic organization. We should note that the properties of structure and demarcation are interrelated"—*The Structure of the Artistic Text*, tr. Ronald Vroon, Michigan Slavic Contributions, No. 7 (1971; tr. Ann Arbor: Dept of Slavic Languages, Univ. of Michigan, 1977), p. 53. Finally, it builds on Robert Martin Adams's definition of "open form," that is, "literary form . . . which includes a major unresolved conflict with the intent of displaying its unresolvedness"—quoted by Richter, *Fable's End*, p. 1, from Adams, *Strains of Discord: Studies in Literary Openness* (Ithaca, N.Y.: Cornell Univ. Press, 1958), p. 13.

[47] Wharton quoted by Irving H. Buchen, "The Aesthetics of the Supra-Novel," in *The Theory of the Novel: New Essays*, ed. John Halperin (New York: Oxford Univ. Press, 1974), p. 107, n. 4 (see, also, Buchen, p. 100); I. A. Richards, "How Does a Poem Know When It Is Finished?" in *Parts and Wholes*, ed. Daniel Lerner (New York: Macmillan, 1963), p. 168; Said, *Beginnings: Intention and Method* (New York: Basic Books, 1975).

[48] Saltykov-Shchedrin's novel is—according to Milton Ehre—"organized around death. Dying is the true action of *The Golovlyovs*. As a result the pressures of actual circumstance ebb into insignificance. The novel does not end because the lines of a plot have been tied together and its enganglements resolved. It ends simply because its rhythms have been exhausted. The Golovlyovs fade one by one, and when there are none—as in the child's jingle of the ten little Indians—the book is over"—"A Classic of Russian Realism: Form and Meaning in *The Golovlyovs*," *Studies in the Novel*, 9 (1977), 7.

[49] I reserve the term, "allusion," for the relationships established between a preexistent biblical, historical, legendary, literary, or mythological narration when a later (or older) author brings it into the current creation. References to my work on the subject are given in chapter 3, n. 32. Excellent analyses of historical realities exploited in poetic allusions are to be found in David Lee Rubin's *Higher, Hidden Order: Design and Meaning in the Odes of Malherbe*, Univ. of N. C. Studies in the Romance Languages and Literatures, No. 117 (Chapel Hill: Univ. of N. C. Press, 1972); and in his more recent *The Knot of Artifice: A Poetic of the French Lyric in the Early Seventeenth Century* (Columbus: Ohio State Univ. Press, 1981), especially chapter 1. For an example of an allusion to a myth, see Robert J. Niess's very fine study of *L'Oeuvre*, where Zola made effective use of the Pygmalion story: *Zola, Cézanne, and Manet: A Study of L'Oeuvre* (Ann Arbor: Univ. of Michigan Press, 1968), pp. 211-49.

## Chapter 3

[1]*Middlemarch*, 3 vols. (London: Hawarden Press, 1899), I, 2.

[2]*Noé*, in vol. 3 of *Oeuvres romanesques complètes*, ed. Robert Ricatte, Bibliothèque de la Pléiade (Paris: Gallimard, 1974), p. 642.

[3]Northrop Frye, "The Archetypes of Literature," in *Myth and Literature: Contemporary Theory and Practice,* ed. John B. Vickery (Lincoln: Univ. of Nebraska Press, 1966), p. 93.

[4]I previously discussed this usage (and the accompanying concept) of "image" in relation to Proust: *The Color-Keys to A la recherche du temps perdu* (Geneva: Droz, 1976), pp. 8-19.

[5]E.g., Jean Ricardou, "Naissance d'une fiction," in *Nouveau Roman: Hier, aujourd'hui,* II, 393-417; Alain Robbe-Grillet, "An Interview with Alain Robbe-Grillet," by Beverly Livingston, *Yale French Studies*, No. 57 (1979), 235. Still, despite Ricardou's and Robbe-Grillet's repeated insistence on the reader's liberty, their violent response to Jean Alter's study "Perspectives et modèles" (*Nouveau Roman: Hier, aujourd'hui*, I, 35-73), was indeed so categorical that Alter was led to wonder about "the terrorism in literature [which] tends to believe that one single explanation, that one single attitude delivers the only admissible meaning" (p. 72).

[6]See, e.g., Jean Ricardou's studies of Simon's *La Route des Flandres* and Soller's *Parc—Problèmes du nouveau roman* (Paris: Seuil, 1967), pp. 44-66, and Barthes' analysis of *Mobile*, "Littérature et discontinu," *Essais critiques* (Paris: Seuil, 1964), pp. 175-87.

[7]*Kabbalah and Criticism* (New York: Seabury, 1975), p. 46.

[8]*L'Oeuvre ouverte*, tr. C. Roux de Bézieux and A. Boucourechliev (Paris: Seuil, 1965), pp. 34-35. The same "closure" seems to exist in other formulations of "open works." For Heinrich Wölfflin, "The style of open form everywhere points out beyond itself and purposely looks limitless, although, of course, secret limits continue to exist, and make it possible for the picture to be self-contained in the aesthetic sense"— *Principles of Art History: The Problem of the Development of Style in Later Art,* tr. M. D. Hottinger, 7th ed. (New York: Dover, n.d.), p. 124. For Sharon Spencer, an open work collects "a variety of complementary and perhaps contradictory perspectives on the same subject"—*Space, Time and Structure in the Modern Novel* (Chicago: Swallow Press, 1971), p. 4. In such cases, the convergence would encourage closure. Another common definition has to do with a plot which projects beyond the confines of the novel. Not infrequently, the point of the accompanying study is to demonstrate that the work in question has no closure—e.g., Alan Friedman, "Suspended Form: Lawrence's Theory of Fiction in *Women in Love,*" in, Stephen J. Miko, ed., *Twentieth Century Interpretations of Women in Love: A Collection of Critical Essays* (Englewood Cliffs, N.J.: Printice-Hall, 1969), pp. 40-49. On considering the primary source, however, closure appears. In *Women in Love*, to turn to the instance Friedman studies, the novel ends when the pattern and the quality of possible relationships have been firmly established. As Hermann Broch put it, in respect to his own *Die Schlafwandler*, "After the material for character construction already provided, the reader can imagine it for

himself"—quoted from Spencer, *Space,* pp. 95-96. Charles Altieri's article, "Objective Image and Act of Mind in Modern Poetry," *PMLA*, 91 (1976), 101-14, provides penetrating insights into other varieties of modern closure in the midst of apparent openness.

[9]I return to *Composition No. 1* for a more developed discussion in chapter 8.

[10]*Pour un nouveau roman,* p. 20.

[11]Allan H. Pasco, "*Nouveau où Ancien Roman*: Open Structures and Balzac's *Gobseck,*" *Texas Studies in Literature and Language*, 20 (1978), 15-17.

[12](Princeton: Princeton Univ. Press, 1975).

[13]*Oeuvres complètes,* vol. 24 (Paris: Club de l'Honnête Homme, 1956), p. 81.

[14]John Bayley has discussed modern character as consciousness with acuity—"Character and Consciousness," *New Literary History,* 5 (1974), 225-35. Mary McCarthy has pointed out that one might even claim, on viewing modern characters, "[T]here are no people any more . . .—only human vectors with acceleration and force"—"Characters in Fiction," in *Critical Approaches to Fiction*, eds. Shiv K. Kumar and Keith McKean (New York: McGraw Hill, 1968), p. 80. In regard to Céard, see "Un Document retrouvé. 'M. Zola et *Germinal*' de Henry Céard," ed. Albert J. Salvan, *Cahiers Naturalistes*, No. 35 (1968), p. 58.

[15]Julia Kristeva, *Le Texte du roman: Approche sémiologique d'une structure discursive transformationnelle* (The Hague: Mouton, 1970), pp. 129-33. Neither Kermode—*The Sense of an Ending*, pp. 138-39—nor Culler—*Structuralist Poetics*, p. 218—would agree that fiction remains possible in such a case.

[16]Note appended to *Scènes de la vie privée, La Comédie humaine,* Bibliothèque de la Pléiade, XI (Paris: Gallimard, 1965), 165. Although he mentioned "certain minds [who] could reproach him for having so often dwelled at length on seemingly superfluous details" in the preface to this edition of the *Scènes de la vie privée* (p. 164), the insistence on detail in the note is senseless unless he means, as it seems, to stress the primary importance of description in creating the "picture."

[17]*Gobseck,* in *La Comédie humaine*, vol. 2 (Facsimile of the 1842 Furne edition corrected by Balzac; rpt. Paris: Les Bibliophiles de l'Originale, 1965), p. 375. All further references to *Gobseck* will be to this edition.

[18]"Les États successifs d'une nouvelle de Balzac: *Gobseck,*" *Revue d'Histoire Littéraire de la France*, 47e année (1947), p. 87.

[19]*Balzac* (Paris: Hachette, 1913), pp. 84-85, n. 1. Balzac's style continues to cause controversy, though of a different kind. See, my "Balzac in the Exegetic Mode... Alas!" *Virginia Quarterly Review*, vol. 53 (1977), pp. 160-65.

[20]For this summary, the following references have been particularly helpful: Mircea Eliade's *Patterns of Comparative Religion* (London: Sheed and Ward, 1958), and

his *Images and Symbols: Studies in Religious Symbolism* (London: Harvill, 1961); Paul Diel, *Le Symbolisme dans la mythologie grecque* (Paris: Pagot, 1952); Jean Chevalier and Alain Gheerbrant, *Dictionnaire des symboles: Mythes, rêves, coutumes, gestes, formes, figures, couleurs, nombres* (Paris: Robert Laffont, 1969).

[21] *La Clef des songes* (Paris: la Sirène, 1921), p. 149.

[22] *Rest Days: A Study in Early Law and Morality* (New York: Macmillan, 1916), p. 247.

[23] Diel, *Le Symbolisme*, p. 172. Jean-Pierre Richard discusses the symbolic implications of Gobseck's gold from a Marxist viewpoint—*Etudes sur le romantisme* (Paris: Seuil, 1970), p. 122, n. 21.

[24] Pp. 377, 379, 397, 419. I would not, however, dispute Pierre Abraham's further insight that Balzac frequently accompanied such qualities as cupidity, criminal passion, avarice, usury, and materialism with yellow—*Recherches sur la création intellectuelle. Créatures chez Balzac* (Paris: Gallimard, 1931), e.g., p. 163 and figure 5.

[25] *L'Esthétique du roman balzacien* (Paris: P.U.F., 1950), p. 129. Several years earlier, M. Bernard had stated: "Gobseck's name, with the harsh, grim ending, seems at first glance to derive from *gobe-sec*, arranged to square with the heartless, unscrupulous usurer's Dutch origins." He ends, however, by preferring the biographical explanation that Balzac was influenced by the name of the musician François-Joseph Gossec—"Autour de la *Comédie humaine*: Les Noms de personnes," *Études Classiques*, vol. 10 (1941), p. 347.

[26] "On Balzac's *Goriot*," *Symposium*, 8 (1954), 68-75; "Balzac's Frenhofer," *MLN*, 69 (1954), 335-38; "La Composition de *La Fille aux yeux d'or*," *Revue d'Histoire Littéraire de la France*, 56e année (1956), pp. 535-47; "Vautrin et ses noms," *Revue des Sciences Humaines*, fasc. 95 (1959), pp. 265-73.

[27] P. 378. Adrian Cherry quite properly emphasizes the similarity between the life of a nun and of Gobseck—"Balzac's 'Gobseck': A Character Study of a Usurer," *Language Quarterly*, 5 (1967), 6.

[28] P. 389. As Jean-Luc Seylaz suggests, the work insists on "society's blindness before Gobseck's exceptional traits"—"Réflexions sur Gobseck," *Etudes de Lettres*, 1 (1968), 301.

[29] I would consequently disagree with B. Lalande who considers Fanny a useless, though cleverly disguised, leftover from former versions—"Les Etats," *Revue d'Histoire Littéraire de la France*, 46e année (1939), p. 186; 47e année (1947), p. 70.
    Elsewhere, while pointing to the tight narrative structure of Gobseck—Prologue, Story 1, Interruption 1, Story 2, Interruption 2, Story 3, Epilogue—R. J. B. Clark argues persuasively for considering the story as a thematic opposition: order-disorder. I shall suggest below, however, that this and other related oppositions are subordinated to the image of Gobseck—"*Gobseck*: Structure, images, et signification d'une nouvelle de Balzac," *Symposium*, 31 (1977), 290-301.

[30]*Balzac lu et relu* (Neuchâtel: La Baconnière, 1965), p. 188.

[31]E.g., Claude Lévi-Strauss, *Structural Anthropology*, Anchor (Garden City, N.Y.: Doubleday, 1967), pp. 205-06, and *The Raw and the Cooked* (New York: Harper & Row, 1969), pp. 15-16. Octavio Paz expands the position to include poems, again in their fully recounted form—*Claude Lévi-Strauss o el nuevo festin de Esopo,* Volador (Mexico: Joaquín Mortiz, 1967), pp. 56-57. For an interesting application of the hypothesis, see, Djelal Kadir, "A Mythical Re-Enactment: Cortázar's *El Perseguidor,"* *Latin American Literary Review,* 2 (1973), 63-73.

[32]"A Study of Allusion: Barbey's Stendhal in 'Le Rideau cramoisi,' " *PLMA,* 88 (1973), 461-71; "Marcel, Albertine and Balbec in Proust's Allusive Complex," *Romanic Review,* 62 (1971), 113-26.

[33]Though I sympathize with the historicist Frederic R. Jameson's essay against ill-considered attacks on realism, I clearly cannot accept his blanket statement: "To prove Dickens was really a symbolist, Flaubert the first modernist, Balzac a myth-maker, and George Eliot some Victorian version of Henry James if not even of Dostoevsky, is an intellectually dishonest operation that skirts all of the real issues"— "Beyond the Cave: Demystifying the Ideology of Modernism," *Bulletin of the MMLA,* 8 (Spring 1975), 6.

[34]Ricardou is, of course, opposing such a simplification—*Nouveau Roman: Hier, aujourd'hui,* II, 43.

[35]Vol 9 of the previously cited Bibliophiles de l'Originale edition of *La Comédie humaine,* p. 237.

[36]J.-K. Huysmans, *Là-Bas* (1891), in *Oeuvres complètes,* t. 12, vol. 2 (Paris: Crès, 1930), p. 108.

[37](New York: Evergreen, 1966), p. 221.

[38]In the previously cited vol. 11 of the Pléiade edition of *La Comédie humaine,* p. 165.

[39]"The Fantastic in Fiction," tr. Vivienne Mylne, *Twentieth Century Studies,* No. 3 (1970), p. 88.

[40]For an introduction to this subject, vastly more complicated than my summary, see, e.g., Nigel Calder, *The Mind of Man* (New York: Viking Press, 1970), pp. 243-52; Norman Geschwind, "Language and the Brain," *Scientific American,* 226 (April 1972), 76-83; Doreen Kimura, "The Asymmetry of the Human Brain," *Scientific American,* 228 (March 1973), 70-78; Niels A. Lassen, David H. Ingvar and Erik Skinhøj, "Brain Function and Blood Flow,"*Scientific American,* 239 (October 1978), 62-71.

[41]Critics since Lessing's *Laokoön* (I think most notably of Apollinaire) have used time to distinguish between poetry and prose. Poetry, it is frequently argued, is atemporal, for it describes, while narrative prose is dominated by time and chronology.

Thus, description and narration are considered opposites. See, Marie-Jeanne Durry's discussion in *Guillaume Apollinaire: Alcools*, II (Paris: SEDES, 1964), 204-05. A related idea is clearly present in more recent critics who hitch the novel firmly to "action"— e.g., Philip Stevick's conclusion: "The history of the genre ever since [*Pamela, Clarissa, Joseph Andrews,* and *Tom Jones*] has tended to confirm the idea that a novel is a novel insofar as it is an action and as it ceases to be an action it becomes not a novel but something else"—"Introduction" to his ed. of *The Theory of the Novel*, p. 4. In a brilliant study, first published in 1945, Joseph Frank traces "the evolution of form in modern poetry and, more particularly, in the novel. For modern literature, as exemplified by such writers as T.S. Eliot, Erza Pound, Marcel Proust, and James Joyce, is moving in the direction of spatial form; and this tendency receives an original development in Djuna Barnes's remarkable book *Nightwood*. All these writers ideally intend the reader to apprehend their work spatially, in a moment of time, rather then as a sequence"— quoted from Frank's *The Widening Gyre: Crisis and Mastery in Modern Literature* (New Brunswick, N.J.: Rutgers Univ. Press, 1963), pp. 8-9. Frank gives a helpful history of the concepts under consideration here as they appeared in criticism, though I would suggest that image, or what he calls spatial, structure was by no means original with twentieth-century literature.

[42] In *Dictionary of World Literature*, ed. Joseph T. Shipley (New York: Philosophical Library, 1953), p. 93.

[43] "Frontières du récit," *Communications,* No. 8 (1966), p. 157.

[44] *Problèmes du nouveau roman,* p. 93.

[45] "L'Effet de réel," *Communications,* No. 11 (1968), p. 85.

[46] Ibid., pp. 84-89.

[47] "Fonction de la description romanesque: La Description de Rouen dans *Madame Bovary," Revue des Langues Vivantes*, 40 (1974), 132-49. This fact has been recognized with more frequency since Jean Ricardou's paper, "Naissance d'une fiction," in *Nouveau Roman: Hier, aujourd'hui*, II, 393-417, where the author claimed that his *La Prise/Prose de Constantinople* was "generated" by the elements which would appear on the cover when published by Les Editions de Minuit. Considerable attention has also been paid to one or more of a system of elements external to a text, which may be more or less integrated into the final version, but which form its nucleus. I think, for example, of the importance of Delacroix's *Entrée des croisées à Constantinople* to Ricardou's novel just cited or of the way Pierodi Cosimo's *The Death of Procris* becomes an integral part of the New Novelist's "Play"—see, Lynn Anthony Higgins, "Typographical Eros: Reading Ricardou in the Third Dimension," *Yale French Studies*, No. 57 (1979), pp. 180-94.

# Chapter 4

[1] Marcel Proust, *A la recherche du temps perdu,* I. 85.

[2] *Teoria y praxis de la novela* (Paris: Ediciones Hispanoamericanas, 1970), p. 31.

[3] *Zola et son temps: Lourdes—Rome—Paris* (Paris: Les Belles Lettres, 1961), pp. 57-58. For similar conclusions, see, e.g.: Gerhard Gerhardi, *"Germinal:* Mass Action and the Psychology of the Individual," *Studi di Letteratura Francese* (Florence: Biblioteca dell' 'Archivum Romanicum,' Serie I, vol. 123), 3 (1974), 155-56; Aimé Guedj, "Les Révolutionnaires de Zola," *Cahiers Naturalistes,* 14 (1968), 137; Jules Lemaître, "Emile Zola" (14 mars 1885), rpt. in *Les Contemporains: Etudes et portraits littéraires,* 1<sup>re</sup> série (1884 et 1885) (Paris: Boivin, n.d.), p. 279, where despite some hesitation, he concludes that the novel "does not contain an atom of hope or illusion." Guy Robert, *Émile Zola: Principes et caractères généraux de son oeuvre* (Paris: Belles Lettres, 1952), pp. 100-01, concludes that the destructive catastrophe will be followed by rebirth, a conclusion echoed by Jean-Louis Vissière, "Politique et prophétie dans *Germinal,"* *Cahiers Naturalistes,* 8 (1962), 167; Henri Marel, "A propos de *Germinal* et des *Rougon-Macquart,"* *Cahiers Naturalistes,* 19 (1973), 96; and Roger Ripoll, "L'Avenir dans *Germinal:* Destruction et renaissance," *Cahiers Naturalistes,* No. 50 (1976), 115-33. André Vial reminds us that "The novel is titled 'Germinal' in memory of an event which took place during the first Republic: on the 12th day of the month of Germinal during the year III, the famished people invaded the Assembly shouting, 'Bread, and the Constitution of '93' "—Germinal *et le 'socialisme' de Zola* (Paris: Editions Sociales, 1975), p. 90. For other references to critics who see the conclusion of *Germinal* in the bleakest of terms, see, e.g., Ripoll, "L'Avenir," pp. 115-16, n. 1; D. Sandy Petrey, "The Revolutionary Setting of *Germinal,"* *French Review,* 43 (1969), 61-62; and Elliott M. Grant, *Zola's* Germinal: *A Critical and Historical Study* (Leicester: Leicester Univ. Press, 1962), pp. 123, 124, 126.

[4] Grant, *Zola's* Germinal, p. 39. For similar opinions, see, e.g., Claude Abastado, *Émile Zola:* Germinal: *Analyse critique* (Paris: Hatier, 1970), p. 56; Pierre Aubéry, *Pour une lecture ouvrière de la littérature* (Paris: Editions Syndicalistes, 1969), p. 45; William Berg, "A Note on Imagery as Ideology in Zola's *Germinal,"* *Clio,* 2 (1972), 45; Patrick Brady, "Structuration archétypologique de *Germinal,"* *Cahiers Internationaux de Symbolisme* Nos. 24-25 (1973), p. 87; Marcel Girard, "L'Univers de *Germinal,"* *Revue des Sciences Humaines,* fasc. 69 (1953), 76; Martin Turnell, *The Art of French Fiction* (London: Hamish Hamilton, 1959), p. 135; Melvin Zimmerman, "L'Homme et la nature dans *Germinal,"* *Cahiers Naturalistes,* 18 (1972), 213.

[5] E.g., Irving Howe, "Zola, the Genius of *Germinal,"* *Encounter,* 34, No. 4 (April 1970), 57; Joseph Sungolowsky, "Vue sur *Germinal* après une lecture de *La Peste,"* *Cahiers Naturalistes,* No. 39 (1970), 47-48; Emile Tersen, "Sources et sens de *Germinal,"* *La Pensée,* 95 (1961), 88.

[6] Henry James, "Preface to *The Portrait of a Lady,"* in *The Art of the Novel: Critical Prefaces* (New York: Charles Scribner's Sons, 1950), p. 53.

[7]Girard, "L'Univers de *Germinal*," pp. 59-76; Philip Walker, "Prophetic Myths in Zola," *PMLA*, 74 (1959), 444-52; Girard's subsequent *"Germinal" de Zola* (Paris: Hachette, 1973), covers some of the same ground as his earlier article.

[8]"Univers," pp. 67-68.

[9]*Germinal*, in *Les Rougon-Macquart*, Bibliothèque de la Pléiade, III (Paris: Gallimard, 1964), 1249. All other references to this edition will be indicated parenthetically in the text.

[10]Jean-Pierre Davoine, "Métaphores animales dans *Germinal*," *Études Françaises*, 4 (1968), 392. William Berg notes that "as the strike progresses the animal imagery reveals a definite change in the miners—the 'herd' is seen as 'stampeding,' and comparisons with ferocious animals, particularly wolves, are far more frequent"—"A Note on Imagery," p. 44. Of the animals used to emphasize man's lot, the horses are doubtless the most important, and, as Carl G. Jung's comments on horses make clear, that is no accident. Horses are traditionally believed to have a close relationship with man. Jung puts it this way: " 'Horse' . . . [a]s an animal . . . represents the non-human psyche, the sub-human, animal side, and therefore the unconscious. This is why the horse in folklore sometimes sees visions, hears voices, and speaks . . . .As an animal lower than man it represents the lower part of the body and the animal drives that take their rise from there"—"Dream-Analysis in its Practical Application," in *Modern Man in Search of a Soul* (London: Kegan Paul, Trench, Trubner, 1941), p. 29. Perhaps this explains the choice of Chaval's name, for, as Rachelle A. Rosenberg points out, it is very close to the French word for horse—cheval—"The Slaying of the Dragon: An Archetypal Study of Zola's *Germinal*," *Symposium*, 26 (1972), 357. In an outstanding study of "The Function of Zola's Souvarine," which sheds light on the whole of *Germinal*, David Baguley suggests that the rabbit, Pologne, "is the martyred victim of the primordial, bacchanal instincts in man . . . . The rabbit, here the archetypal sacrificial victim of allegory (the *pharmakos*), as in Golding's tale, ends in the ultimate demonic process: cannibalism"—*Modern Language Review*, 66 (1971), 794.

[11]Zola's intuition that men, and not animals, are capable of imagination would be accepted by at least some current authorities. See, e.g., Paul Chauchard, "Comment fonctionne le cerveau humain," *Paris-Match*, No. 1185 (22 janvier 1972), p. 39.

Zola's insistence on the difference between men and animals is evident elsewhere as well. See, e.g., my article, "Literary History and Quinet in the Meaning of *La Faute de l'abbé Mouret*," *Forum for Modern Language Studies*, 14 (1978), 208-16.

[12]E.g., pp. 1277, 1380.

[13]Pp. 1339, 1376.

[14]E.g., pp. 1161-62.

[15]Pp. 1148-49, 1327, 1357.

[16]Pp. 1255, 1342-43, 1409.

[17]"Prophetic Myths," p. 450. Walker would, I think, have been more convincing had he extended his argument to include the Gigantomachy. He also believes that Zola's reference to Ceres in relation to Mme Hennebeau (p. 1304) is ironic. It seems to me that it should be read as a straightforward parallel. Ceres was sterile, and the world suffered, while Proserpina was hidden in the depths of the underworld. Mme Hennebeau is sterile, and she is a representative of the bourgeois class. The fact of her isolation from the people and her oblivion to them makes her a symbolic reincarnation of Ceres cut off from her soul-partner.

[18]E.g., Elliott M. Grant, *Zola's* Germinal, pp. 108-09; F. W. J. Hemmings, *Émile Zola,* 2nd ed. (Oxford: Oxford Univ. Press, 1966), p. 192.

[19]*Theogony,* in *Hesiod: The Homeric Hymns and Homerica,* tr. Hugh G. Evelyn-White, Loeb Classical Library (Cambridge, Mass.: Harvard Univ. Press, 1959), v. 633. Other quotations refer to this edition and make use of Evelyn-White's translation.

[20]*The Library,* tr. James George Frazer, Loeb Classical Library (Cambridge, Mass.: Harvard Univ. Press, 1939), I, vi, 1-2. Further references to Apollodorus will be to this edition; I use Frazer's translation.

[21]I quote Eliade from Walker's footnote discussion: "The *Ébauche* of *Germinal,*" *PMLA,* 80 (1965), 583, n. 36. Of course, the pattern is so common as to constitute a topos, if not an archetype. Albert B. Smith studies the "Variations on a Mythical Theme: Hoffmann, Gautier, Queneau and the Imagery of Mining," *Neophilologus,* 63 (1979), 179-86. He is interested in the hero leaving our world for the underworld, from which the *figura* returns victorious, full of new power. In addition to the archetypal pattern, Smith mentions several significant motifs. He is particularly drawn to the imagery of mining in Hoffmann, Gautier, and Queneau, but he also points to the "forbidding desolation" around the mines of *Die Bergwerke zu Falun* (1819). Readers of *Germinal* will also be struck by Gautier's "Pays Vert," which however exists below ground in *Le Preneur de rats de Hamelin.* In Zola's novel, of course, the *Côte-Verte* sits "like a miracle of eternal spring" in the middle of the burned out wasteland above Tartaret (p. 1395).

[22]Mircea Eliade, *Patterns in Comparative Religion,* p. 160.

[23]Pp. 1379-80. With considerable perspicacity, Colin Smethurst discusses the wide importance of their lovemaking, "clearly intended to be life-giving and liberating," which is contrasted to the sterile passions of the bourgeoisie and "linked emotionally with the notion of the miners becoming the seed of the future revolution"—*Emile Zola:* Germinal (London: Edward Arnold, 1974), pp. 51-52.
Several scholars have made what seems to me the incontrovertible suggestion that Etienne is here in a womb—Richard B. Grant, "Zola's *Germinal,*" *Explicator,* 18, No. 1 (Oct. 1959), item 37; Rosenberg, "Slaying of the Dragon," p. 358.

[24]P. 1328, see, also, 1460.

[25]Pp. 1279, 1339-40, 1380.

[26]"Prophetic Myths," p. 449.

[27]*The Metamorphoses,* tr. Rolfe Humphries (Bloomington: Indiana Univ. Press, 1963), Book I, p. 10.

[28]René Canat, *La Renaissance de la Grèce antique (1820-1850)* (Paris: Hachette, 1911); Charly Clerc, *Le Génie du paganisme* (Paris: Payot, 1926); E. Egger, *L'Hellénisme en France*, 2 vols. (Paris: Dider, 1896); Henri Peyre, *Bibliographie de l'Hellénisme en France: 1843-1870* (New Haven: Yale Univ. Press, 1932); Philip Walker, "Zola's Hellenism," *The Persistent Voice: Essays on Hellenism in French Literature*, ed. Walter Langlois (New York: New York Univ. Press, 1971); pp. 61-77.

[29]Ovid, *Metamorphoses*, Bk. III, p. 59. I refer to the Cadmus story rather than Jason, who also planted serpent's teeth, because of the thrashing death of Mars' snake. Given Zola's seeming love of Ovid, however—Philip Walker, "Zola, Myth, and the Birth of the Modern World," *Symposium,* 25 (1971), 214—it is not impossible that he also remembered the vivid episode of Jason dropping the serpent's teeth in the plowed ground behind the Colchian bulls:

> They grew, took on new forms, the way a baby
> Grows in the womb, in its slow time, and only
> Comes forth when fully formed, so, in the earth,
> Their pregnant mother, these forms of men were growing,
> And when they rose, they rose on teeming soil,
> Hundreds and hundreds, and what is even stranger
> Rose in full armor, brandishing their weapons,
> And the people saw them, aiming spears at Jason,
> And their hearts shook and faces paled. . . .
> But Jason, hurling a giant rock among them,
> Turned their fury from him to each other,
> And the earth-born brothers wounded and killed
> Each other.
>
> > *(Metamorphoses,* Bk. VII, p. 157)

[30]"Remarques sur l'image du serpent dans *Germinal,*" *Cahiers Naturalistes,* No. 31 (1966), 84-85. The relevant passages occur on pp. 1161, 1169, 1273, 1367, 1368, 1400, 1402, 1405, 1406, 1567.

[31]Zola said essentially the same thing in a letter of December 1885: "Be on guard, look under the ground, see these wretched people who work and suffer. There is perhaps still time to avoid the final catastrophes. But hurry up and be just; otherwise, this is the peril: the earth will open and nations will be swallowed up in one of the most frightful upheavals of History"—*Oeuvres complètes,* ed. Henri Mitterand, t. XIV (Paris: Cercle du Livre Précieux, 1970), p. 1449.

[32]Bibliothèque Nationale, Nouvelles acquisitions françaises, no. 10307, folio 421, quoted from the "Ébauche" or "Draft" published by Elliott Grant, *Zola's Germinal*, p. 177. See, also, the quotation in n. 31.

[33]Anchor Books (Garden City, N.Y.: Doubleday, 1957), p. 452.

[34]Bibliothèque Nationale, N.A.F. 10308, folio 358. See Elliott M. Grant's "Quelques précisions sur une source de *Germinal*: La Question ouvrière au 19ᵉ siècle, par Paul Leroy-Beaulieu," *Cahiers Naturalistes*, No. 22 (1962), 249-54.

[35]Pp. 1209, 1360-61.

[36]Pp. 1397, 1547. Cf., "And Jesus said unto them, See ye not all these things? Verily I say unto you, There shall not be left here one stone upon another, that shall not be thrown down" (Matt. 24: 2), and, *Germinal's* "Yes, it would be . . . the same frightful mob . . . sweeping the old world away beneath their overflowing, barbarian pressure. Fires would flame; not one stone of the cities would remain standing" (p. 1437).

[37]N. A. F. 10308, folio 352. While the resemblance which Zola perceived on reading is not explicitly in Laveleye, Paul Leroy-Beaulieu's *La Question ouvrière au XIXᵉ siècle* (Paris: Charpentier, 1872), which as the dossier indicates (N. A. F. 10308, fols. 357-63) Zola also read with care, makes the analogy at some length (pp. 12-15).

[38]P. 1591. For a study of the theme of germination, see, e.g., Pierre Moreau, *Germinal d'Émile Zola: Epopée et roman*, Les Cours de Sorbonne (Paris: Centre de Documentation Universitaire, 1954), p. 35; Abastado, *Émile Zola*, pp. 57-58.

[39]P. 1380. In this regard, one should perhaps consider Patrick Brady's suggestion: "The principal equine inhabitant of this hell is Bataille, a 'large white horse,' which may represent the pale horse of the Apocalypse, a presage of death"— "Structuration archétypologique," p. 91.
   Such Messianic prophecy as Souvarine's, cited in the next few lines of the text is, of course, common in the biblical prophets. Likewise, the specific injustices that so enrage Étienne are frequently named by the prophets: e.g., "Woe unto them that decree unrighteous decrees, and that write grievousness which they have prescribed, To turn aside the needy from justice, and to take away the right from the poor of my people, that widows may be their prey, and that they may rob the fatherless! And what will ye do in the day of visitation, and in the desolation which shall come from far? To whom will ye flee for help? And where will ye leave your glory?" (Isaiah 10: 1-3).

[40]"From the beginning, the end of the novel is not designed as a closure; it must open into the future, a menacing future for society, despite the momentary defeat of the workers . . . . Zola's preparatory work was in actual fact governed by an intention to show the future"—"L'Avenir dans *Germinal*," pp. 118-19.

[41]N. A. F. 10307, folio 496, quoted from Grant, *Zola's Germinal*, pp. 204-05.

[42]"Fonction narrative et fonction mimétique: "Les Personnages de *Germinal*," *Poétique*, No. 16, (1973), 482.

[43]Roland Barthes, *S/Z* (Paris: Seuil, 1970), pp. 26, 215-16, et passim.

44Victor Chklovski [Shklovsky], *Sur la théorie de la prose,* tr. Guy Verret (1929; tr. Lausanne: L'Âge d'Homme, 1973), pp. 211-44; Tomashevsky, "Thematics," in Lee T. Lemon and Marion J. Reis, eds. *Russian Formalist Criticism: Four Essays* (Lincoln, Neb.: Univ. of Nebraska Press, 1963), pp. 61-95.

45Maurice Z. Shroder, "The Novel as a Genre," in Stevick's *Theory of the Novel,* pp. 14, 16-17.

46Lawrence Harvey, "The Cycle Myth in *La Terre* of Zola," *Philological Quarterly,* 38 (1959), 89-95; Guy Robert, *La Terre d'Émile Zola: Étude historique et critique* (Paris: Les Belles Lettres, 1952), pp. 377-91.

47Bruce Morrissette's analysis of *La Jalousie* is seminal—*Les Romans de Robbe-Grillet* (Paris: Eds. de Minuit, 1963), pp. 111-47—though one should add the insight of Olga Bernal that the terminal mention of 6:30, being the time when A... and Franck left together, indicates that the narrator is about to begin again to relive the obsessive images of his jealous passion—*Alain Robbe-Grillet ou le roman de l'absence* (Paris: Gallimard, 1964), pp. 152-53.

48"*Nana*: Symbol and Action," *Modern Fiction Studies,* 9 (1963), 157-58. For another version of mirror structure, consider the two legs of Boule de Suif's trip, as analyzed in Mary Donaldson-Evans's remarkable article, "The Decline and Fall of Elisabeth Rousset: Text and Context in Maupassant's 'Boule de suif,'" *Australian Journal of French Studies,* 18 (1981), 16-34.

49The famous quotation, which Stendhal attributes to Saint-Réal (erroneously, authorities agree), concerns the realism of the novel—*Le Rouge et le noir,* ed. Henri Martineau (Paris: Garnier, 1960), p. 76.

## *Chapter 5*

1"André Gide," *Contemporary Literature,* 10 (1969), 118-19.

2The first editions carried the rubric "Novel," which, in 1911, Gide removed, apparently because his conception of the novel had changed. In 1910, he had written in a "Projet de Préface pour *Isabelle,*" "Why I took the care to entitle this little book a 'story' ['*récit*']? It was simply because it does not correspond to the idea I have of a novel—no more than *La Porte étroite* or *L'Immoraliste*—and I would not like people to be fooled. A novel, as I recognize or conceive it, bears a diversity of points of view, submitted to the diversity of characters that it puts on stage. In essence, it is a deconcentrated work"—*Oeuvres complètes d'André Gide,* ed. L. Martin-Chauffier, 15 vols. (Paris: N.R.F., 1932-39), VI, 361-62. Subsequent references to this edition will be cited, *O.C.* In his diary for June 17, 1923, he returned to the difficulty: "What I would like a novel to be? An intersection, a rendezvous of problems"—Gide, *Journal: 1889-1939,* Bibliothèque de la Pléiade (Paris: Gallimard, 1951), p. 760. Further references to this edition will be preceded by *J* I.

3*Portrait of André Gide* (New York: Knopf, 1953), p. 169. See, also, *J* I, p. 111.

[4]*O.C.*, IV, 187.

[5]*L'Immoraliste,* in *Romans, récits et soties, Oeuvres lyriques,* ed.Yvonne Davet and Jean-Jacques Thierry, Bibliothèque de la Pléiade (Paris: Gallimard, 1958), p. 368. Further references to this edition will be cited parenthetically.

[6]The first quotation is from *J* I, p. 132, the second from *J* I, p. 134.

[7]Published in, *O.C.*, IX, 331.

[8]Jean Hytier, *André Gide* (Paris: Charlot, 1945), p. 170.

[9]*O.C.*, XIII, 439-40.

[10]E.g., *J* I, p. 437.

[11]Jones, *L'Ironie dans les romans de Stendhal,* p. 66.

[12]W. Wolfgang Holdheim has convincingly argued that this opposition resides at the center of Gide's artistic theory and practice: *Theory and Practice of the Novel: A Study on André Gide* (Geneva: Droz, 1968).

[13]I summarize from Gide's important discussion of this problem in "Les Limites de l'art," *O.C.*, III, 399-409.

[14]J. C. Davies, *Gide: L'Immoraliste and La Porte étroite*, Studies in French Literature (London: Edward Arnold, 1968), p. 43.

[15]Stephen Ullmann, "The Development of Gide's Imagery," *The Image in the Modern French Novel: Gide, Alain-Fournier, Proust, Camus* (Cambridge: Cambridge Univ. Press, 1960), p. 30.

[16]*Gide* (New Brunswick, N.J.: Rutgers Univ. Press, 1963), p. 125.

[17]Since the publication of an abbreviated version of this study in 1973—"Irony and Art in Gide's *L'Immoraliste*," *Romanic Review*, 64 (1973), 184-203—three very interesting readings have appeared which insist that Michel is reliable, not a hypocrite, and not responsible. In "The Generativity Crisis of Gide's *Immoraliste*," *French Forum*, 2 (1977), 58-69, Laurence M. Porter argues that the "structural ordering principles of the *récit* express the inexorable logic of unconscious drives rather than Michel's defensive creation of a simulated fatality which can be blamed for his misdoings" (p. 66). Elsewhere he suggests that "the tight structure of *L'Immoraliste* reflects not hypocrisy, as some critics have misleadingly claimed, but rather, helplessness"—"Autobiography versus Confessional Novel: Gide's *L'Immoraliste* and *Si le grain ne meurt,*" *Symposium*, 30 (1976), 152. John T. Booker, "*The Immoralist* and the Rhetoric of First-Person Narration," *Studies in Twentieth Century Literature,* 2 (1977), 18, centers on the heavy, terminal use of the present tense, which he views as a "direct re-living of the recent past that underlines the increasing *reliability* of Michel as narrator. . . . Michel's gradual surrender to an unstructured re-creation of scenes in the present tense strips away the smooth veneer of his earlier narration and reveals

the real Michel." It seems to me that neither critic gives sufficient consideration to the fact that at the time *L'Immoraliste* was written, the devices especially in such dense clusters appearing in the work are incapable of gaining credence from the sophisticated reader for whom Gide wrote. The use of the present tense to increase immediacy is, of course, a device like the others. Furthermore, if what Porter calls the "implied author" is responsible for the structure—here I do not refer to Gide's markers but the diegesis itself—and hyperstylization, one wonders why, as I shall suggest further on, the pattern of symbols subverts the structure. The crux has to do with the degree of Gide's complexity. I would say that he was either extremely clumsy and amaturish (which I do not believe) or he was extraordinarily knowing, in which case one must investigate the possibility that a deeper reading will be rewarded.

The benefit of such a rich reading is evident in Arthur E. Babcock's fine study, *Portraits of Artists: Reflexivity in Gidean Fiction, 1902-1946* (Columbia, S.C.: French Literature Publications, 1982). His remarkable analyses demonstrate, I think conclusively, that the kind of sophisticated irony I find in *L'Immoraliste* (what he calls "reflexivity") represents "one of the sustaining principles of Gide's fiction."

[18]*Design and Truth in Autobiography* (Cambridge, Mass.: Harvard Univ. Press, 1960), pp. 189-90.

[19]Hermine de Saussure, *Rousseau et les manuscrits des Confessions* (Paris: Boccard, 1958), pp. 265-69; cf., Jean Starobinski, *Jean-Jacques Rousseau: La Transparence et l'obstacle* (Paris: Plon, 1957), p. 216; P. Moreau, "Remarques sur le style du 6$^e$ livre des *Confessions*," *Revue Universitaire*, 66 (1957), 81; and Charly Guyot, "Du manuscrit de Neuchâtel au manuscrit de Genève: Etude de quelques variantes du texte des *Confessions*," in, *Jean-Jacques Rousseau et son oeuvre: Problèmes et recherches: Commemoration et Colloque de Paris (16-20 octobre 1962) organisés par le Comité National pour la Commemoration de J.-J. Rousseau* (Paris: Klincksieck, 1964), pp. 33-46.

[20]The claim by itself is enough to arouse suspicions, as Boris Tomashevsky pointed out: "A system of realistic motivation quite often includes a denial of artistic motivation. The usual formula is, 'If this had happened in a novel, my hero would have done such and such, but since it really happened, here are the facts. . .' But the denial of the literary form in itself asserts the laws of artistic composition"— "Thematics," in, Lee and Reis, *Russian Formalist Criticism*, p. 85.

[21]Davies, *Gide*, pp. 40-51; Martin Turnell, *The Art of French Fiction: Prévost, Stendhal, Zola, Maupassant, Gide, Mauriac, Proust* (New York: New Directions, 1959), pp. 272-82; and Ullmann, *Image*, esp. pp. 2-4, 24, 30. Ullmann, who gives a bibliography of studies dealing with Gide's style (p. 3, n. 1), suggests pertinently, in respect to *L'Immoraliste*, "It could of course be argued that the novelist . . . could legitimately aim at a . . . style which would correspond to the narrator's character but would be transposed into a purer and more artistic key. Yet such a solution, whatever its advantages, is bound to affect verisimilitude, 'that willing suspension of disbelief for the moment, which constitutes poetic faith'" (p. 30). Ernst Bendz mentions *L'Immoraliste*'s numerous imperfect subjectives which "jar"—*André Gide et l'art d'écrire* (Paris: Messageries du Livre, 1939), p. 56.

[22]Such stylization is highly significant, as Rousseau well knew. He would have deleted the phrase. He did so in a similar case: "Mon style inégal et naturel, tantôt rapide et tantôt diffus, tantôt sage et tantôt fou, tantôt grave et tantôt gai fera lui-même partie de mon histoire" ["My uneven and natural style, sometimes rapid and sometimes diffuse, sometimes well-behaved and sometimes crazy, sometimes serious and sometimes gay will itself be a part of my story"]—Jean-Jacques Rousseau, *Oeuvres complètes,* Bibliothèque de la Pléiade, I (Paris: Gallimard, 1959), 1154. Rousseau apparently felt that the alternating, intertwined ternary and binary rhythms, perfectly rounded off and marked by the strong alliteration in [t], betrayed a master artist in perfect control of his media, rather than the sincere, truthful, artless soul he wished to portray. In any case, it does not appear in later versions of *Les Confessions.*

[23]Hytier, *Gide,* p. 184. Georges Kassaï, "Forme de phrase et forme de récit dans *l'Immoraliste,"* *Lettres Nouvelles,* septembre-octobre 1973, p. 163, notes that Michel starts from a point of fixity and, after his rise and fall, finds, if not fixity, at least the desire for it. Manfred Kusch, "The Gardens of *L'Immoraliste,"* *French Forum,* 4 (1979), p. 207, proposes viewing "the three segments of the story as stages in the formulation of an ideology: an ideology intuitively arrived at in part one, consciously defined in part two, and radically applied in part three."

[24]Elaine D. Cancalon sees, I think correctly, Michel's constant traveling as the symbol of "his quest for a personality created by multiple experience." The "vertigo" of his rapid trip south represents the failure of his ideal and "the complete disintegration of his character"—"Symbols of Motion and Immobility in Gide's Twin 'Récits,' " *Modern Language Review,* 66 (1971), 799. Marshall Lindsay sees *L'Immoraliste* as Michel's quest for life in the present, empty of either past or future—"Gide's Ethic of the Moment: *L'Immoraliste,"* *Nottingham French Studies,* 23 (1984), 24-36.

[25] *Gide,* pp. 34, 57.

[26]O.C., IV, 616. This was not the only time Gide was to make a similar statement about one of his characters. In reference to Edouard, he said, "I must carefully respect everything in Edouard that causes his inability to write his book. . . . True commitment is almost impossible for him. He is a dabbler [*amateur*], a failure" (*O.C.,* XIII, 42). This statement has always left me uneasy for I see nothing in *Les Faux-Monnayeurs* to make me believe that, indeed, Edouard cannot write his novel. For me, where Gide did not succeed in accomplishing his stated intention in his later novel, he succeeded admirably in *L'Immoraliste.* Still, if only because the letter to Scheffer was written after the publication of *L'Immoraliste,* Gide's a posteriori statement of intention should not be accepted without question. All too frequently, Gide's opinions and memories of his own works were to change as the years went by. Perhaps the most convincing evidence that Gide meant *L'Immoraliste* to appear artificial may be found in the work itself.

[27]*Art of French Fiction*, p. 257.

[28]Pierre Lafille, *André Gide romancier* (Paris: Hachette, 1954), p. 23.

[29]*O.C.*, III, 407-09.

[30]*O.C.*, XIII, 440.

[31]*Theory*, pp. 190-212.

[32]*André Gide* (Cambridge, Mass.: Harvard Univ. Press, 1951), p. 99.

[33]Robert Goodhand, "The Religious Leitmotif in *L'Immoraliste*," *Romanic Review,* 57 (1966), 274-76.

[34]Neither the word, "unconscious" nor the psychic phenomenon it represents were unknown to French psychology or letters prior to the period in which Gide wrote *L'Immoraliste*. See, Elizabeth Czoniczer, *Quelques antécédents de "A la recherche du temps perdu": Tendances qui peuvent avoir contribué à la cristallisation du roman proustien* (Geneva: Droz, 1957), pp. 75-81. Although Germaine Brée uses different vocabulary, she has pointed to the same conflict by emphasizing the importance of Michel's subconscious—*Gide*, pp. 124, 128, 137, 138.

[35]See Gide's comments, e.g., *J* I, pp. 1051-52. In a letter to Pastor Ferrari, Gide talked of the dissolution of Saul's personality in *Saül* and Michel's "surrender *to* self, which is precisely the opposite of that surrender *of* self that the Gospel teaches"— *O.C.*, XV, 532.

[36]Gide returns again and again to the question of "influence"—e.g., *J* I, p. 739; *O.C.*, XIII, 440-43. Before the publication of *L'Immoraliste,* Gide became acquainted with the work of Nietzsche and Dostoevski, to name but two. Affinities with these authors and others are evident in *L'Immoraliste*. One even wonders whether the influence of the Greek and Latin tradition has not been as important in this *récit* as his religious training. Gide himself suggested: "The big influence that perhaps I *underwent* is that of Goethe, and I am not certain whether my admiration for Greek literature and Hellenism would not have even sufficed to counterbalance my early Christian formation" (*J* I, p. 859).

[37]For a more comprehensive study of Gide's names, see: A. H. Pasco and Wilfrid J. Rollman, "The Artistry of Gide's Onomastics," *MLN*, 86 (1971), 523-31.

[38]E.g., the discussion between the narrator-protagonist and Angèle about symbols in *Paludes,* in *Romans, récits et soties,* p. 94, and Carola's delightfully ubiquitous cufflinks emblazoned with four encircled cats' heads. From Lafcadio, after going full circle, one of them returns to him.

[39]For the symbology in the following pages, the most helpful references have been: Carl G. Jung, et al., *Man and His Symbols;* Jung, *Psychology and Alchemy*; J. E. Cirlot, *A Dictionary of Symbols*; Paul Diel, *Le Symbolisme dans la mythologie grecque*; Ernst and Johanna Lehner, *Folklore and Symbolism of Flowers, Plants and Trees*; Harold Bayley, *The Lost Language of Symbolism,* 2 vols. (London: Williams and Norgate, 1912); and, of course, the extremely important works by Nietzsche, esp., *The Birth of tragedy, Beyond Good and Evil, On the Genealogy of Morals,* and *Thus Spoke Zarathustra,* all in Walter

Kaufmann's translations. For further work on Gide's symbols, see Robert F. O'Reilly's excellent article, "Ritual, Myth, and Symbol in Gide's *L'Immoraliste*," *Symposium,* 28 (1974), 346-55.

[40]Pp. 387, 396, 467.

[41]Pp. 397, 467.

[42]P. 371. Nietzsche's reverberating echoes are impossible to ignore in conjunction with the light and darkness imagery and Michel's adhesion to the night. Consider Zarathustra's temptation, thirst, rather, for the night: "Light am I; ah, that I were night! But this is my loneliness that I am girt with light. Ah, that I were dark and nocturnal! How I would suck at the breasts of light! . . . But I live in my own light; I drink back into myself the flames that break out of me. I do not know the happiness of those who receive; and I have often dreamed that even stealing must be more blessed than receiving. This is my poetry, that my hand never rests from giving; this is my envy, that I see waiting eyes and the lit-up nights of longing. Oh, wretchedness of all givers! . . . A hunger grows out of my beauty: I should like to hurt those for whom I shine; I should like to rob those to whom I give; thus do I hunger for malice"—*Thus Spoke Zarathustra: A Book for All and None,* trans. Walter Kaufmann (New York: Viking, 1966), pp. 105-06.

[43]Critics have made a great deal of the number three in *L'Immoraliste*. There is no question about its importance, but it should also be noted that one and two appear more frequently. Four, five, six, eight, twelve, fifteen, twenty and one hundred occur a significant number of times. Gide's use of numerology deserves a monograph. His understanding of the symbolic import of numbers is revealed throughout his work. Lafcadio says, for example, "Thirty-four Verneuil street, . . .four and three, seven— the number is good" (*Les Caves du Vatican,* in *Romans, récits et soties*, p. 732). Indeed it is. Seven, the number Lafcadio reaches through mystic addition, symbolizes perfect order. As Germaine Brée pointed out, this number occurs frequently in *Le Voyage d'Urien (Gide,* p. 47).

[44]Pp. 406, 408.

[45]Pp. 406, 408, 410.

[46]Pp. 467, 468, 469, 470.

[47]P. 387. In this regard, I would agree with Hippolytus Dority who links the brown skin of the children to the earth-colored water—"Les Images de la nature dans *L'Immoraliste,*" *Études Littéraires,* 2 (1969), 315.

[48]Pp. 453, 459, 461, 465.

[49]"Religious," p. 276.

[50]"Generativity," p. 66.

[51]*O.C.*, III, 405.

[52]Martin Turnell makes a similar admission, joining Porché and myself: "I can think of no other work of comparable length which requires quite the same desperate effort to 'get through.' The truth is that there is a monstrous element which makes parts of it unbearable" (*The Art of French Fiction*, p. 257).

[53]*O.C.*, XIII, 439-40.

## Chapter 6

[1]Quoted from Victor Erlich, *Russian Formalism: History-Doctrine*, 3rd ed. (The Hague: Mouton, 1969), p. 252.

[2]Thomas S. Kuhn, *The Structure of Scientific Revolutions,* 2nd ed., Vol. II, no. 2 of the *International Encyclopedia of Unified Science* (Chicago: Univ. of Chicago Press, 1970).

[3]*J.-K. Huysmans devant la critique en France (1874-1960)* (Paris: Klincksieck, 1970), p. 177.

[4]Robert Baldick, *The Life of J.-K. Huysmans* (Oxford: Clarendon, 1955); Marcel Cressot, *La Phrase et le vocabulaire de J.-K. Huysmans* (Paris: Droz, 1938).

[5]Victor Brombert, "Huysmans et la Thébaïde raffinée, "*La Prison romantique: Essai sur l'imaginaire* (Paris: José Corti, 1975), pp. 153-74; François Livi, *J.-K. Huysmans*: *A rebours et l'esprit décadent* (Paris: Nizet, 1972).

[6]"J.-K. Huysmans' *A Rebours*: A Study of Structure, Metaphor and Artifice," unpublished Ph.D. Dissertation: Columbia University, 1966, p. 24. The opinion is repeated in her "Structural Techniques in *A rebours,"* *French Review*, 49 (1975), 222-33. Of course, Weinreb is not alone in this opinion: see, e.g., H. Brunner and J. L. de Coninck, *En marge d'A rebours* (Paris: Dorbon-aîné, 1929), p. 75; and David Mickelson, "*A rebours*: Spatial Form," *French Forum*, 3 (1978), 49-51.

[7]*Travaux de linguistique et de littérature,* 11, No. 2 (1973), 61-70.

[8]Issacharoff, *Huysmans devant la critique*, pp. 16, 78-82.

[9]Lucien Descaves, "Note" to *En rade* by J.-K. Huysmans, *Oeuvres complètes de J.-K. Huysmans,* vol. 9 (Paris: Crès, 1929), p. 275.

[10]*Joris-Karl Huysmans* (New York: Twayne, 1968), pp. 67-68. Some have pointed to the growing spirituality which will mark the later Catholic—e.g., Marcel Lobet, *J.-K. Huysmans ou le témoin écorché* (Lyon: E. Vitte, 1960), p. 57. Others emphasize its naturalistic traits. For Ernest Seillière, "It is a return to the driest and most trifling naturalism"—*J.-K. Huysmans* (Paris: Grasset, 1931), p. 113. The baron continues on the same page to scold Huysmans from aristocratic heights for the bad taste of the ptomaine sequence. Léon Daudet—*A propos de J.-K. Huysmans* (Paris: Cadran, 1947), p. 15—and Italo Gotta—"Introduction," *A vau-l'eau* by Huysmans (Rome: Angelo Signorelli, 1956), p. 33—consider it a sort of "regression." Some seem to find this

renewed naturalism its only virtue. Henry R. T. Brandreth believes that "Huysmans' description of the delapidated château, although an exaggeration of its actual state and even more so of the dwelling des Esseintes remembers as a youth, is a masterpiece"—*Huysmans* (New York: Hillary House, 1963), p. 42—while, for Maxwell A. Smith, "The only interest of this work, which mitigates at times its yawning ennui, is its sombre atmosphere of horror, enhanced by the sinister description of a ruined castle, the nocturnal apparition of the terrifying bats [*sic*; read: owls] . . . the pathological disease of Mme Marles, and finally the grim death struggle of the cat, not one of whose convulsions we are spared"—"Joris Karl Huysmans (1848-1907)," *French Review*, 11 (1938), 297-98. Aside from the rage to categorize *En rade*, these comments reveal a dominant interest in the subject matter of the book, Huysmans did not mince words in respect to others of the same disposition, e.g., those who wrote the "Manifeste" against Zola's *La Terre*: "They begin again the stupidity of discussions about subjects, about words, because . . , in short, it is the fart and word shit which offends them!"—Letter 53, dated "[around 20 August 1887]" by Pierre Lambert in his edition of *Lettres inédites à Emile Zola* (Geneva: Droz, 1953), p. 129. It matters not at all that one *appreciates* the book for such elements as the castle, the owls, the convulsions. The heart of the novel lies elsewhere. It is more accurate, if one is interested in trends and influences, to suggest that Huysmans was struggling for his own style. The result in *En rade* has overtones of naturalism and of Baudelaire—see, Pierre Cogny, *J.-K. Huysmans à la recherche de l'unité* (Paris: Nizet, 1953), pp. 110-11. In addition, it foreshadows surrealism—Pierre Cogny, "Introduction" to Lambert's edition, *Lettres inédites à Emile Zola*, p. xi; J. H. Matthews develops the point in "J.K. Huysmans: *En rade* (1887)," in his *Surrealism and the Novel* (Ann Arbor: Univ. of Mich. Press, 1966), pp. 28-40. It should, however, be pointed out that neither Cogny nor Matthews feel Huysmans achieved this integration in *En rade*—Cogny, *A la recherche de l'unité*, pp. 116-17; Matthews, "*En rade* and Huysmans' Departure from Naturalism," *L'Esprit Créateur*, 4 (1964), 93.

[11]E.g., Ridge, *Huysmans*, p. 68; Smith, "Joris Karl Huysmans," p. 301; Seillière, *J.-K. Huysmans*, p. 113; Albert Thibaudet, *Histoire de la littérature française de 1789 à nos jours* (Paris: Stock, 1936), p. 378.

[12]E.g., P. Cogny speaks of "a crisis of depression"—*A la recherche de l'unité*, p. 115; Brandreth of "unreleaved gloom"—*Huysmans*, p. 43; Gotta of "the theme of the most pessimistic despondency"—*A vau l'eau*, p. 33; Seillière of "the constantly heart-rending . . . impression"—*J.-K. Huysmans*, p. 113; and Henri Bachelin of a "song of nihilism"—*J.-K. Huysmans: Du naturalisme littéraire au naturalisme mystique* (Paris: Perrin, 1926), p. 181.

[13]In his edition of the *Lettres inédites à Jules Destrée* (Geneva: Droz, 1967), p. 110, n. 3.

[14]*Lettres inédites à Émile Zola*, p. 12. Dated by Lambert "[about June 2, 1887]."

[15]*Surrealism*, p. 32.

[16]*Lettres inédites à Jules Destrée*, p. 100. Dated by Vanwelkenhuyzen "[end Nov. 1886]." Later, he tells Gustave Guiches, "*En rade* has just been a great passion for me. I sank in it with intoxication, in the garbage of souls and the nothingness of things, but

it's all over! I don't want any more of naturalism's pigsty!"—quoted from Emmanuel
Malbay, "J.-K. Huysmans et l'alchemie," *Bulletin de la Société J.-K. Huysmans,* no. 45-46
(1963), p. 31. Huysmans's affair with *En rade* does indeed seem a passion, excluding
neither excitement, obsession, complacency, nor disgust. See, also, his letters of 17
October 1886 and 2 December 1886 to Destrée, *Lettres inédites à Jules Destrée,* pp. 90,
102.

[17]Paul Valéry, *Tel Quel,* in vol. II of *Oeuvres,* p. 557.

[18]Matthews, "Huysmans' Departure," p. 91; *Surrealism and the Novel,* p. 35.

[19]P. 94 of the edition cited in n. 9. All references to *En rade* will be to this edition.

[20]Françoise Gaillard shares this view: "The bedroom is for Jacques Marle[s], as
for all Huysmansian heros, the place of autoregulation, a model of domestic economy
that secures one against the disordered expenditure of the great social machine.
Reduce exchanges to a minimum, live at low temperatures beside a fire which you
economize by covering it with cinders, such is the unsatisfactory solution of a lower
middle class person who organizes his survival on what is undoubtedly the fringes of
the system, but on fringes created by the system"—"*En rade,* ou le roman des énergies
bloquées," in *Le Naturalisme,* ed. Pierre Cogny, Colloque du Centre Culturel International
de Cerisy-La-Salle [30 juin-10 juillet 1976] (Paris: 10/18, 1978), pp. 275-76. In a
fascinating study of water imagery, Mireille Favier-Richoux reaches a similar
conclusion in regard to Jacques's goals and his failure in achieving them—"Le Thème
de l'eau dans *En rade* de Huysmans," *Bulletin de la Société J.-K. Huysmans,* 16 (1978), 42-
60. As I shall make clear, I view these conclusions as excellent descriptions of Jacques
Marles's state at the beginning, but not at the end, of his stay at the château de Lourps.

[21]The following works have been particularly helpful: Chevalier and Gheerbrant,
*Dictionnaire des symboles*; J. E. Cirlot, *A Dictionary of Symbols,* tr. Jack Sage (New York:
Philosophical Library, 1962); Ernst and Johanna Lehner, *Folklore and Symbolism of
Flowers, Plants and Trees* (New York: Tudor, 1960); Edward A. Armstrong, *The Folklore of
Birds: An Enquiry into the Origin & Distribution of some Magico-Religious Traditions,* 2nd ed.
(New York: Dover, 1970); Carl G. Jung, et al., *Man and His Symbols* (New York:
Doubleday, 1964); Jung, *Psychology and Alchemy,* vol. 12 of *The collected Works of C. G. Jung,*
tr. R. F. C. Hull (London: Routledge, 1953); Mircea Eliade, *Myths, Dreams and Mysteries*
(London: Harvill, 1960); Isaac Myer, *Qabbalah: The Philosophical Writings of Solomon Ben
Yehudah Ibn Gebirol or Avicebron* (1888; rpt. New York: Ktav, 1970); Eliphas Lévi, *Dogme et
rituel de la haute magie,* 2 vols. (Paris: Baillière, 1856); his *La Clef des grands mystères* (Paris:
Baillière, 1861); his *Histoire de la magie* (Paris: Baillière, 1860); his *Fables et symboles avec
leur explication* (Paris: Baillière, 1862); his *La Science des esprits* (Paris: Baillière, 1865);
Frédéric Portal, *Des couleurs symboliques dans l'antiquité, le moyen-âge et les temps modernes*
(Paris: Treuttel et Würtz, 1837); Martin Anton Del Rio, *Les Controverses et recherches
magiques,* tr. André Duchesne (Paris: I. Petit-Pas, 1611); Paracelsus, *Selected Writings,* ed.
Jolande Jacobi (New York: Pantheon, 1951); Adolphe Franck, *La Kabbale ou la
Philosophie des Hébreux,* (Paris: Hachette, 1843).

[22]Arthur Symons, who dates Huysmans's symbolism from *En route,* has an
interesting discussion of its meaning and importance to "The Later Huysmans": "In
*La Cathédrale* Huysmans does but carry further the principle which he had perceived in

*En route*, showing, as he does, how inert matter, the art of stones, the growth of plants, the unconscious life of beasts, may be brought under the same law of the soul, may obtain, through symbol, a spiritual existence. He is thus but extending the domain of the soul while he may seem to be limiting or ignoring it; and Durtal may well stand aside for a moment, in at least the energy of contemplation, while he sees, with a new understanding, the very sight of his thoughts, taking life before him, a life of the same substance as his own. When is Symbolism if not an establishing of the links which hold the world together, the affirmation of an eternal, minute, intricate, almost invisible life, which runs through the whole universe? Every age has its own symbols; but a symbol once perfectly expressed, that symbol remains, as Gothic architecture remains the very soul of the Middle Ages. To get at the truth which is all but the deepest meaning of beauty, to find that symbol which is its most adequate expression, is in itself a kind of creation; and that is what Huysmans does for us in *La Cathédrale*. More and more he has put aside all the profane and accessible and outward pomp of writing for an inner and more severe beauty of perfect truth. He has come to realize that truth can be reached and revealed only by symbol. Hence, all that description, that heaping up of detail, that passionately patient elaboration: all means to an end, not, as you may hastily incline to think, ends in themselves"—*The Symbolist Movement in Literature*, 2nd. ed. (London: Constable, 1911), pp. 145-46.

[23]*A rebours*, vol. 7 of his *Oeuvres complètes* (Paris: Crès, 1929), p. xi.

[24]For a very fine article which demonstrates the potential of such an approach, see, Angela Nuccitelli, "*A rebours*'s Symbol of the 'Femme-Fleur': A Key to des Esseintes's Obsession," *Symposium*, 28 (1974), 336-45.

[25]Claire Wade remarks that in Huysmans's decadent novels, by which she means *A rebours*, *En rade*, and *Là-Bas*, "Although the concrete elements of the visual world still retained their force and dynamism, they came to serve primarily as a springboard for the imagination and sensitivity of the human being observing them"—"The Contribution of Color and Light to Differing Levels of Reality in the Novels of Joris-Karl Huysmans," *Symposium*, 28 (1974), 371.

[26]*Dogme et rituel*, I, 120.

[27]In another context, Ricardou discusses the ways of joining two sequences. If one makes use of a formula like "A week later," the hiatus is effectively hidden. "*Passing the hiatus in silence is less slipping one over than pointing it out*. Far from receiving the buffer of a few intermediary words between them, the two joined sequences remain separated by an abrupt emptiness that the text crosses only by knocking one against the other. *It is a process for discontinuity*"—*Le Nouveau Roman*, p. 77.

[28]Although the Book of Esther, including precious stones, columns, etc., seems the most convincing source, scholars have attempted to go elsewhere. Seillière suggests: "The dreams . . . seem to be the reminiscences of Flaubert's *Saint-Antoine* and of the bizarre visions that unroll there"—p. 113. For Helen Trudgian, on the other hand, "It appears possible, if not probable, that Hello furnished Huysmans with the essential and perhaps ostentatious décor for this palace"—*L'Esthétique de J.-K. Huysmans* (Paris: Conard, 1934), p. 205. Cogny, as already noted, proposes Baudelaire—*A la recherche*, pp. 111-12.

[29]Porphyrius, *On Abstinence from Animal Food*, bk. ii, § 53, in *Select Works of Porphyry,* tr. Thomas Taylor (London: Thomas Rodd, 1823), p. 85.

[30]Ibid., bk. ii, § 41, p. 78.

[31]Paracelsus, *Selected Writings*, p. 209.

[32]Bronze, as well, symbolizes unity, for it represents the marriage of sun and moon, water and fire. As with most symbols, it also has the negative side. See, e.g., Hesiod's account of the bronze race: *The Works and Days*, vv. 140-56.

[33]*Histoire de la magie*, p. 62.

[34]*Les Mystères du verbe* (Paris: Chacornac, 1908), pp. 159-60.

[35]Eliade, *Patterns in Comparative Religion*, p. 173.

[36]Huysmans went to some trouble to make the moon of the dream correspond to the lunar information of the day. See, Pierre Lambert, "Un Homme est allé dans la lune en 1886!...Mais c'était J.-K. Huysmans, et il rêvait," *Figaro Littéraire*, 11 January 1958, pp. 1, 7.

[37]*On the Homeric Cave of the Nymphs*, § 13, in the previously cited *Select Works*, p. 194.

[38]The strangely garbed creature is prepared by a print Jacques saw at Antoine's (p. 198).

[39]Portal, *Couleurs*, p. 300.

[40]Huysmans will, of course, exploit much of this imagery again. In *Là-bas* (1891), for example, Des Hermies and Durtal, while going up in the towers of Saint-Sulpice to visit Carhaix, "found themselves on a wooden ledge above an empty space on the plank curb of a double shaft, one of which was bored beneath their feet and the other raised above them"—Huysmans, *Là-bas*, I, 48. In some cases *En rade* contains only a mention of what will later function as a central image. *En rade*, for example, has a bell, "but its clapper did not strike the metal, and yet strange sounds could be heard reflected back by the tower's echoes" (p. 217). Jacques does not understand the bell which communicates divine will. In *Là-bas*, however, the bells have enormous importance, as is widely recognized, and Carhaix says, among other things, "At one time in the forbidden sciences [i.e., cabalism and alchemy] bells played a role. The art of predicting the future with their sounds is one of the most unknown and most abandoned branches of the occult"—*Là-bas*, i. 114. On other occasions, *Là-bas* contains a mere mention of an image which Huysmans previously exploited. Des Hermies points out, for instance, to Gévigney and Durtal that "Paracelsus was one of the most extraordinary practitioners of occult medicine. He knew the now forgotten mysteries of blood, the still unknown medical effects of light. Professing, like the cabalists moreover, that human beings are composed of three parts: of a material body, a soul, and a perisprit (also called an astral body), he especially looked after the latter and reacted against the carnal, exterior envelope by procedures that have either lost their standing or become incomprehensible. He treated wounds by caring not for

the tissues but for the blood which came out"—*Là-bas*, ii, 230. Although Paracelsus receives only passing mention in *En rade* (p. 228), the cabalists' idea of the three centers is, as this chapter attempts to demonstrate, the basis for the novel's metaphorical structure.

[41] Eliphas Lévi, *Fables et symboles*, pp. 294-95.

[42] Especially in respect to those who pay little attention to entire contexts (i.e., the whole work), Huysmans's practice encourages the grossest kind of error. Gaston Bachelard, for example, who treats the materials of literature as symbolic representations of the artist's psyche, devotes a large portion of a chapter of *La Terre et les rêveries de la volonté* (Paris: José Corti, 1948), pp. 205-20, to *En rade*. He formulates, he says, "[T]he material dialectics that Huysmans vivified with these two terms: pus and slag" (ibid., p. 206), directing his attention primarily to the second dream where Jacques and Louise wander on the moon. According to Bachelard, "By softening Huysmans's pages somewhat, we would find real impressions, genuine dreams once again" (ibid., p. 209). Since an experienced psychologist "can . . . recognize [in the lunar dream] a 'Medusa complex,' a desire for the evil kind of hypnotism that with a word or look could control others at the very source of their beings" (ibid., p. 208), Bachelard does not hesitate to apprehend Huysmans's "ill-intentioned desire to project his hostility, . . .*mute fury, petrified anger*, blocked suddenly at the instant of its excess" (ibid., pp. 208-09).

Bachelard feels no need to integrate the elements that interest him into the whole, nor indeed does he hesitate to elevate passages above the level of importance indicated by the text. He states, for example, "In using the very terms of Huysmans, we can say that the root of the petrified vine is 'a subterranean thread functioning in the obscurity of the soul' and that by following its path the dreamer 'suddenly [sees] his forgotten cellars [illuminated], tying together the storerooms that have been unoccupied since childhood' " (ibid., p. 219). It seems worth mentioning that this is *not* Huysmans speaking, rather one of his creations and that this represents but one of Jacques's speculations, neither more nor less important than the others (cf., pp. 55-62). In addition, it should be pointed out that Bachelard's conclusions correspond poorly with the witnesses still available from Huysmans's day—excepting, of course, the less than trustworthy remarks of people like Léon Bloy and Remy de Gourmont.

[43] *Maximen und Reflexionen*, no. 1047, quoted from, Kurt Weinberg, *On Gide's Prométhée* (Princeton, N.J.: Princeton Univ. Press, 1972), p. 12.

## Chapter 7

[1] Marcel Proust, *A la recherche du temps perdu*, eds. Pierre Clarac and André Ferré, 3 vols., Bibliothèque de la Pléiade (Paris: Galliimard, 1954), I, 382.

[2] "Marcel Proust: Witness to a Dissolving Dream," *The Christian Science Monitor*, 10 July 1971, p. 9.

[3] *Correspondence générale*, vol. 3 (Paris: Plon, 1932), p. 306. Similar statements are to be found in *A la recherche*, II, 397; III, 899.

[4]Howard Moss, *The Magic Lantern of Marcel Proust* (New York: Macmillan, 1962), p. 2.

[5]Gaëtan Picon, *Lecture de Proust* (Paris: Mercure de France, 1963), pp. 9-10.

[6]In my *The Color-Keys to A la recherche du temps perdu* (Geneva: Droz, 1976), pp. 5-6.

[7]*Marcel Proust: The Fictions of Life and of Art* (New York: Oxford Univ. Press, 1965), p. 212.

[8]*Le Symbole littéraire: Essai sur la signification du symbole chez Wagner, Baudelaire, Mallarmé, Bergson et Marcel Proust* (Paris: Corti, 1941), p. 169.

[9]*Sur Proust: Remarques sur A la recherche du temps perdu,* Bibliothèque Médiations (Paris: Denoël-Gonthier, 1970), p. 33.

[10]Albert Feuillerat's attempt to reconstruct an "original" version, free of the seeming irrelevancies, was predicated on the belief that the novel, as published, included large quantities of unnecessary material—*Comment Marcel Proust a composé son roman* (New Haven, Conn.: Yale Univ. Press, 1934). Robert Vigneron likewise discusses the "compromised" order of the published text—"Structure de *Swann*: Combray ou le cercle parfait," *Modern Philology*, 45 (1948), 190—and Henri Peyre states that the *A la recherche* we know is "liberally encumbered with digressions and extraneous accretions"— *French Novelists of Today* (New York: Oxford Univ. Press, 1967), p. 76.

[11]Letter 161, 22 July 1922, in *Marcel Proust et Jacques Rivière: Correspondance: 1914-1922,* ed. Philip Kolb (Paris: Plon, 1955), p. 265.

[12]Marcel Proust, "Journées de lecture" (1905), rpt. in *Contre Saint-Beuve; Précédé de Pastiches et mélanges; Et suivi de Essais et articles*, eds. Pierre Clarac and Yves Sandre, Bibliothèque de la Pléiade (Paris: Gallimard, 1971), p. 178. Subsequent references to materials published in this edition will be preceded by *CSB*.

[13]E.g., II, 949, III, 553-54.

[14]I have discussed this character and her ramifications in: "Albertine's Equivocal Eyes," *Australian Journal of French Studies*, 5 (1968), 257-62; and in: "Marcel, Albertine and Balbec in Proust's Allusive Complex," *Romanic Review*, 62 (1971), 113-26.

[15]*Sur Proust*, p. 34.

[16]Chapter x of my previously cited *The Color-Keys*. For "Verdurin," Gérard Genette, "Proust et le langage indirect," *Figures II: Essais* (Paris: Seuil, 1969), p. 243, has suggested *"via Duras."*

[17]See, J. Wayne Conner, "On Balzac's Goriot," *Symposium*, 8 (1954), 70.

[18]Anna Louise Frey, *The Swan-Knight Legend* (Nashville, Tn.: George Peabody College, 1931), pp. 5-6.

[19]*Sur Proust*, p. 199. Similar opinions are to be found in such early critics as Paul Souday: "It seems to us that the thick volume by M. Marcel Proust is not composed and that it is as excessively long as it is chaotic, but that it encloses some precious pieces with which the author could have formed an exquisite little book," and "Certain murky episodes do not have the excuse of being necessary"—*Marcel Proust* (Paris: Kra, 1927), pp. 11 and 13 respectively.

[20]E.g., Jean Rousset, *Forme et signification: Essais sur les structures littéraires de Corneille à Claudel* (Paris: J. Corti, 1962), pp. 135-70; Louis Bolle, *Marcel Proust ou le complexe d'Argus* (Paris: Bernard Grasset, 1967), pp. 216-42; Michel Raimond, "Note sur la structure du *Côté de Guermantes*," *Revue d'Histoire Littéraire*, 71[e] année (1971), pp. 854-74; Jean-Yves Tadié, *Proust et le roman* (Paris: Gallimard, 1971), esp. pp. 236-92; Gérard Genette, "Métonymie chez Proust, ou la naissance du récit," *Poétique*, No. 2 (1970), pp. 156-73; Jean Ricardou, " 'Miracles' de l'analogie (Aspects proustiens de la métaphore productrice)," *Etudes Proustiennes*, No. 2 (1975), esp. pp. 233-39.

[21]Fasquelle's reader who was largely responsible for the publisher's rejection of *Du côté de chez Swann*, provides a good example: Jacques Madeleine, "Lecteur chez Fasquelle, n'aimant pas *A la recherche du temps perdu*... Il fut le Madeleine de Proust." See Henri Bonnet in *Le Figaro Littéraire*, no. 1077 (8 déc. 1966), p. 15.

[22]*Louis Lambert, La Comédie humaine*, vol. 16 (Facsimile of Balzac's corrected Furne edition of 1846; Paris: Bibliophiles de l'original, 1967), p. 121.

[23]"La Bibliothèque de l'homme de l'an 2440 selon L. S. Mercier," *French Review*, 45 (1972), 579.

[24]*Problèmes du nouveau roman* (Paris: Seuil, 1967), p. 178. Pascal Ifri, who focuses specifically on *A la recherche* and, in particular, on the *narrataire* (the one whom the narrator addresses), says, "The *narrataire* gives the narrator's enterprise the entirety of its meaning"—*Proust et son narrataire dans A la recherche du temps perdu* (Geneva: Droz, 1983), p. 200.

[25]III, 257-58. See, also, III, 569-72, 885, 890.

[26]The above quotations are to be found in the Bibliothèque Nationale. Nouvelles Acquisitions Françaises, MS. 16648, fol. 52v; MS. 16652, fol. 100v; MS. 16694, fol. 46v; MS. 16693, fols. 13v and 18v; MS 16683, fol. 58v; MS 16668, fol. 16v, in that order.

[27]N.A.F. 16654, fols. 8r-16r.

[28]N.A.F. 16668, fol. 68r.

[29]N.A.F. 16648, fol. 52v; *A la recherche*, I, 49-50, 120-21.

[30]N.A.F. 16648, fol. 52v.

[31]N.A.F. 16693, fol. 9v.

[32] *Louis Lambert,* p. 113.

[33] "The Philosophy of Composition," *The Works of Edgar Allan Poe* (London: J. C. Hotten, 1872), p. 662.

[34] Roger Shattuck's discussion of the necessity of "forgetfulness" is excellent: *Proust's Binoculars: A Study of Memory, Time and Recognition in A la recherche du temps perdu* (New York: Random House, 1963), pp. 65-68.

[35] N.A.F. 16668, fol. 33r.

[36] When a work of art is incapable of provoking discovery, that is, when it has been thoroughly analyzed, it "dies." Albertine, the narrator tells us, "guessed that at the third or fourth execution [of a musical work], my intelligence having reached all the parts, having consequently put them at the same distance, and no longer having any activity to exert for them, had reciprocally extended and immobilized them on a uniform plane." Of course, "at the moment when my intelligence had succeeded in dissipating the mystery of a work, it was very rare that it did not, in the course of its destructive task, pick up some profitable reflection by compensation" (III, 372).

[37] *Journal d'un inconnu* (Paris: Grasset, 1953), p. 153.

[38] Louis Martin-Chauffier, "Proust et le double 'je' de quatre personnes," rpt. Jean Prévost, ed., *Problèmes du roman* (Lyon: Confluences, 1943), p. 60.

[39] *Bulletin de la Société des Amis de Marcel Proust et des Amis de Combray,* No. 9 (1959), esp. pp. 80-82.

[40] N.A.F. 16696, fol. 8r.

[41] Numerous passages across *A la recherche* suggest the importance of universals: e.g., I, 861-62; III, 895, 900, 904, 905, 907. Gilles Deleuze, in the material added to the second edition of his provocative *Proust et les signes* (Paris: P.U.F., 1970), would agree that Proust's fragmented world can communicate, though he would deny the degree to which this communication may go beyond the simple effect of involuntary memory to the conception—exact and detailed—of the whole, of the author's essence and of the reader's self.

[42] See, above, n. 10.

[43] *Aesthetic Function, Norm and Value as Social Facts,* pp. 91-92.

## Chapter 8

[1] *La Jalousie* (Paris: Minuit, 1957), p. 11.

[2] "Order and Disorder in Film and Fiction," tr. Bruce Morrissette, *Critical Inquiry,* 4 (1977), 8.

[3]*The Novels of Robbe-Grillet* (1963; tr. Ithaca: Cornell Univ. Press, 1975), p. 123.

[4]Lucien Goldmann, *Pour une sociologie du roman* (Paris: Gallimard, 1964), p. 187.

[5]See, Morrissette, *Novels*, p. 130.

[6]Interview, by B. Knapp, tr. Alba Amoia, *French Novelists Speak Out*, p. 141.

[7]*Composition No. 1* (Paris: Seuil, 1962). The leaves are unnumbered and printed only on the recto side. I have had several dozen unshuffled copies from differing lots compared and found consistent order. Folio 1 then starts with: "La rue défile," fol. 50 with: "L'escalier qui mène," fol. 100; "Les cierges dressent," and fol. 149: "Dagmar en manteau." I shall refer to the folios in this order. These comparisons just mentioned occur on fols. 4, 8, 110.

[8]*Rayuela* (1963); rpt. Buenos Aires: Editorial Sudamericana, 1968), ch. 56. I quote Gregory Rabassa's translation: *Hopscotch* (New York: Pantheon, 1966).

[9]As Ken Holsten has it in an otherwise helpful article—"Notas sobre el 'Tablero de Dirección' en Rayuela de Julio Cortázar," *Revista Iberoamericana*, Nos. 84-85 (julio-diciembre 1973), p. 684.

[10]"In Quest of a Newer New Novel: Ricardou's *La Prise de Constantinople,*" *Contemporary Literature*, 14 (1973), 300.

[11]Jean Ricardou, *La Prise de Constantinople* (Paris: Eds. de Minuit, 1965). I have followed Jones's lead and, for purposes of identification, numbered the pages beginning with the front cover. The passage just quoted then appears on p. 256.

# Index